ONE-HUNDRED-AND-ONE
JEWISH READ-ALOUD
STORIES

ONE-HUNDRED-AND-ONE
JEWISH READ-ALOUD
STORIES

Edited and retold by
Barbara Diamond Goldin

BLACK DOG
& LEVENTHAL
PUBLISHERS
NEW YORK

A Match Made in Heaven; Dona Gracia Nasi; Ketsele's Gift- First Published in Cricket, the Magazine For Children Peru, IL April 1989 Volume 16, Number 8 Even In The Darkest Places; Right Side Up- First Published in A Hanukkah Treasury Edited by Eric A.Kimmel Henry Holt and Co., New York 1998 Brave Like Mordecai- First Published in Highlights for Children Honesdale, PA March 1992 volume 47, number 3, Issue No. 487; Don't Blow Out the Candles- First Published in Highlights for Children Honesdale, PA December 1998 Volume 53, Number 12, Issue No. 566; Never Too Quiet- Based On a Hasidic Story First Published in Cricket, the Magazine for Children Peru, IL September 1993 Volume 21, Number 1

Copyright © 2001 Black Dog & Leventhal

Published by
Black Dog & Leventhal Publishers, Inc.
151 West 19th Street, New York, NY 10011

Distributed by
Workman Publishing Company
708 Broadway, New York, NY 10003

Extensive searches of copyright registration and renewal records have been conducted for all previously published materials included in this book. The editor and publisher apologize for any inadvertent oversight and will include an appropriate acknowledgments in all future editions.

K'tonton Arrives by Sadie Rose Weilerstein Copyright © 1980 by Sadie Rose Weilerstein. Reprinted by permission of the Jewish Publication Society of America. Sabbath in Paradise by Jane Yolen Copyright © 1996 by Jane Yolen. Reprinted by permission of G.P. Putnam's Sons. The Cave of Shimon Bar Yohai by Howard Schwartz Copyright © 1993 by Howard Schwartz. Reprinted by permission of Oxford University Press. Mountains of Blintzes by Sydney Taylor Copyright © 1974 by the Board of Jewish Education of Greater New York. Reprinted by permission of the Board of Jewish Education of Greater New York. A Tale of Three Wishes by Isaac Bashevis Singer Copyright © 1984 by Isaac Bashevis Singer. Reprinted by permission of Farrar Straus & Giroux. The Pan of Oil by Chaver Paver. Copyright © 1976 by the Jewish Publication Society of America. Reprinted by permission of the Jewish Publication Society of America. The Magician by Y.L. Peretz. Copyright © 1947 by the B. Manischewitz Co. Honi and the Carob Tree by Eric Kimmel Copyright © 2001 by Eric Kimmel. Poems from I Never Saw Another Butterfly by U.S. Holocaust Memorial Museum edited by Hana Volavkova Copyright © 1978, 1993 by Artia. Reprinted by permission of Shocken Books, a division of Random House, Inc.

Design by Liz Trovato

ISBN: 1-57912-212-4

Manufactured in the US

Library of Congress Cataloging-in-Publication Data

Goldin, Barbara Diamond.
One-hundred-and-one-read-aloud Jewish stories : ten minute readings from the world's best loved Jewish literature / collected and retold by Barbara Diamond Goldin.
p. cm.
Summary: A collection of Jewish tales, Bible stories, legends, and real life accounts from Jews from every generation and many lands.
ISBN 1-57912-212-4
1. Jews—Literary collections. [1. Jews—Literary collections.] I. Title.

PZ5.G58 On 2001

808.8'9824—dc21   2001037685

CONTENTS

Introduction	9
BIBLE	11
The Beginning	12
In The Garden of Eden	14
Noah	17
Abraham and Sarah	20
Isaac and Rebecca	23
Jacob and Esau	27
Jacob, Leah and Rachel	31
Joseph and His Brothers	34
Pharaoh's Dreams	37
Moses and the Burning Bush	41
The Ten Plagues	44
Crossing the Sea	50
The Ten Commandments	53
The Golden Calf	55
David and Goliath	59
David and Michal	62
Jonah	65
Naomi and Ruth	68
TALMUD AND MIDRASH	71
The Alphabet and the Creation of the World	72
Am I My Brother's Keeper?	75
The Tower	77
The Idol Smasher	79
Shifra and Puah	82
Why Moses Stuttered	84
Why God Chose Moses	87
Aaron's Rod	90

The Field of Brotherly Love   93
King David and the Frog   96
While Standing on One Foot   99
Rabbi Yochanan's Lesson   103
This Too Is For the Best   106
The King and the Two Glasses   110
The Witches of Ashkelon   113

FROM THE KABBALAH AND HASIDIM   117
The Ari and the Hidden Saint   118
The Kabbalah   121
The Prince Who Thought He Was A Rooster   124
The Treasure   127
Only the Story   130
The Window and the Mirror   133
A Game of Hide and Seek   136
The Holy Goat   138
Hannah Rachel Werbermacher   141
The Wealthy Man and the Mud   145
A Match Made in Heaven   148

JEWISH TALES FROM AROUND THE WORLD   153
King Solomon and the White Eagle (*Palestine*)   154
King Solomon and the Bee (*Palestine*)   157
If It Pleases God (*Palestine*)   160
The Slave (*Palestine*)   163
The Power of Prayers (*Palestine*)   165
The Horseman (*Iraq*)   168
The Midwife and the Cat (*Kurdistan*)   173
Which Is The Sweetest of All Melodies (*Afghanistan*)   176
The Bewitched Donkey (*Tunisia*)   179
Rabbi Haim and the King (*Morocco*)   181
Cats and Mice (*Ethiopia*)   184

Dona Gracia Nasi (*Portugal and Turkey*)   187
Rabbi Loew and the Golem of Prague, Part 1 (*Eastern Europe*)   189
Rabbi Loew and the Golem of Prague, Part 2 (*Eastern Europe*)   192
It Could Always Be Worse (*Eastern Europe*)   197
The Coachman Who Was a Rabbi (*Eastern Europe*)   201
The Golden Shoes (*Chelm, Eastern Europe*)   203
Count Your Blessings (*Eastern Europe*)   207
Yonkel's Visit to Warsaw, (*Chelm, Eastern Europe*)   210
Hershel from Ostropol (*Eastern Europe*)   214
Hershel's New Coat (*Eastern Europe*)   217
Ketsele's Gift (*United States*)   220

ISRAEL STORIES   225
Eliezer Ben Yehuda   226
Theodor Herzl   229
Joseph Trumpeldor   233
Golda Meir   236
Neve Shalom/Wahat al-Salam   239

HOLIDAY TALES   243
The Sabbath   244
Joseph the Sabbath Lover   245
Sabbath in Paradise *by Jane Yolen*   248
Rosh Hashanah   251
To Heaven? If Not Higher!   252
The Shofar   256
Yom Kippur   259
The Rabbi Was Late   260
The Shepherd's Prayer   262
Sukkot   265
Never Too Quiet   266
A Tale of Three Wishes *by Isaac B. Singer*   271
Rough or Smooth?   277

K'tonton Arrives *by Sadie Rose Weilerstein*   281

Hanukkah   284

That Day in Modin (Day One)   285

Soldiers Become Builders (Day Two)   289

Adding to the Light (Day Three)   294

The Pan of Oil *by Chaver Paver* (Day Four)   297

Even In the Darkest Places (Day Five)   301

Right Side Up (Day Six)   304

In Honor of Judith, Rosh Hodesh Hanukkah (Day Seven)   309

Don't Blow Out the Candles (Day Eight)   314

Tu B'Shvat   318

Honi and the Carob Tree *by Eric Kimmel*   319

Purim   322

Esther   323

Brave Like Mordecai   327

Passover   330

Passover Herbs   331

The Magician *by Y.L. Peretz*   334

Yom Hashoa   339

At Terezin   340

The Butterfly   341

On a Sunny Evening   342

Hannah Senesh   343

Yom Ha'atzmaut: Israel's Birthday   346

Lag B'Omer   350

The Cave of Shimon Bar Yohai *by Howard Schwartz*   351

Shavuot   353

Mountains of Blintzes *by Sydney Taylor*   354

Bibliography   359

INTRODUCTION

I work in the youth department of a small public library, but for over twenty years I was a teacher. One day, a woman came into the library and asked me how she could get her eight-year-old daughter to read. "I'm very worried about her," the woman said. "She has to be forced to pick up a book."

"Read to her," I said. "The more you read to her, the greater the chance you'll hit on something she really likes, and then she'll probably start to read books like that one on her own for enjoyment."

I went on to tell her how my own mother read to me constantly when I was little, and I grew up to love books. Then in fourth grade, my teacher, Mrs. Chambeau, had a wonderful classroom library full of books fourth graders really liked. It was in her class that I really began to read on my own. After that year, my mother had to beg me to put my book down, shut off the light, and go to sleep!

Not only does reading aloud to children inspire their love of books, words, and stories, and make them better readers themselves, it also provides a warm sharing time for parents and children. In addition, it gives children and parents a common base of stories they can talk about together and to which they can relate their real life experiences and values.

Reading aloud to children doesn't have to stop when they learn to read themselves. Families can keep reading aloud and continue to discover the wealth of stories in children's literature and beyond. One is never too old to hear a good story and to share it!

ABOUT THE SELECTIONS

The 101 stories in this collection are but a small sampling of Jewish stories from earliest Biblical times to the present, and from all corners of the globe. All the stories have been retold in language true to the originals, in a way that can be readily understood by contemporary readers. These are not just stories by Jews or about Jews. These are stories that contain Jewish values, history, humor, traditions, and ways of looking at the world and at God.

In this collection, you will find famous Bible stories like the ones about Garden of Eden and David and Goliath. Then there are stories told by rabbis 2000 years ago who were trying to find hidden meaning in the Bible and answers to their own questions. Why did Cain kill his brother? How did King Solomon know where to build the Holy Temple? There are teaching tales by Hasidic rabbis of the 1700s and 1800s. And tales from all over the Jewish world, from all different time periods including our own. You'll read a cautionary tale from Ethiopia, funny ones from Eastern Europe about the town of fools, and mysterious stories that will give you goosebumps like "Rabbi Loew and the Golem of Prague." There are biographies of people who helped found the State of Israel, lots of holiday stories—including one for each night of Hanukkah, plus stories by famous Jewish writers like Issac B.Singer. I hope you will enjoy this sampling of Jewish stories throughout the ages and then go on to read more!

BIBLE

THE BEGINNING

God created the heavens and the earth from nothingness. The earth was unformed and void and there was darkness over the surface of the deep. God sent a wind sweeping over the waters, and said, "Let there be light." And there was light. God saw that the light was good and separated the light from the darkness, calling the light Day, and the darkness Night. And so there was evening and there was morning on the first day of Creation.

Then God said, "Let there be a separation in the waters." And there was a separation and God called this separation sky. And so there was evening and there was morning on the second day of Creation.

Next God said," Let the water below the sky be gathered so that dry land may appear." And there was dry land. God called this dry land Earth, and the waters God called Seas. God saw that this was good. God said, "Let this Earth grow vegetation, plants that bear seeds and trees that produce fruits of every kind." And God saw that this too was good. So there was evening and there was morning on the third day of Creation.

Again God spoke. "Let there be lights in the sky to separate day from night. These lights will serve as signs for the days and years, and will shine upon the earth to illuminate it." And it was so. God created two great lights, the greater light to shine in the day and the lesser light to shine in the night. God also made the stars. God set these lights in the sky to separate light from darkness. God saw that this was good. And there was evening and there was morning on the fourth day of Creation.

Then God spoke these words. "Let the waters bring forth living creatures, and let there be birds that fly above the earth across the sky." God created the great sea monsters and swarms of living creatures that creep and swim and fly. God saw that this was good and blessed them all. "Be fertile and multiply, fill the seas and the skies." And there was evening and there was morning on the fifth day of Creation.

God spoke, "Now let the earth bring forth every kind of creature, cattle and creeping things and wild beasts." And it was so. God created all these and saw that this too was good.

And God said, "I will make people in My image. They will rule the fish of the sea, the birds of the sky, the cattle and creeping things of the earth, all the earth." So God made man and woman and blessed them. "Be fertile and multiply, fill the earth and rule over it, over the fish of the sea and the birds of the sky, over all the things that creep upon the earth. See how I give you these seed-bearing plants and trees with fruit for food. And to all the animals of the land, the birds of the sky and the fish in the sea, everything which has the breath of life, I give all the green plants for food." And it was so. God saw all that God had made and found it very good. And there was evening and there was morning on the sixth day of Creation.

Now the heavens and the earth were complete and all that filled them. On the seventh day God finished all this work and rested. And so God blessed this seventh day and said it was holy.

IN THE GARDEN OF EDEN

God formed man from the dust of the earth and blew the breath of life into his nostrils so that man became a living being. God planted a garden in the east, in Eden, and placed man there. In this garden, God caused every kind of tree to grow that was pleasing to look at with fruit that was good to eat. God put the Tree of Life in the middle of the garden, and the Tree of Knowledge of Good and Evil.

God made a river with four branches to water the garden, one branch called Pishon, one Gihon, the others the Tigris and the Euphrates. God put man in the garden to work it and care for it. And God said to the man, "You are free to eat of every tree in this garden except for the Tree of Knowledge of Good and Evil. If you eat of this tree, you will die."

Then God brought all the creatures of the land and the sky and the sea to man so he could name them.

God said, "It is not good for man to be alone so I will make a helpmate for him." As none of the creatures God had brought to man to name made a fitting helpmate, God caused man to fall into a deep sleep. While man slept, God took a rib from man, closing up the spot afterwards, and made this rib into woman.

Man and woman lived together in the garden and, though they wore no clothes, they were not ashamed. They enjoyed the garden, eating of the fruit of all the trees except for the one which God had said they should not eat of.

Now of all the creatures which God made, the serpent was the shrewdest. One day this serpent said to woman, "Did God tell you that you cannot eat of any tree of the garden?"

"God said we may eat the fruit of any of the trees in the garden except that which is in the middle, the Tree of Knowledge of Good and Evil. Of that one we may not eat or we will die," answered woman.

"You will not die," said the serpent. "God does not want you to eat of it for if you do, your eyes will open. You will become like God and will know good and evil."

And woman was not afraid of the fruit of the Tree of Knowledge any-more. She picked a fruit from this forbidden tree and ate it, and picked another, and gave it to man to eat. Both their eyes were opened, and they saw that they wore no clothes. They were ashamed and sewed clothes from fig leaves to cover themselves.

They heard the sound of God moving about the garden carried by the breezes but for the first time, they hid from God among the trees.

"Where are you?" God called out to them.

"I heard You moving in the garden," said man, "but I was naked and afraid and hid from You."

"Who told you that you were naked?" asked God. "Did you eat any fruit from the tree which I told you was forbidden to you?"

"The woman You placed here with me gave me the fruit to eat," said man.

"What have you done?" God said to woman.

"The serpent tricked me into eating of the fruit of the forbidden tree," she said.

So God punished the serpent, making it crawl always on its belly and eat dirt all the days of its life, and making it an enemy of man and woman.

God punished woman by giving her pain on bearing her offspring.

And God punished man saying, "By the sweat of your brow you shall eat." Now man would have to work very hard with the soil to eat from it, and he would face the many challenges of farming like weather and insects. In the Garden of Eden, all the plants and fruit grew of themselves and man just picked what he wished and ate of it.

"For dust you are and to dust you shall return," God said to man and woman. He named man Adam, for God had taken him from the earth—*adamah*—and God named the woman Eve, for she was the mother of all living beings. God clothed them in garments of skins and banished them forever from the garden so that they would never be able to eat from the Tree of Life and live forever. God stationed cherubim and the ever-turning sword of fire to guard the way to the garden so that man and woman could never return.

NOAH

od looked at the earth and saw that the people's wicked ways were increasing. God regretted creating people, and said, "I will destroy this humanity along with the animals and birds."

Only Noah of all his generation found favor with God.

"I have decided to put an end to all beings on the earth," God said to Noah. "For the earth is filled with lawlessness. Make yourself an ark of cypress wood, and divide it into compartments. Cover the inside and outside with pitch."

God gave Noah the exact dimensions of this ark he was to build. It was to be three hundred cubits in length, fifty cubits wide and thirty cubits high. It was to have a skylight, a door in the side and three decks.

"I am bringing a flood," said God. "All that is on land will perish. But I am making this promise to you, Noah, that you will come into this ark you are to build. You and your wife Naamah, your sons and your sons' wives will come into it.

"After you build this ark, you are to bring two of each kind of creature into the ark to live with you. Male and female. Also take with you all the food that you and your family and these creatures will need and keep it in storage. In seven days' time, I will bring rains upon the earth, and it will rain for forty days and forty nights."

And Noah did exactly as God commanded him to do.

He built the ark. He brought his family, and pairs of every creature of the earth and sky, and food for all onto the ark.

On the seventh day after God had instructed Noah, the rains began. On that day, the wellsprings of the seas burst forth, and the floodgates of the heavens broke open. It rained for forty days and forty nights.

The ark drifted on the waters as they rose higher and higher, covering the land. Even the highest mountains were covered with water. All living creatures on the earth perished, all the flying creatures and land animals and all the people, too. Only Noah and those in the ark with him survived the flood.

Then God remembered Noah, and made a gentle wind to blow on the earth, and the waters slowly subsided. At the end of one hundred and fifty days, the waters receded.

In the seventh month, on the seventeenth day, the ark came to rest on the Ararat Mountains. And in the tenth month, the tops of the mountains around the ark were visible.

After forty days, Noah opened the ark's window to release a raven which flew back and forth, back and forth looking for dry land. Noah also released a dove, but, like the raven, it could not find any land on which to rest. So it returned to the ark. Noah waited for seven days more, and sent out the dove again. This time the dove returned with an olive leaf in its beak. Now Noah knew there was dry land on the earth. In another seven days, Noah released the dove once more. But this time the dove did not return.

So Noah opened the ark's door, and saw the dry land for himself.

God said to Noah, "Leave the ark, you and your wife, your sons and their wives. Take out all the animals that they may walk on the earth again and fly above it, filling it with life."

And Noah did as God said.

Noah and his wife Naamah, his sons and their wives, and every creature both male and female left the ark to walk on the earth or fly above it.

Then Noah built an altar, and made sacrifices to God to show his gratitude. God smelled the fragrances of these offerings, and said, "Never again will I bring such a curse on the land. As long as the earth shall last, seedtime and harvest, summer and winter, day and night shall never cease."

God blessed Noah and his family, saying, "Be fruitful and multiply and fill the earth. All the beasts of the land and the birds of the sky and the creatures of the sea will be afraid of you. I have placed them in your hands.

"I am making a covenant with you and your offspring after you, and with all the living creatures on the earth, all that have come out of the ark, that never again will all life be cut short by the waters of a flood. Here is a sign of this covenant for all generations."

Noah and Naamah, their sons and their sons' wives, looked up at the sky and saw this sign that God had sent. It was an arc of many colors that arched across the heavens, a rainbow.

ABRAHAM AND SARAH

N ow one of the descendants of Noah was named Abram and his wife was Sarai. They lived in Haran and, much to their sorrow, had no children.

God spoke to Abram saying, "Go from your homeland to the land that I will show you. I will make of you a great nation, and I will bless you. I will make your name great."

Abram did as God had said. He took his wife Sarai and his brother's son Lot, many other people and animals and all that he owned with him to the land God showed him, to Canaan. Abram built an altar to God and pitched his tent near the place which came to be called Bethel, the house of God.

Over the years that passed, Abram grew rich in livestock, silver and gold. Abram's nephew Lot also had sheep and cattle and tents. Abram's herdsmen and Lot's herdsmen began to argue and it was difficult to share the lands. So Abram said to Lot, "We are brothers. Let's not have this friction between us. There is no need with all this land before us. If you go to the left, I will go to the right. If you take the right, then I will go to the left, and we will separate our flocks and tents."

Lot chose the entire Jordan Plain for himself while Abram lived in the land of Canaan. After Lot left, God spoke to Abram, "Raise your eyes, and from the place where you are now standing, look to the north, the south, east and west. All this land which you see I will give to you and your descendants forever. I will make your offspring as numerous as the grains of dust of the earth."

From Bethel, Abram later moved to Hebron and there built another altar to the One God. Abram continued to act in righteous ways and be loyal to the One God.

But there was something that worried Abram. He and Sarai did not have any children. Who would be heir to their household? How could his descendants be as numerous as the grains of sand as God had said?

By way of answer, God told Abram to come outside his tent. "Look at the sky and count the stars," God said. "That is how numerous your offspring will be."

God also told Abram, "Their future will not always be an easy one. They will be strangers, even slaves, in a land that is not theirs for 400 years. But know that in the end, I will bring judgment against the nation that oppresses them and they will leave with great wealth."

After God spoke to Abram, and the sun went down, it became very dark. Before Abram, on the altar that he had built and placed his offerings to God, there appeared a smoking furnace and a flaming torch. Abram understood these to be signs of what God had told him to expect for his descendants, of their oppression and then the freedom and light that would follow.

Time passed and still Abram's wife Sarai did not bear any children. So Sarai took her Egyptian maid Hagar and brought her to Abram for a wife so that she could bear him children in Sarai's stead. When Hagar became pregnant, she began to gloat over Sarai. Sarai could not bear the disrespect and was mean to Hagar, who then ran away from Sarai into the desert.

An angel of God encountered Hagar by a spring in the desert. He told her to return to her mistress, that she would bear a son whom she should call Ishmael. He would be the father of many descendants. And so Hagar did as the angel of God told her to do.

After more years had passed, God spoke to Abram once again, and Abram fell on his face before God. "From this time on," God said, "you'll be called Abraham and your wife will be called Sarah. You must keep My covenant, you and your descendants. And I will bless Sarah who will bear you a son."

"Can a man as old as I am and a woman as old as Sarah have a son?" said Abraham.

"Yes, and when Sarah bears you this son at this time next year, you will call him Isaac. And do not worry about your other son. I will bless Ishmael and make him into a great nation, too."

Abraham was ninety-nine years old when he and all the men in his household were circumcised, as a sign of this covenant that he had agreed to before God.

ISAAC AND REBECCA

When Abraham was old he called Eliezer, his oldest servant, and instructed him to go to his native land, to his birthplace, and find a wife for his son Isaac.

"What if the woman does not want to come back with me to live here?" said Eliezer. "Should I bring Isaac to live there?"

"Beware. Do not take my son back there! God took me from my father's house and the land of my birth, and told me to go to this land which God would give me and my descendants," answered Abraham. "Don't worry. God will send an angel before you to help you in your mission."

Then Eliezer took ten camels and many fine things that Abraham owned to give as gifts and set out on his journey to the city of Nahor.

When he came near Nahor, Eliezer let the camels rest near the well outside the city. It was evening, the time when the women went to the well to draw water.

Eliezer prayed, "Oh God, be with me today and grant this favor to Your servant Abraham. Here I stand by the well, and the women come. If I say to one, 'Please, lower your pitcher that I may drink' and that one answers, 'Drink and I will give your camels water to drink also,' let this one be the one You mean for Isaac to marry."

He had not yet finished speaking when a beautiful young woman carrying a jug on her shoulder approached the well. She bent down, filled her jug, and stood up again.

"Please, if you would," Eliezer said, "give me a sip of water from your jug."

"Drink, sir, " she said, and lowered her jug to give him a drink.

When Eliezer finished drinking, the young woman said, "Let me draw water for your camels also." Then she emptied the water in her jug into the trough and ran to the well to draw more water.

Eliezer stood there staring at her, watching her water all his camels, wondering if indeed this was to be the wife for Isaac.

Eliezer took out a gold ring and golden bracelets as gifts for this young woman, and said, "Tell me, whose daughter are you? And is there a place in your parents' house for us to spend the night?"

"I am Rebecca, the daughter of Bethuel, son of Milcah, wife of Nahor," said the woman. "We have plenty of straw and feed for your camels and room for you also."

"Thank you," said Eliezer. And he knew that God had guided his mission because Nahor was brother to his very own master Abraham. Eliezer bowed his head and prayed to God in gratitude for God's guidance and kindness.

And Rebecca ran to tell her mother about the visitor.

Rebecca's brother Laban heard her story while she was telling it to their mother, and he also noticed the ring and bracelet Eliezer had given her. Laban went to see this stranger at the well and invite him to come to stay.

Laban led Eliezer and his camels to the house, and gave the camels straw and food. Then he gave Eliezer and his men water to drink and wash with. They were served food, but Eliezer said he would not eat until he had spoken.

"Speak," said Laban.

"I am Abraham's servant. God granted my master many blessings, and he has prospered with sheep and cattle, silver and gold, camels and donkeys. In her old age, my master's wife Sarah gave birth to a son. Isaac is grown now and his father does not want him to take a wife from the Canaanite people, but to marry a woman from where he was born. That is why I have journeyed here. To find Isaac a wife from his kinsmen."

He went on to relate the whole story of meeting Rebecca at the well and how she gave him a drink and his camels also. Then Eliezer said, "Now tell me what you want to do."

"This is something decreed by God," both Laban and Bethuel said. "We give you permission to take Rebecca to be wife to your master's son as God has spoken."

Eliezer was overjoyed and gave many gifts of gold and silver jewelry and clothing to Rebecca and other valuable gifts to her mother and brother. He and all his men ate and drank and spent the night. The next morning, Eliezer wished to leave with Rebecca and begin the return journey right away. But Laban and Bethuel protested. "Please let her stay with us for a year before she goes."

Eliezer was eager to bring her back to Abraham and Isaac sooner, so Bethuel suggested they call Rebecca and ask her what she wanted to do.

When Rebecca heard their question, she did not hesitate. "I will go," she said.

Rebecca and her attendants mounted camels and joined Eliezer's caravan. She left her home with her relative's blessings.

Time passed and one day toward evening, Isaac went out into a field to meditate. When he raised his eyes, he saw a caravan approaching. Rebecca happened to look up at the same time and when she saw Isaac, she almost fell off the camel.

"Eliezer, who is that coming toward us in the field?" she asked.

"That is my master, Isaac," Eliezer answered, "The man you will marry."

When they came closer, Eliezer told Isaac all that had happened. Isaac did marry Rebecca and he loved her, and the joy which had left when his mother Sarah died, again returned to fill Isaac's house and his heart.

JACOB AND ESAU

hen Rebecca became pregnant, she could feel two babies struggling within her, and she prayed to God.

"Two nations are in your body," God said. "The one shall be stronger than the other. And the elder one shall serve the younger."

When the time came, Rebecca gave birth to twin boys. The firstborn was ruddy of complexion and hairy all over, and they called him Esau, the hairy one. The younger brother was born with his hand holding onto Esau's heels, and they called him Jacob, one who holds by the heel.

As he grew up, Esau became a skilled hunter, while Jacob was a quiet man who stayed in the camp. Isaac had a taste for the meat Esau hunted and prepared, and he favored Esau. Rebecca favored Jacob.

One day, Jacob was preparing a stew when his brother Esau came in very hungry and tired from working in the fields.

"Give me a swallow of that red stuff you are cooking," he said to Jacob. "I am starving!"

"First sell me your birthright," said Jacob.

"I am at the point of dying of hunger," Esau said. "What good is my birthright to me right now?"

Jacob said, "Swear to me first."

And Esau swore to give Jacob his birthright for some stew.

Jacob gave his brother bread and stewed lentils, and Esau ate of them, rose and went on his way.

Time passed and Isaac was weak with age and nearly blind. He called to Esau.

"My son."

"Here I am."

"I am old and may die any day. Take your bow and arrows and bring back some game for me. Make me a tasty dish of it, and bring it to me so I can bless you before I die."

Now Rebecca was nearby and heard what her husband said to Esau, her eldest. She went to Jacob and told him what she had heard.

"I command you," she said, "go to the flock and bring me two choice young goats. I will make them into a tasty dish for your father that he will love. You will bring it to your father so that he may bless you before he dies."

Jacob answered, "But my brother is a hairy man while I am smooth of skin. If my father should touch my skin, he will know I am deceiving him, and I will bring a curse onto myself not a blessing."

"Let any curse for you fall on me, my son. Obey me and bring what I ask you."

So Jacob brought the two young goats to his mother who made of them a tasty dish. Then Rebecca took some of Esau's best clothes and put them on Jacob. She also placed the young goats' skins over Jacob's arms and neck.

She handed the dish and some bread she had baked to Jacob who brought them to Isaac.

"Father."

"Yes. Who are you, my son?"

"It is I, Esau, your first born," answered Jacob. "I have done as you asked. Please sit up and eat of this dish so that you may give me your blessing."

"How did you find this game so quickly, my son?" asked Isaac.

"Because the Lord, your God, was with me," said Jacob.

"Come closer that I may feel you, my son—to tell whether you are really Esau or not."

So Jacob came closer and Isaac touched him.

"The voice is Jacob's but the hands are Esau's," said Isaac. Isaac was just about to give Jacob the blessing when he hesitated yet again.

"Are you really my son, Esau?"

"I am."

"Then serve me the food you have brought. I will eat the game my son trapped and bless you."

So Jacob served his father, and Isaac ate. And he brought his father wine and Isaac drank. Then Isaac said, "Come close and kiss me, my son."

And Jacob went over and kissed Isaac.

Isaac could smell Jacob's clothes. "Ah the smell of my son's clothes is like the smell of the fields that God has blessed," Isaac said. And he gave Jacob the blessing meant for Esau.

"May God grant you the dew of heaven and the fat of the earth, an abundance of grain and wine. Let nations serve you and governments bow down to you. May you be master over your brothers. Cursed be those who curse you, and blessed by they who bless you."

No sooner had Isaac finished his blessing and Jacob left his father's presence, than Esau came back from hunting. After preparing the dish for his father, Esau brought it to him.

"Let my father get up and eat this venison that I hunted and prepared for you so that you may bless me," said Esau.

"Who are you?" asked Isaac.

"I am Esau, your first born!"

On hearing these words, Isaac began to tremble violently. "Who was it then who just brought me the stew he hunted and prepared? I ate it all before you came, and I blessed him. The blessing must remain his."

When Esau heard these words from his father, he let out a wild and bitter scream.

"Please, father, bless me too," Esau pleaded.

"Your brother came and tricked me and took your blessing."

"He has deceived me twice. First he took my birthright, and now he took my blessing!" Then Esau added, "Don't you have a blessing for me too, father?"

"But I made him like a lord over you, over all his brothers. And I have given him the blessing for abundance of grain and wine. What can I still do for you, my son?"

"Have you only one blessing? Please, father, bless me too!" And Esau wept out loud.

His father said, "The fat places of the earth can still be your dwelling place, and you can still have the dew of heaven. But by your sword shall you live. You may still have to serve your brother, but you shall be able to throw his yoke from off your neck."

And Esau was furious at Jacob because of the blessing that his father had given him. "The days of mourning for my father are near," he said. "Then I will kill my brother Jacob."

These words of Esau's were reported to Rebecca and she called for Jacob. "Your brother Esau plans to kill you. You must flee to my brother Laban in Haran. Stay with him until Esau's anger has subsided, and he forgets what you have done to him. I will send you word when your brother has calmed down and you can return."

To Isaac, Rebecca said, "Jacob must not take a wife from the Hittite women."

So Isaac called Jacob, and charged him to go to the house of his maternal grandfather Bethuel and take a wife from the daughters of his uncle Laban.

JACOB, LEAH AND RACHEL

**A**nd Isaac said to his son Jacob, "You must not take to wife a daughter of the Canaanites. Go to Paddan Aram, the house of Bethuel, your mother's father, and take a wife from the daughters of Laban, your mother's brother. May God bless you and make you fruitful."

So Jacob left Beer-Sheba and began his journey. When the sun set, he stopped for the night. He gathered some stones to place under his head, and lay down on the ground to sleep. During the night he had a dream, of a ladder with its bottom standing on the earth and its top reaching to heaven. Angels of God were going up the ladder and coming down.

Then Jacob saw God standing over him in the dream. God said to him, "I am the One, the God of Abraham and Isaac. This land on which you rest I will give to you and your descendants who will be numerous and spread out to the west, the east, the north and the south. I will be with you, and guard you wherever you go. I will bring you back into this land, for I will not leave you until I have done that which I have promised to you."

Jacob woke up from his sleep, and was filled with fear and wonder. "God is in this place and I did not know it," he said. "How awesome is this place! This must be God's Temple, the gate to Heaven!"

He took the stone from under his head and set it up as a pillar. He poured oil over it and named the place Bethel, the House of God. Then Jacob made a vow. "If God remains with me and protects me on this journey, gives me food to eat and clothing to wear, and if I return safely to my father's house, then I will dedicate myself to God. Then this stone which I have set up as a pillar shall be God's house, and of everything that You give me, I will set aside a tenth of it all for You."

Jacob continued on his journey, his steps swifter with the promise of his dream. He came to a place where there was a well in the field with flocks of sheep nearby. There was a very large stone over the well. When all the flocks had gathered, then the stone would be rolled off and the sheep watered.

Jacob walked over to the shepherds and asked them if they knew of Laban, his mother's brother.

"Yes, we know him," they answered.

"Is he well?"

"He is well," they answered. "And there is his daughter Rachel coming with the sheep."

When Jacob saw Rachel, he himself went over to the well, rolled the stone off the well's mouth, and watered the flock that belonged to his mother's brother, Laban. Then Jacob kissed Rachel and wept. He told her that he was Rebecca's son, and she ran to tell her father that their kinsman Jacob was near.

On hearing the news about Jacob, Laban ran to the well to greet his sister's son. He embraced Jacob and kissed him and took him to his house where Jacob stayed for a month's time.

While Jacob stayed with Laban, he also worked alongside him, and Laban said to Jacob, "Just because you are my kinsman doesn't mean you should work for no wages. Tell me what your wages should be."

Now Laban had two daughters. The older one was named Leah, and the younger, more beautiful one was Rachel. Jacob had fallen in love with Rachel when he met her at the well, and he said to Laban, "I will work for you for seven years for Rachel, your younger daughter."

"Better she marry you than someone else," said Laban. "Stay with me."

Jacob worked the next seven years for Rachel, and because he truly loved her, it seemed like no more than a few days. After the seven years had passed, Jacob said to his uncle, "It is time. Give me my bride and let me marry her."

Laban gathered everyone for a wedding feast, but instead of bringing Rachel, he brought his oldest daughter Leah veiled like a bride to Jacob. It wasn't until the morning light that Jacob saw he was with Leah and not Rachel!

He was angry and ran to his uncle Laban. "How could you do this to me?" he demanded. "Didn't I work all those seven years for Rachel? Why did you deceive me like this?"

"It is not our custom to give the younger sister in marriage until the elder is married," said Laban. "Let us finish this week of the wedding celebrations, then I will give you Rachel to marry in return for the work you will do for me for another seven years."

And Jacob did so. He completed the week of the wedding celebrations for his marriage to Leah, and then married Rachel. Jacob loved Rachel more than Leah, and worked another seven years for Laban.

JOSEPH AND HIS BROTHERS

ow, Jacob, with all his wives and children and all that belonged to him, left Laban to return to his father Isaac, to the land of Canaan. When he neared the place of his birth, Jacob prayed to God to deliver him from the anger of his brother Esau. He sent a gift of goats and sheep, camel, cattle and donkeys ahead to Esau, and that night an angel came to him and wrestled with him. Until the break of day did they wrestle, and Jacob was spared. His name was changed to Israel because he struggled with God and man, and lived. Jacob, who was now named Israel, called this place Peniel—God's face—"Because I have seen God face to face and yet my life has been spared." And when Jacob, now called Israel, met Esau, the two brothers embraced and wept.

Then Jacob settled in the area where his father had lived in the land of Canaan. He had twelve sons, and of them all, he loved Rachel's son Joseph the most. He called him the son of his old age.

Joseph was seventeen years of age, and tended his father's sheep with his brothers. Sometimes he brought bad reports about his brothers to his father.

Now because of his love for Joseph, his father made him a long colorful coat. When his brothers realized that their father loved Joseph more than any of his other sons, they began to hate Joseph, and could not speak a friendly word to him.

Then Joseph had a dream, and when he told it to his brothers, they hated him even more. "Listen to this dream I had," he said to his brothers. "We were binding sheaves in the field. My sheaf suddenly stood up tall, and your sheaves formed a circle around mine and bowed low to it."

"Do you mean to rule over us?" they said.

Then Joseph had another dream and told this one, too, to his brothers.

"I just had another dream," he told them. "The sun, the moon, and eleven stars were bowing down to me."

When he told this dream to his father and brothers, his father said, "What kind of dream is this? Am I and your mother and your brothers to come and bow down on the ground to you?"

His brothers grew ever more jealous of Joseph and angry with him. And his father thought about Joseph's words.

Joseph's brothers left to tend their father's sheep in Shechem. His father sent Joseph to them saying, "Go and see how your brothers are doing. See how the flocks are and bring me back word."

Joseph was wandering in the fields at Shechem, looking for his brothers, when he met a man who told Joseph that his brothers had gone on to Dothan. So Joseph followed his brothers to Dothan and found them there.

Before he reached his brothers, they saw him coming and began plotting to kill him. "Here comes the dreamer," they said to one another. "Now we have the chance. Let's kill him and throw him into one of these wells. We can say a wild beast devoured him. Then we'll see what becomes of his dreams!"

But when Reuben, the eldest of the brothers, heard this, he tried to save Joseph.

"Let's not kill him! Don't shed blood. Cast him into the well but do not touch him yourselves," said Reuben, who was planning to rescue Joseph later from the pit and return him to their father.

When Joseph reached his brothers, they took off his colorful coat and threw him into the pit. It was an empty pit with no water in it.

Then the brothers sat down to eat a meal. When they looked up, they saw a caravan of Ishmaelites coming from Gilead. The camels were transporting spices and perfumes to Egypt.

Judah said to his brothers, "What will we gain if we kill our brother and cover his blood? Come, let's sell him to these Ishmaelites and not harm him with our own hands. After all he is our brother, our own flesh and blood." And his brothers agreed. They pulled him out of the well and sold him for twenty pieces of silver to the merchants.

When Reuben returned to the well and saw that Joseph was no longer there, he tore his clothes in grief. He returned to his brothers. "The boy is gone! What am I to do now?"

So they took Joseph's colorful coat, killed a young goat and dipped the coat in the blood. They sent the coat on to their father. When they returned home, they explained to their father that they found this coat. "Is it your son's coat or not?" they asked him.

He immediately recognized it. "My son's coat!" he said. "A wild beast devoured him!" Jacob rent his clothes in grief and observed mourning for his son for many days. All his sons and daughters tried to comfort him, but he would not be comforted.

Meanwhile the merchants arrived in Egypt and sold Joseph to Potiphar, who was Pharaoh's chief steward.

PHARAOH'S DREAMS

N ow Joseph was cast into prison because of a wicked deception by Potiphar's wife. But God was with Joseph, and he found favor with the chief jailer who placed all the prisoners under Joseph's care.

Soon after this, Pharaoh's cupbearer and baker offended him, and Pharaoh had them arrested. They were placed in the same prison as Joseph, and the chief jailer assigned Joseph to look after them.

One night, both the cupbearer and the baker had dreams. When Joseph came to them in the morning, he saw they were distressed. "Why do you look so worried today?" he asked.

"We each had a dream," they told him. "But there is no one here who can interpret them for us."

"Interpretations belong to God, but you can tell me your dreams if you would like."

The cupbearer told Joseph, "In my dream there was a grape vine in front of me. It had three branches. It had barely grown buds when out came blossoms, and its clusters ripened into grapes. I held Pharaoh's cup in my hand. I took the grapes, squeezed them into Pharaoh's cup, and gave the cup to him."

"The three branches are three days," said Joseph. "In three days,

Pharaoh will give you back your position. You will again place Pharaoh's cup into his hand, as you did before. Think of me when things are going well with you again, and say something about me to Pharaoh when you have the chance, so I can be freed from this place. I was stolen out of the land of the Hebrews and brought here, and I did not do anything that warranted my being thrown into this prison."

The baker saw that Joseph gave a good interpretation to the cupbearer, and so he told Joseph, "I also saw myself in a dream. There were three baskets of white bread on my head. The top one had the kinds of baked goods Pharaoh eats. Birds were eating from this top basket."

"The three baskets are three days," Joseph said. "In three days, Pharaoh will have you hung on a gallows."

The third day happened to be Pharaoh's birthday, and he made a feast for all his officials. He restored the cupbearer to his position, but the baker he ordered hung, just as Joseph had interpreted.

The cupbearer forgot all about Joseph.

Two years passed and Pharaoh had a dream. He was standing near the Nile River when seven handsome, healthy looking cows suddenly emerged from the water and grazed in the marsh grass nearby. Then seven other cows, who were ugly and lean, came and stood next to the healthy cows, who were already on the riverbank. These ugly lean ones ate up the seven fat cows. Pharaoh woke up from this dream.

When he fell asleep again, he had another dream. He saw seven fat, good ears of grain growing on one stalk. Suddenly seven ears of grain that were empty and scorched by the east wind grew behind these. They swallowed up the seven good fat ears.

The next morning, Pharaoh was upset about his dreams and summoned all his wise men. He told them his dreams, but not one could give him a satisfactory interpretation.

Pharaoh's cupbearer spoke up. "When Pharaoh was angry with us, he placed me in prison along with the chief baker. We each dreamed a dream one night. There was a young Hebrew there. When we told him our dreams, he interpreted them for us. Everything was just as this man said it would be."

Pharaoh sent messengers to have Joseph brought to him. Joseph had his hair cut, and changed his clothes to appear before Pharaoh.

Pharaoh told Joseph he had dreamt two dreams, but that no one could interpret them for him. "I heard that when you hear a dream, you can interpret it," Pharaoh said.

"It is not by my own power," Joseph said to Pharaoh. "But God may provide an answer concerning your dreams."

So Pharaoh told his dreams to Joseph.

"Your dreams have a single meaning," Joseph told Pharaoh. "God has told you what you are to do. The seven healthy cows and the seven healthy ears represent seven good years. It is the same dream. The seven ugly cows and the seven empty ears of grain represent seven years of famine.

"There will be seven years of plenty in the land of Egypt. After these will come seven years of famine. Since Pharaoh has had the same dream twice, this means God will bring this soon.

"Select a man of wisdom and set him over the land of Egypt. Select overseers and organize the land so that during the seven years of plenty, some of the food will be gathered to be set aside in cities and stored there. These reserves of food will be guarded under Pharaoh's authority. When the seven years of famine come, you and all the people in Egypt will have this food that has been held in reserve."

Joseph's plan pleased Pharaoh and all his advisors. Pharaoh said to his advisors, "Could we find anyone else who has God's spirit in him as this Joseph does?"

So Pharaoh said to Joseph, "Since God has made all this known to you, there is no one with as much wisdom as you. You shall be in charge of my court and your command will direct the people. Only by the throne will I outrank you." Then Pharaoh took off his ring and placed it on Joseph's hand. He had him dressed in the finest garments and placed a gold chain around his neck. Joseph rode in his royal chariot, and they cried before him, "Kneel!"

Pharaoh said to Joseph, "I am Pharaoh. But without your say, no one will lift a hand or foot in all of Egypt."

MOSES AND THE BURNING BUSH

When Moses was a young man and had to flee from Pharaoh, he came to the land of Midian where he married Zipporah, daughter of Jethro. While Moses was in Midian, the burdens of the Israelites in Egypt worsened, and they cried out to God for help. God heard their groaning and remembered the covenant with Abraham and Isaac and Jacob.

At this time, Moses was tending his father-in-law Jethro's sheep. He led them to the edge of the desert and came to God's mountain, in the area of Horeb. An angel of God appeared to Moses in the heart of a fire that was in the middle of a thornbush. As he looked, Moses could see that the bush was on fire, but it was not burning up.

Moses thought, *I must go there and see this wonderful thing. Why doesn't the bush burn all up in this fire?*

God saw that Moses had noticed the burning bush and come to see it. God called out, "Moses! Moses!"

Moses answered, "Here I am."

God said, "Do not come closer. Take your sandals from off your feet for this ground on which you stand is holy. I am the God of your father, the God of Abraham, the God of Isaac, and the God of Jacob."

When he heard these words, Moses hid his face for he was afraid to look at God.

God said, "I have seen the suffering of My people in Egypt. I have heard how they cry out because of their cruel taskmasters. I have come down to rescue them from out of Egypt and bring them to a land flowing with milk and honey, the region of the Canaanites.

"Now you must go. I am sending you to Pharaoh to bring My people out of Egypt."

"Who am I that I should go to Pharaoh?" said Moses. "And how can I bring the Israelites out of Egypt?"

God said, "I will be with you. There will be proof that I have sent you when you succeed in getting the people out of Egypt. Then you and all the people will become my servants on this mountain."

"But when I come to the Israelites, and I say that the God of your ancestors has sent me to you, they will ask me what Your name is, and then what shall I say to them?"

"I will be who I will be," God said. "Tell them I Will Be sent you to them. They will listen to you. Then you and the elders of Israel will go to Pharaoh and say that the God of the Israelites is with you. Request a three day journey into the desert to offer sacrifices to God.

"I know this Pharaoh will not allow you to leave unless he is shown a greater might, so I will stretch out My hand and show Egypt various wonders. After that, they will let you go. And when you go, you will not go empty handed. You will take with you objects of silver and gold and clothing."

"But they will not believe me. They will say You never appeared to me."

"What is that in your hand?" said God.

"A staff."

"Throw it onto the ground."

So Moses threw the staff onto the ground, and it turned into a snake. Moses ran away from it.

"Reach out and grasp its tail," God said.

So Moses reached out and grasped its tail, and the snake turned back into a staff in his hand.

"This is so that they will believe that God appeared to you. Now put your hand inside your robe where your chest is."

When Moses placed his hand in his robe and took it out again, his hand was white as snow, as if he had leprosy.

"Place your hand inside your robe again," said God.

When Moses did so, and pulled his hand out again, it was not white, but it was as it had been before.

"If they still do not take you seriously with these two signs, then you will take some water from the Nile and spill it on the ground. It will turn to blood."

Moses continued to plead with God. "I am not one who is good with words. I have difficulty speaking."

"Who is it that gave you a mouth? Is it not I? God? Go and I will be with your mouth and teach you what to say."

"Please, God, send someone else," begged Moses.

God became angry with Moses. "Your brother Aaron the Levite knows how to speak. He is setting out to meet you. When he sees you, he will be glad. You will be able to speak to him and tell him what to say. And I will be with you and with Aaron your brother when you speak, and I will teach you what to do. He will speak for you to the people. And take with you this staff that you may perform the signs."

THE TEN PLAGUES

M oses took his wife and sons, mounted them on a donkey, and traveled back to the land of Egypt. He carried the rod God had given him in his hand.

His brother Aaron met him in the wilderness, and Moses told him of all that God had said to him and of the signs.

Then Moses and Aaron gathered all the elders of the Israelites. Aaron spoke all the words that God had said to Moses. He performed the signs before them, and they believed.

Moses and Aaron went to Pharaoh and said, "This is what God says, 'Let My people go so that they may have a celebration for Me in the wilderness.'"

But Pharaoh said, "Who is God that I should do this and let the Israelites go? I do not know God, and I will not let Israel go."

"The God of the Hebrews has been revealed to us. Please, let us go for a three-day journey into the desert and sacrifice to our God. Or God may strike us down with the plague or the sword."

Pharaoh answered, "Why do you distract the people from their tasks? Get back to your labors!"

That same day, Pharaoh ordered the taskmasters to no longer provide the Israelites with straw for making bricks. "Let them go and gather their own straw. But they must still make the same number of bricks as they did before, for they are lazy and that is why they want to go into the desert to celebrate for three days."

The taskmasters told this to the people who had to spread out all over Egypt to gather grain stalks for straw.

Now that their work was even harder than before, the people complained to Moses. "You have made us even more hateful in Pharaoh's eyes. You have put a sword in their hands for them to slay us with."

Moses returned to God and said, "Why do you mistreat Your people? Why did you send me?"

"You will see what I will do to Pharaoh," said God. "He will be forced to let them go.

"I am God. I revealed Myself to Abraham, to Isaac and to Jacob. I have heard the groaning of the Israelites and remember my covenant. Tell the Israelites that I will take them out of Egypt and free them from their slavery. I will deliver them with a demonstration of My power. I will take you to Myself as a nation, and you will know that I am the Lord your God. I will bring you into the land that I promised to Abraham and Isaac and Jacob, and give it to you as a heritage."

Moses told all that God had said to the Israelites, but, because of their suffering, they would not listen to him.

God spoke to Moses again. "You must repeat all that I command you, and your brother Aaron shall speak to Pharaoh to let the Israelites go. But I will make Pharaoh obstinate, and I will show many miraculous signs and wonders in Egypt. With great acts of judgments I will bring My people out of bondage, and Egypt will know that I am God.

"When Pharaoh speaks to you, he will ask you to prove yourself with a sign. Tell Aaron to throw down his rod, and it will become a snake."

Moses and Aaron came before Pharaoh, and did exactly as God

instructed them. Aaron threw down his rod, and it became a snake.

Pharaoh summoned his magicians and wise men. They in turn did the same. But Aaron's rod swallowed theirs. Yet Pharaoh's heart stiffened, and he did not listen to Moses and Aaron, as God had said.

"Go to Pharaoh in the morning when he goes out to the water," God said to Moses. "Take your rod with you, and stand on the banks of the Nile to meet him. Say to him again to let My people go so they may serve Me in the wilderness. And say that since you have not listened, God says that I am to strike the water in the Nile with this rod and it will turn to blood. The fish in the river will die, and no one will be able to drink its water."

Moses and Aaron did as God had said, and the Nile's water was transformed into blood. However, Pharaoh's magicians were able to do the same thing, and Pharaoh would not pay attention to Moses and Aaron, as God had said.

Seven days passed, and God said to Moses, "Go to Pharaoh and say to him, 'You should let My people go or I will strike your land with frogs. The Nile will swarm with frogs. They will enter your palace, your bedroom, and even into your bed. They will fill the homes of your people, their ovens and kneading bowls. They will be all over you!'"

So Aaron held his hand over the waters of Egypt, and the frogs came and covered the land.

Pharaoh's magicians were able to do the same thing and make frogs come onto the land.

Then Pharaoh called for Moses. "Please, plead with your God to get these frogs away from me and my people, and I will let the Israelites go serve God in the wilderness."

So Moses prayed to God, and the frogs in the houses and courtyards and fields died. But when Pharaoh saw that the land was quiet once again, he hardened his heart, and would not listen to Moses, as God had said.

God said to Moses, "Tell Aaron to hold out his rod, and strike the dust of the earth. It shall turn to lice throughout the land of Egypt." They did so, and the lice appeared, attacking man and animal. Pharaoh's magicians tried to produce lice, but they could not.

"It is the finger of God," the magicians told Pharaoh. But still Pharaoh was stubborn, and would not listen, as God had said.

God said to Moses, "Get up early in the morning, and present yourself to Pharaoh when he goes to the water. Say in My name, 'Let My people go and serve Me. If you do not, I will send swarms of harmful creatures to attack you and your people. But Goshen, where My people live, will not be harmed. Then you will know I am God.'"

God did this, and through all of Egypt, the land was devastated by the creatures.

Pharaoh called for Moses and Aaron. "I will let you go for three days, but do not go far. Plead for me!"

"I will plead with God that tomorrow the swarms of harmful creatures leave Egypt," said Moses. He did this and God removed the swarms of harmful creatures, but again Pharaoh hardened his heart, and would not let the people go.

God said to Moses, "Go to Pharaoh and say to him that if he doesn't let My people go to worship Me, I will strike all the livestock that is in the field with disease."

When Pharaoh refused, God sent the plague on the livestock of Egypt, the horses, the donkeys, the camels, cattle and sheep. Yet Pharaoh remained stubborn and would not let the people go.

God said to Moses and Aaron, "Take handfuls of soot from the furnace. Let Moses throw it upward in Pharaoh's sight. It shall become a fine dust which will settle all over the land and cause boils to form on both man and beast." They did this, and even the magicians were afflicted, but still Pharaoh would not let the people go.

God told Moses to tell Pharaoh that the next day God would cause a very heavy hail to rain down on the land. And God sent thunder and hail. Fire, too, streamed down to the ground. Only in Goshen, where the Israelites lived, was there no hail.

Pharaoh sent for Moses and Aaron. "Plead with God to end this thunder and hail. I will let you go."

Moses went outside the city, and spread his hands out to God. The thunder and hail stopped. But when Pharaoh saw that it had ended, he became stubborn, and he would not let the Israelites go.

Then Moses and Aaron went to Pharaoh and said, "If you refuse to let the people go, tomorrow God will bring locusts onto the land, and they shall eat away all your trees that grow in the field, and fill your houses."

"Let the men go to worship God," said Pharaoh.

"We will all go," said Moses. "Young and old, sons and daughters, flocks and herds for we must observe God's festival."

And Moses and Aaron were expelled from Pharaoh's presence.

So Moses held his rod over the land, and the Lord drove an east wind day and night that brought the locusts. They invaded all of Egypt in a thick mass, and darkened it. They ate up all the grasses and all the fruit of the trees that the hail had left, so there was nothing green.

Again Pharaoh called Moses, and again Moses pleaded with God to end the plague. But God made Pharaoh stubborn, and he would not let the people go.

Then God told Moses to lift his arm toward the sky that a great darkness would fall upon the land, a darkness that could be touched. Moses held out his arm toward the sky, and the darkness descended on the land for three days.

Pharaoh said to Moses, "Go! Worship the Lord! Even your children may go, but leave your flocks behind."

"We must bring our flocks for the sacrifice to God," Moses answered.

"Be gone from me then," said Pharaoh. "The moment you look upon my face again, you shall die!"

"I shall not see your face again!" said Moses.

"I will bring but one more plague upon Pharaoh and Egypt," said God. "Then Pharaoh will let you go. Toward midnight I will go among the Egyptians, and every first-born in the land will die, from the first-born of Pharaoh who sits on the throne to the first born of the slave, and the cattle. There shall be a loud cry in Egypt.

"But you must speak to the whole community of Israel, and tell them that each household must take a lamb and kill it. Take the blood and place it on the two doorposts and on the beam above the door of their houses. And they shall eat of it with unleavened bread and bitter herbs. None of you shall go outside the door of the house until morning. The blood on your houses will be a sign. When I see it, I will pass over you so that no plague will destroy you. You shall remember this day and celebrate it as a festival to God throughout the ages."

And the Israelites did just as God had commanded.

In the middle of the night, God struck down all the first-born in the land of Egypt. There was such a loud cry in the land that Pharaoh called for Moses and Aaron in the night. He told them to leave with all the Israelites and all their flocks.

The people took their dough before it had leavened, their kneading bowls wrapped in their cloaks on their shoulders, and left Egypt.

CROSSING THE SEA

When the Israelites left Egypt, they journeyed from Raamses to Succot, about six hundred thousand adult males, three million people in all, with sheep and cattle. And they baked unleavened cakes of the dough they had carried out of Egypt. The Israelites had been in Egypt for four hundred and thirty years.

And Moses said to the people, "Remember this day as the day you left Egypt, the place of slavery, when God brought you out with a mighty hand. You shall eat no leaven bread. When God brings you into the land of the Canaanites, Hittites, Amorites, Hivites and Yebusites, to a land flowing with milk and honey, as God promised your ancestors, you will observe this practice. For seven days you will eat unleavened bread and on the seventh day make a festival to God."

Now God led the Israelites by way of the desert to the Red Sea to avoid the land of the Philistines. In this way, the people would not have to fight, and perhaps have a change of heart and want to return to Egypt.

Moses brought Joseph's remains out of Egypt with him.

And God went before them by day in a pillar of cloud to guide them, and in a pillar of fire by night to give them light. And they traveled both in the day and in the night.

When Pharaoh was told that the Israelites had fled, his heart changed. "What have we done?" he said. "How could we release Israel from serving us?"

Pharaoh harnessed his chariot, and took his people with him, the entire chariot corps of Egypt and the infantry. They overtook the Israelites while they were camping by the sea. When the Israelites looked up, they saw the Egyptians, and they became very frightened.

"Weren't there enough graves in Egypt?" the people cried out to Moses. "Why did you bring us here to die in the desert? It would have been better to stay and be slaves in Egypt than to die in the desert!"

"Don't be afraid," Moses answered them. "Stand firm. You might be seeing the Egyptians today, but you will not see them tomorrow. God will fight for you."

Then God told Moses to tell the Israelites to move forward, and to lift his rod and extend his hand over the sea. God's angel that had been traveling in front of the Israelites, moved and went behind the camp. Thus the pillar of cloud moved behind the people, between them and Pharaoh. There was cloud and darkness that night, and the Egyptians and Israelites could not see each other or come near one another.

Moses extended his hand over the sea. God drove back the sea with a strong east wind all that night, and turned the seabed into dry land. The waters split, and the Israelites entered the sea on dry land. The water was on their right and on their left like two walls.

The Egyptians pursued them. All of Pharaoh's horses, chariots and cavalry went into the middle of the sea. Toward the end of that night, God struck at the Egyptian army with the pillar of fire and cloud. The Egyptian army panicked, and its chariot wheels bogged down in the seabed.

"Let us flee from the Israelites," the Egyptians called out.

God said to Moses, "Extend your hand over the sea, and the waters will come back to cover the Egyptians."

Just before morning, Moses extended his hand over the sea, and the waters returned as they had been. They covered all the Egyptians. Not a single one remained. But the Israelites marched through the sea onto dry ground. Thus God rescued the Israelites, and they saw the great power of God.

Then Moses and the Israelites sang a song to God:

I will sing to God for God has triumphed

Horse and rider God has thrown into the sea

My strength and song is God

God is my deliverance.

Who is like You, God

Majestic in holiness

Doing wonders

God will reign forever and ever!

And Miriam the prophetess, Aaron's sister, took a drum in her hand, and all the women followed her with dancing and drumming. Miriam led them in singing, "Sing to the Lord, for God has triumphed, horse and rider has God hurled into the Sea."

THE TEN COMMANDMENTS

I n the third month after the Israelites left Egypt, on the first day of the month, they entered the wilderness of Sinai, and camped there in front of the mountain. Moses went up to God, and God called to him, "Say to the people, 'You have seen what I did to the Egyptians, how I bore you on eagles' wings, and brought you to Me. If you obey Me and keep My covenant, you shall be beloved to Me and a holy people.'"

Moses summoned the elders and told them what God had said. And the people answered, every one, "All that God has said, we will do."

When Moses told this to God, God said, "I will come to you in a thick cloud, so that all the people will hear when I speak to you, and they will believe in you. Tell the people to wash and purify themselves, for on the third day, I will descend on Mount Sinai before all the people. Set boundaries all around so the people do not touch the border of the mountain or go up it. When the ram's horn sounds a long blast, then they may go up the mountain."

Moses went down to the people. He warned them to stay pure and wash their clothes. On the third day, there was thunder and lightning in the morning. A heavy cloud lay on the mountain. A loud blast of the ram's horn pierced the air and the people trembled. Moses led the people out of the camp to meet God. They stood at the foot of the mountain.

Mount Sinai was covered with smoke because of the presence of God. God was in the fire. And the whole mountain shook violently. The sound of the ram's horn grew louder and louder. Then Moses spoke, and God answered with these words, "I am God, your God, who brought you out of the land of Egypt, out of slavery.

"You shall have no other Gods before Me nor make for yourselves a graven image. You shall not bow down to them or serve them.

"You shall not swear falsely by the Name of God.

"Remember the Sabbath day and keep it holy. For six days you shall labor and do all your work, but the seventh day is a Sabbath to the Lord, and you shall not do any work. For in six days, God made heaven, and earth, and sea, and all that is in them. On the seventh day, God rested. So God blessed the seventh day and made it holy.

"Honor your father and mother that you will live long on the land that God is giving you.

"You shall not murder.

"You shall not commit adultery.

"You shall not steal.

"You shall not testify falsely against your neighbor.

"You shall not be envious of your neighbor, or of anything that belongs to your neighbor."

"You speak to us and we will obey," they said to Moses. "But don't let God speak to us anymore or we may die."

"Do not be afraid," said Moses. "God has only come to raise you up, and so that you will not wander astray."

The people stayed at a distance while Moses entered the glowing mist where God was.

THE GOLDEN CALF

ater, after the people witnessed the thunder and lightning, and heard the voice of God speak to them, God said to Moses, "Come up to Me, to the mountain, and stay there. I will give you the stone tablets on which I have inscribed the teachings and commandments to instruct the people."

Moses and his attendant Joshua set out. Moses said to the elders, "Wait here for us until we return. Aaron and Hur are with you. If anyone has a problem, go to them."

And Moses went up on God's mountain. As soon as he reached the mountaintop, the cloud covered the mountain. To the Israelites, the Presence of God on the mountain was like a devouring flame. Moses went into the cloud and remained on the mountain forty days and forty nights.

The people began to see that Moses was taking a long time to come down from the mountain, and they gathered around Aaron. "Make us a god to lead us. We don't know what happened to Moses, who led us out of Egypt."

"Take off the gold rings that are on the ears of your wives and sons and daughters, and bring them to me," said Aaron.

The people took off their rings and brought them to Aaron. He had them molded into the form of a calf. Some of the people said, "This is your god who brought you out of Egypt."

When Aaron saw this, he built an altar before it, and said, "Tomorrow will be a festival to the Lord."

Early the next morning, the people made offerings on the altar, and sat down to eat and drink.

God said to Moses, "Hurry back down for the people you brought out of Egypt have left the path that I have shown them. They have made for themselves a golden calf and bowed down to it. They are saying it is this calf who has brought them out of Egypt."

Moses turned around and went down the mountain with the two tablets of stone in his hands. The tablets were God's work, and the writing was God's writing.

Joshua, who waited for Moses, heard the sound of the people, and when he saw Moses coming down the mountain, said to him, "It sounds as if a war is going on in the camp."

"No, I think it is the sound of singing," Moses answered.

As Moses came closer to the camp, and actually saw the golden calf and the dancing, he grew very angry. He lifted up the tablets and threw them, shattering them to pieces at the base of the mountain. Then he took the calf that the people had made, and burned it in a fire. He ground what was left into a fine powder, and made the people drink it.

"What did the people do to you, that you allowed them to commit such a great sin?" Moses said to Aaron.

"Do not be angry," said Aaron. "You know that the people have bad tendencies. They asked me to make them a god to lead them since they did not know what happened to you. I asked them who had gold, and collected it, and made this calf."

Moses realized that the people were out of control, and that Aaron had actually only done a small part of what some of the people had demanded.

Moses stood at the gate of the camp and said, "Whoever is on the side of the Lord, come to me." And all the sons of Levi gathered to him. Moses instructed them to put on their swords, and kill all those involved in the making of the false god, the golden calf. They did as Moses said, and Moses gave the sons of Levi a special blessing. The next day Moses told the people, "You have committed a terrible sin by making this idol. Now I will go back up the mountain to God and ask for God's forgiveness."

When Moses went up the mountain again, God told him that he would send an angel to lead the people to the land flowing with milk and honey, but that God would not go with them on the journey because of their stubbornness. When the people heard this news, they began to mourn.

Moses took his tent and set it outside the camp. He called it the meeting tent. Whoever sought God would go there. Whenever Moses went out to the tent, all the people would stand near their own tent, watching him. When he entered the tent, a pillar of cloud would descend at the tent's entrance, and God would speak to Moses, just as a person speaks to a close friend.

Moses went into the Tent of Meeting and pleaded with God to stay among the people. "Unless You go in the lead, do not make us leave this place."

"I will do this thing that you have asked," God said, "because you have truly gained My favor. I will lead you. My presence will lighten your burden."

"Please, let me see Your Presence," begged Moses.

"I will make My goodness pass before you, and reveal to you My Name. But you cannot see My face. People cannot see My face and live. There is a special place where you can stand on the mountain. I will shield you until I have passed by. And you will behold a glimmer of Me.

"Before you come up the mountain, carve two stone tablets like the first set. I will write on these the same words that were on the first tablets that you broke."

So Moses carved the two tablets as God had said, and in the morning, he climbed up the mountain to see God.

God came down in a cloud and passed before Moses. And Moses quickly bowed his head in homage to the One.

After forty days and forty nights, when God wrote upon the tablets the words of the commandments, Moses came down from the mountain. He did not realize that his face shown with a brilliant light because God had spoken to him. But Aaron and all the Israelites saw this radiance on Moses' face.

And Moses told the people all that God commanded them to do.

DAVID AND GOLIATH

T he Philistines assembled their forces for battle on one hill, and Saul, King of Israel, and his men massed and encamped on the opposite hill. There was a ravine between them. Then a Philistine, huge like a giant with a bronze helmet on his head, a bronze breastplate, a javelin and spear stepped forward.

He called out to the soldiers of Israel. "I am the Philistine champion. Choose one of your men and let him come against me. If he bests me in battle and kills me, then we will become your slaves. If I best him and kill him, you shall be our slaves and serve us. I defy you, ranks of Israel. Get me a man and let's fight it out!"

When Saul and all Israel heard this Philistine's words, they were terrified. The Philistine stepped forward morning and evening and announced his challenge for forty days.

Now Jesse of Bethlehem had eight sons, and three of them were serving with King Saul in the war with the Philistines. David, the youngest of the sons of Jesse, went back and forth from his home where he was a shepherd to the encampment to bring provisions to his brothers.

One time, when David reached the camp where his brothers were, he left the provisions with the man in charge and ran toward the battle line to greet them. While he was talking to them, Goliath, the Philistine champion, stepped forward. David heard his words.

"Who is that Philistine that he dares to defy the soldiers of the living God?" David asked the terrified men around him.

"That giant comes out to defy Israel," they told him. "The man who kills Goliath will be rewarded by the King with great riches. He will also give him his daughter in marriage."

The things that David said among the men were reported to Saul who called David over to him.

"Let no man's courage fail him," David said to the King. "Your servant will go and fight that Philistine!"

"But you are only a boy," said the King. "He has been a warrior from his youth!"

"Your servant has been tending his father's sheep," answered David. "If a lion or a bear came and carried off an animal from the flock, I would go after it and fight it and rescue the animal from its mouth. If it attacked me, I would grab it by the beard and strike it down. I have killed both lion and bear. The Philistine will end up like one of them for he has defied the living God. The Lord who saved me from lion and bear will also save me from the Philistine."

"Then go," said Saul. "May the Lord be with you!"

Saul clothed David in his own garments and placed a bronze helmet on his head. He fastened a breastplate on him and gave him a sword. David tried to walk, but couldn't. He was not used to all these pieces of armor.

He took them off. Then he picked up his stick and walked to the nearby wadi where he chose a few smooth stones. He put these in the pocket of his shepherd's bag. Sling in hand, he went to meet the Philistine.

When the Philistine caught sight of David, he mocked him saying, "Am I a dog that you come against me with sticks? Come closer and I will give your flesh to the birds of the sky and the beasts of the field."

"You come against me with sword and spear and javelin," said David. "But I come against you in the name of the Lord of Hosts. This very day, God will deliver you into my hands"

As the Philistine advanced, David ran up to the battle line to face him. David put his hand in his bag. He took out a stone and slung it. It struck the Philistine in the forehead and he fell face down on the ground. David, who had no sword, had killed the giant.

When the Philistines saw that their champion was dead, they ran away. The men of Israel pursued them all the way to the gates of Ekron.

DAVID AND MICHAL

After David killed the giant Goliath, Saul would not let him return to his father's house. David went out with Saul's troops and was successful on every mission on which the King sent him. Saul put him in command of all the soldiers.

When the troops returned home from the battles with the Philistines, the women of all the towns of Israel came out dancing and singing to greet the King.

They sang, "Saul has slain his thousands, David his tens of thousands."

Saul became very jealous of David, and from that day on watched him carefully. "All he lacks is the kingship," Saul said.

Now Michal, daughter of Saul, fell in love with David, and this was reported to the King. Saul was pleased. *She can serve as a snare for David,* Saul thought, *so that the Philistines may kill him.*

To David, Saul said, "You may become my son-in-law and marry my daughter Michal. I desire no other bride price than that you kill one hundred Philistines and bring me proof of this deed." Secretly Saul hoped that David would be killed at the hands of the Philistines.

So David went out with his men and killed two hundred Philistines, and Saul gave him his daughter Michal in marriage. When Saul realized that the Lord was with David and that his daughter truly loved her husband, he grew even more afraid of David.

Saul's son Jonathan was very fond of David, and when the King told Jonathan and all his courtiers to kill David, Jonathan went to tell David. "My father means to kill you," he said. "Be careful tomorrow. Go to a secret place and hide. I will go out and stand next to my father in the field near where you will be hiding. I will speak to him about you. If I learn anything, I will tell you."

So Jonathan went to his father and spoke well of David to him, and Saul agreed not to have David put to death. Jonathan told David the news, and brought him to his father where David served the King as he had before.

Once again fighting broke out with the Philistines, however, and David was victorious against them. The Philistines fled before him. When he returned, David went to Saul to play the harp for the King, as he was used to doing. But the King's jealousy rose in him when he saw David because of all his victories and popularity with the people. Saul reached for the spear that was near him and tried to pin David to the wall with it. David fled and got away.

That night, Saul sent messengers to David's home to keep watch there and kill David in the morning. David's wife Michal said, "Do you see the my father's men in hiding around the house? You must run for your life tonight or you will be killed tomorrow."

So Michal let David down by the window, and he was able to escape. Then she took a statue and laid it on the bed. She covered it with a cloth. At its head she put a net of goat's hair.

When Saul sent his messengers to seize David, she said,"He is sick. He cannot come with you."

Saul sent the messengers back to see David for themselves. "Bring him up to me in the bed," Saul said. "So he may be put to death."

The messengers returned to David's house. When they went to the bed, they found the statue with the net of goat's hair at its head.

Saul was very angry when he heard of the trick Michal had played on him. "Why did you do this and let my enemy get away safely?"

Michal lied to her father, and said, "I did this because David said he would kill me if I didn't help him."

With Michal's help, David had enough time to make good his escape from Saul. He came to the Prophet Samuel at Ramah and told him all that Saul had done to him.

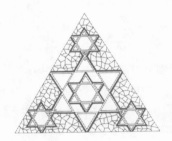

JONAH

T he word of the Lord came to Jonah, son of Amittai. "Go at once to the great city of Nineveh and tell them I know of their wickedness."

Instead of going toward Nineveh, Jonah fled from God's bidding toward Tarshish. In the city of Joppa he found a ship that was going there. He paid for the fare and went aboard to sail away from the service of the Lord.

But God sent a mighty wind onto the sea. Such a great storm came up that the ship was in danger. Because they were frightened, the sailors cried out, each to his own god. They threw all the ship's cargo overboard, trying to make it lighter. In the meantime, Jonah had gone down to the ship's hold where he had fallen asleep.

The captain found him there. "How can you be sleeping so soundly! Get up and call upon your God. Maybe this God will be kind to us and save us."

The sailors said to each other, "Let's cast lots and find out who has caused this misfortune to fall on us."

And so they cast lots, and the lot fell on Jonah.

"Tell us who you are and where you are from, you who have brought this misfortune on us," they said to him.

"I am a Hebrew and worship God who made sea and land."

"What is it you have done?"

Jonah told them that he was fleeing the service of the Lord.

"What must we do then to make the sea calm?" they asked Jonah.

"Throw me overboard," he told the frightened sailors.

Even in their terror, the men were reluctant to do this. They tried once again to row to the shore, but they could not. The sea was growing more and more stormy. Then they cried out, "Oh, please Lord, don't let us die on account of this man's life. Don't hold us guilty of killing an innocent person!" And when they threw Jonah overboard, the sea grew calm.

God provided a big fish to swallow Jonah, and Jonah was in the fish's belly three days and three nights. Jonah prayed to God from the fish's belly, and God heard Jonah. God commanded the fish to spew Jonah out onto dry land.

For a second time, the word of God came to Jonah to go to Nineveh.

Nineveh was a very large city, a three days' walk across. Jonah made his way into the city and shouted, "Forty days more and Nineveh will be overthrown!"

The people in Nineveh believed God and issued a fast. No one ate or drank. They put on mourning clothes and sat in ashes. Even the king of Nineveh did this. Throughout the city, the king's decree was proclaimed. "Let all turn from their evil ways and cry to God. Perhaps then we will not perish."

God saw what they did and did not destroy the city.

But Jonah was displeased. "Oh God, this is why I fled to Tarshish. I know You are a compassionate and forgiving God. And now you have forgiven the people of Nineveh after I have gone through the city warning of their destruction. Please, God, take my life for I would rather die than live."

"Are you that upset?" asked God.

Jonah left the city and found a place to make a shelter. He sat there in the shade to see what would happen to the city. God provided a plant that grew up over Jonah and made shade for his head. Jonah was very happy about the plant. But the next day, God sent a worm that attacked the plant so that it withered and died. When the sun rose, it beat down on Jonah's head and he felt faint. Once again he begged God for death.

"Are you so upset about the plant?"

"Yes," said Jonah.

"You cared about the plant," God said, "which you did not plant and grow, but which appeared overnight and died overnight. Should I not care about Nineveh in which live more than a hundred and twenty thousand persons who do not know their right hand from their left?"

NAOMI AND RUTH

During the time of famine, Elimelech, his wife Naomi, and their two sons left Bethlehem, in Judah, and came to the country of Moab to dwell there. Elimelech died and his two sons married Moabite women. One was named Orpah, and the other Ruth. About ten years later, the two sons died. After this, Naomi heard there was food in Bethlehem. So Naomi and her two daughters-in-law left Moab to travel there.

On the way, Naomi said to Orpah and Ruth, "Turn back, each of you to your mother's house. May God deal kindly with you as you have dealt with my family and me. And may you each find a husband." She then kissed them both farewell.

"No, we want to return with you to your people," they said through tears.

"Why should you go with me?" Naomi said. "I have no more sons to give you to marry."

So Orpah kissed her mother-in-law farewell, but Ruth clung to her.

"Go follow your sister-in-law," said Naomi.

"Do not urge me to leave you, for wherever you go, I will go. Wherever you dwell, I will dwell. Your people will be my people, and your God my God," Ruth said.

Naomi stopped arguing with Ruth, and the two women traveled until they reached Bethlehem, just at the beginning of the barley harvest.

The people of Bethlehem were excited to see Naomi and Ruth

"Can this be Naomi?" they asked.

"Don't call me Naomi," she answered. "Call me Marah because God has made my lot bitter. I went away full and I return empty."

One day Ruth said to Naomi, "I will go to the fields and glean among the ears of grain so that I can bring back something for us to eat."

"Yes, daughter, go," said Naomi.

So Ruth gleaned among the ears of grain, picking up the leftovers after the reapers went through. As luck would have it, the field belonged to Boaz, a kinsman of Naomi's. Boaz saw Ruth gleaning in his fields and asked the reapers who she was.

"She is a Moabite girl who returned to Bethlehem with Naomi," they told him. "She has been on her feet all day gathering among the sheaves behind us. She has rested very little in the hut."

"Listen to me, daughter," Boaz said to Ruth. "You don't need to glean in any other fields. Stay here behind my reapers. None of my workers will harm you. And when you are thirsty, drink some of the water that my workers have drawn."

"Why are you so kind to me when I am a foreigner?" Ruth asked.

"I have heard of your loyalty to my relative Naomi after her husband and sons died," he told her. "May God reward your deeds."

"You are most generous," said Ruth.

Then Boaz told his workers, "You are not only to let her glean among the sheaves, but you must also pull up some stalks of grain and leave them for her to take."

Ruth gleaned in the field until evening.

When Naomi saw how much grain Ruth brought home with her from the fields, she asked, "Where did you glean today? Blessed be he who was so generous to you."

Ruth told her mother-in-law of all that had happened with their kinsman Boaz in his fields, and how kind he had been to her.

"Daughter, I must seek a home for you where you will be happy," Naomi said to Ruth. "Tonight, Boaz will be winnowing barley on the threshing floor to separate the chaff from the grain. Bathe, anoint yourself with oil, and dress in your finest clothes. Then go down to the threshing floor to meet him. Tell him you wish to join his household as his wife."

Ruth did everything her mother-in-law told her to do, and went down to the threshing floor where Boaz saw her.

Boaz was pleased with all that Ruth said to him. "You are indeed loyal! First to Naomi and now to me, your kinsman. You might have turned to younger men, but you have come to me. Have no fear. I will do in your behalf whatever you ask. All the elders here know what a fine woman you are." And Boaz filled her shawl that she was wearing with six measures of barley to take back with her.

"How is it with you, daughter?" said Naomi when Ruth returned from the threshing floor.

"Boaz gave me this barley," she said. "He did not want me to go back to you empty-handed."

"Stay here, daughter," Naomi said, "Boaz will come and tell us his plans."

Boaz did come to see Ruth and Naomi, and Ruth became his wife. Ruth bore a son to Boaz, a grandson to Naomi. Naomi took such delight in the child that she became its foster mother, and the neighbors joked and said, "A son is born to Naomi." That is how close she was with Ruth's child. His name was Obed. He in turn became the father of Jesse, who was the father of David, who became king of Israel.

TALMUD AND MIDRASH

THE ALPHABET AND THE CREATION OF THE WORLD

ust as God was about to create the world, the twenty-two letters of the Hebrew alphabet leapt off God's crown where they were engraved with flaming fire. They were excited. They were going to be used to write the holy Torah and create the world! What an important job! And one of them would be chosen by God to begin the holy Torah and the creation! Which letter would it be? Which one would be first?

The letters clamored for attention! "Choose me! Choose me!" they each cried.

The letter Tav jumped in front of all the others. "Dear God, may it be Your will to create the world and begin the Torah with me," Tav begged. "After all, I begin the beloved word Torah, the very laws You will give Moses on Mount Sinai."

"I'm afraid not," God replied. "Because one day, many years from now when the Second Temple is destroyed, you will be used as a sign of death. I cannot begin Creation and the Torah with a letter that will signify death."

Sadly, the letter Tav withdrew.

The letter Shin came to the front of all the letters.

"Oh, God, please create the world through me. Your own name, Shaddai, begins with me!"

"Yes, but so does the word *sheker*, falsehood," said God. "I cannot begin the world and the Torah with a letter that starts the word for lie. I want to build the world and the Torah on truth."

The letter Raish stepped forward because it had such a strong argument.

"Oh, God, begin the world and the Torah with me! I am the first letter in the word *rachum*, merciful, and the word *rafua* for healing, two very important words."

"Yes, you are a very important letter," agreed God. "But I must point out to you that you also begin the word for evil person, *rasha*, and so I cannot begin with you."

"What about me," called out the letter Kuf. "I begin the word *kadosh*, holy. What a wonderful way to begin the world and the Torah—with holiness."

"Don't you remember that you also begin the word *kelalah* for curse?" answered God.

And so it continued. One by one the letters stepped up to God's throne to give their argument about why they should be first. Mem pointed out how it began the word for *melech*, king, but God said it also began *mechumah*, confusion. Yod was the first letter in *Yah*, God's name, but it also began *yetzer harah*, the evil inclination. Zayin was the first letter in the word *zakor*, remembrance, but it was also the first letter in the word for weapon.

Finally only two letters were left, the Aleph and the Bet. They had been waiting patiently, but were becoming more and more nervous. Which one of them would be chosen to begin creation and the Torah?

Bait stepped forward. "Oh, God, may it be Your will to create the world and the Torah through me. I begin the word *baruch*, blessed, and by beginning with me, Your children will sing your praises every day."

"Yes," God answered the letter Bait. "I will begin the creation of the world and the Torah with you. I want everyone to know that I love each one of them and bless them. And so I will begin with the word *berayshit*, in the beginning."

When the letter Aleph heard God's choice, it quietly walked away, never having argued why it was the best and should be chosen.

"Aleph," called God. "I have not forgotten you."

"Oh, but I am not such an important letter," replied the Aleph.

"That is not so. You will see. Because you were so modest and waited, I will begin the Ten Commandments, which Moses will receive on Mount Sinai, with you. The first words of the Ten Commandments will be *Anochi Hashem*, I am God. See how important you are, Aleph? You are the king of all the letters, for you and I are one!"

AM I MY BROTHER'S KEEPER?

ain was Adam and Eve's oldest son, and Abel was their youngest. As youths, the two brothers often quarreled, so much so that Adam trained them in different occupations. Cain became a worker of the soil and Abel a shepherd.

Real trouble came one day when the brothers were grown and made offerings to God. Abel picked only the best of his flocks to sacrifice to God, while Cain first ate a meal, and then offered some leftovers as his sacrifice to God. God accepted Abel's offering by sending a heavenly fire down to consume it, but God rejected Cain's offering. Cain was angry and sad, and did not understand why God had not accepted his offering also.

God said to Cain, "Why are you so angry and sad? If you do what is right, you shall be happy. If you do not do what is right, you will fall into evil ways. It all depends on whether you listen to the evil inclination and let it be your master, or whether you do not listen to it and so become its master."

But Cain still felt that he had been wronged. His anger seethed inside him, and he quarreled yet again with his brother Abel. "Why did God accept your sacrifice and not mine? That isn't fair."

"If your offering had been the best of your fields, as mine was the best of my flocks, God would have accepted it," Abel tried to explain. But Cain would not hear this.

Cain's anger erupted one day when one of Abel's sheep wandered into a field Cain had planted and trampled it. Cain called out in a rage, "What right do you have to live upon my land and let your sheep pasture on it? Get off!"

"Yes, I live on the land that you tend and my sheep pasture on it, but I let you wear wool from my sheep and eat of their flesh. Pay me for these that you use. Then I will fly off the land as you ask, if I can," answered Abel.

Abel's words only made Cain angrier. He threw himself on his brother and slew him.

Then God called out to Cain. "Where is your brother Abel?"

And Cain answered, "I do not know. Am I my brother's keeper?"

"What have you done?" God said. "Your brother's blood cries out to me from the earth."

"But You are God. Why did you permit me to murder him?"

"I made you with a brain and a soul," God answered. "You would be only a puppet if I were to direct your every action. You are responsible for what you do. As your punishment for this act, you shall be a fugitive from this day on and wander the earth."

Cain argued with God again. "How will I bear such a punishment? I am to be isolated in the world and whoever finds me will kill me. Again You are not fair. I have never seen anyone killed before. How was I to know that the stones I threw at Abel would kill him?"

"I will do this for you," said God. "Since you are the first to shed blood and had no one to instruct you. I will make a mark on you for all to see so that no one, person or beast, will kill you." And God inscribed one letter of God's Holy name on Cain's forehead for this sign.

THE TOWER

In the days after Noah, the people multiplied and filled the earth as God had commanded. All of these peoples spoke the same language.

People came from the east and discovered a valley in the land of Shinar. They settled there. They saw it was a good land, and said to one another, "Let us mold bricks and fire them to make them hard. We will build a magnificent city. Within this city we will construct a tower whose top shall reach the sky. In this way, we can make a great name for ourselves. We will be very powerful and known far and wide."

The rabbis said it was King Nimrod who ordered the tower built with six hundred thousand workers. He wanted his name inscribed on its bricks so he would be remembered forever. King Nimrod and his people were so prosperous that they no longer put their trust in God. They thought they were as good as God, and worthy of dwelling in the heavens themselves. So sure were they of themselves and their power that some of them even suggested setting up their idols in heaven, while others wanted to wage war on the heavens with bows and spears.

King Nimrod planned the tower with steps on the east side by which the people could ascend to the heavens, and steps on the west to go down.

Many, many years passed with the work on the tower. The tower grew so tall that it took a year just to reach the top, and a brick became more precious to the builders than a human life. If a brick fell to the ground, all the workers mourned because it would take a whole year to bring up another one. These workers lived on the tower all their lives, and raised their families on it without ever setting foot on the ground below. And they would shoot arrows toward heaven, thinking they were so powerful that they could conquer it.

God knew all this and went down to look at this city with its tower already reaching higher and higher. God saw these arrogant people and their King Nimrod who believed they could reach the heavens with their bricks and mortar. They were one people who spoke one language and there was nothing they would not try to do. So God decided to confuse their speech. Then one could not understand the other.

When one worker asked for mortar, the other gave him a brick. Then one became angry with the other and they fought.

One said, "Let us put that brick here," and the other would not know if he was talking of bricks or sheep or dinner. They could not plan or give directions to each other. They could not work together. There was so much confusion, such a babel that the people could not finish building the city or the tower. And Nimrod could not become the king of all the world. His tower became the Tower of Babel, abandoned and unfinished in the center of the city.

Then God scattered all of Nimrod's people over the face of the earth. From that time to this, there have been many languages among the peoples, a babel of languages.

THE IDOL SMASHER

When Abraham was still a small boy, and called Abram, he looked up one night at the sky and marveled at how beautiful the stars and the moon were. *They must be gods*, he thought, and bowed down low before them to worship them. But when the dawn came, and he could no longer see the stars and the moon, he thought that the sun with its warmth and light had driven them away. Surely the sun was a god, and he bowed down before the sun to worship it.

Clouds came and hid the sun's light, and Abram realized that these were but part of the wonders of the world. There must be a ruler over all the world, he thought. One who set all these wonders in motion, the stars and the moon, the sun, the clouds and the wind, and all the creatures of the earth. And Abram decided then that he would only worship this One Creator of the universe.

Abram's father Terah made idols for his living out of different materials, wood, silver, gold, and copper. Some looked human and some looked like animals.

After his discovery of the One God, Abram told his father Terah that he would not bow down to these idols any longer. He told him he should stop bowing down to the idols too, but his father would not listen to him.

One day when Terah was ill, he gave Abram a bag of idols to sell in the marketplace. A man came up to Abram wanting to buy one of the idols.

"How much is that big one?" said the man.

"Three coins," said Abram. Then he asked, "How old are you?"

"Thirty years old," said the man, holding out the three coins.

"You are thirty years old and you want to worship this idol which my father made out of wood just yesterday?"

Surprised, the man left quickly, not knowing what to say in response.

Next an old woman came by and wanted an idol too. "Yesterday some thieves came into my house and stole my idol, so now I need to buy another. How much is that one?" she asked, pointing to a fierce beast of an idol.

"That one is five coins," said Abram. "But I want to ask you this. If your idol could not even protect himself, how do you think it could protect you, even if it looks as fierce as this one does?"

And this customer, too, left in a hurry, without buying an idol, not knowing how to answer this idol maker's son.

Next Abram took a rope and wound it around the necks of the idols so he could drag them through the streets crying out, "Who will buy an idol to worship when worshipping it does no good to the idol or the worshipper? This idol has a mouth but cannot speak. It has eyes but cannot see. It has feet but cannot walk. It has ears but cannot hear."

The people all around stood and watched. They did not know what to make of Abram or his words. They had never heard of the One God.

When Abram went back to the idol shop, he took an axe and smashed every single idol, big and little. Then he took the axe and placed it in the hand of the largest idol. When his father came back and saw all the damage, he asked Abram, "Who did this? Who destroyed all the idols?"

Abram pointed to the biggest idol and said, "It was that one. He took the axe and smashed all the ones around him. See, he still has the axe in his hand. If you do not believe me, ask him yourself, and he will tell you this is so."

"Stop making fun of me!" said his father angrily. "You know that idols cannot move, let alone hit each other or tell their story. They are made only of wood and metal and stone."

"That is what I am trying to tell you, father. These idols which you worship have no power! There is only one God Who made the heavens and the earth and has power over all."

SHIFRA AND PUAH

And a new Pharaoh rose up in Egypt who knew not Joseph. He said to his people, "The children of Israel are too numerous and mighty. We must deal wisely with them for if a war were to come, they could join our enemies and fight against us."

The Egyptians set taskmasters over the children of Israel to make them do hard labor and build store-cities for Pharaoh. They would force too heavy a load on the young, or make an old man or woman carry the load that only a strong person in their prime could carry. But the harder they were oppressed, the greater in numbers did they grow. The Egyptians were not able to break the spirit of the Israelites. The Rabbis say that the Israelites did not give up hope because of four things: they did not change their names; they never stopped using their own language; they did not tell on one another to the taskmasters; and they married their own people.

Now, not only was Pharaoh angry that the children of Israel continued to grow numerous, but his advisors told him that they saw a prophecy in the stars. A baby boy would soon be born to the Israelites who would free all the slaves, and lead them out of Egypt.

A dream that Pharaoh dreamt foretold the same event. In the dream Pharaoh sat on his throne. When he lifted up his eyes, he saw all the elders, nobles and great ones of Egypt being tied together. They were placed on one scale of a huge balance while a tender young goat was put on the other scale. Surprisingly the scale with the young goat hung lower than the other scale with all the bound Egyptians. After Pharaoh rose early the next morning, he called all his advisors and told them of this dream. They were frightened.

Balaam the son of Beor spoke. "Pharaoh's dream means a great evil will spring up against Egypt. A son will be born to Israel who will destroy our land and many of its people. He will bring the Israelite slaves out of Egypt to freedom. Pharaoh, you must not let this happen."

So Pharaoh decided to go to the Hebrew midwives Shifra and Puah, who delivered all the babies, and said to them, "You must see to it that no more boy babies are born alive among the children of Israel. If the baby is a boy, kill it; if it is a girl you may let it live. Then tell the mother that you are sorry, but the baby was born dead."

But Shifra and Puah, who some say were really Moses' mother Yocheved and his sister Miriam, did not obey Pharaoh. Instead of killing the babies, they took care of all their needs. If a woman who gave birth was too poor, and did not have any food or drink or clothing, the midwives went to others and collected what they needed. And they were so righteous that they prayed to God saying, "May it be Your will, God, that this child come into the world safe and sound, so that we don't fall under any suspicion that we tried to hurt it in any way."

Seeing that baby boys were still being born by the Israelite women, Pharaoh called the midwives to him. He demanded to know why they weren't carrying out his orders.

"The Israelite women are so strong that they do not need the services of midwives. They have their babies before we even come to help them," the midwives told Pharaoh.

Because of their many good deeds, Yocheved became the mother of the priest Aaron and of the Levite Moses. And Miriam became the mother of the royal house of David.

WHY MOSES STUTTERED

W hen Moses was born, his mother Yocheved and father Amram had to hide him because of the Pharaoh's decree that all baby boys born to the Israelites must be thrown into the Nile River. At all costs, Pharaoh did not want the prophecy to come true—that a baby boy born to the Hebrews would lead his people out of Egypt and slavery.

Yocheved and Amram hid their baby as long as they could. When he grew too big to hide, Yocheved took a basket of bulrushes and covered it with pitch so it would float. Moses' sister Miriam watched over her brother to see what would happen to him when he was placed in the Nile River in his little basket.

Miriam saw Pharaoh's daughter rescue baby Moses from the Nile, and bravely came out from hiding to offer the princess the services of a Hebrew woman to nurse him. Pharaoh's daughter did not know that the woman Miriam brought to her was Moses' own mother. She gave him to Yocheved to nurse, and told her that she would come get the boy when he was finished nursing.

Moses lived for two years with his mother Yocheved, his father Amram, his brother Aaron, and his sister Miriam. Then Pharaoh's daughter came to take Moses to live in the palace with her. Now Pharaoh's daughter loved

Moses as if he were her own son, and often brought him to dine with her father and all the princes of the land.

One evening, when Pharaoh's daughter sat with three-year-old Moses on her lap next to her father the Pharaoh, it happened that Pharaoh bent down to play with Moses. Just then Moses reached up, attracted by the jewels in Pharaoh's crown, and grabbed the crown right off Pharaoh's head. Moses put it on his own head and sat there smiling. But Pharaoh didn't smile, and he didn't think this very funny. He and all the princes of the land were terrified, and interpreted Moses's action as a sign of things to come.

One of Pharaoh's ministers said, "Beware! This boy, though very young, snatches your crown from you. When he grows up, he will snatch away your whole kingdom! Perhaps this is the boy whom your magicians and soothsayers prophesied will take the Israelite people out of Egypt!"

"I agree," said a second minister. "Even though he is a child, he knows exactly what he does. You must kill him now or he will become your dangerous enemy."

Yet another minister said, "Can't you see this Moses is merely a child. He knows not what he does. Your crown is so awesome in splendor that he could not help but be attracted to it and reach for it."

In order to decide what should be done, Pharaoh gathered all the wise ones of Egypt together. The angel Gabriel disguised himself as one of these wise ones and hid amongs them. It was Gabriel who spoke up and suggested a test for Moses.

"If it please the king," he said. "Let a beautiful onyx stone be placed before the child, as well as a coal of fire. If the boy stretches out his hand and grasps the precious onyx, then we will know that this Moses is wise and knows what is valuable, and he will be killed. But if he reaches for the coal of fire, which glitters like your crown, then we will see that he does not know what he does, but is merely playing. Then his life will be spared."

Pharaoh thought this wise one's counsel was good, so he ordered that a valuable onyx stone and some glowing coals be placed before Moses.

Moses began to reach his hand toward the onyx because he knew its value, but the angel Gabriel guided his hand away from it, toward the coal, in such a way that no one saw the angel's motion. Moses lifted the coal and automatically put it to his mouth. It was so hot that it burnt part of his lips and tongue. For all the rest of his life, he would be slow of speech and stutter, but in this way his life was spared.

As soon as the king and all the princes and wise ones saw Moses chose the coal, they knew that he had not acted with any knowledge when he grabbed Pharaoh's crown. He had only been attracted to its glitter and shining jewels. And so the child Moses lived.

WHY GOD CHOSE MOSES

hen Moses lived in Midian and tended Jethro's sheep, Moses watched over the flocks with loving care. He always led the youngest animals to pasture first so they could eat the tender, juicy grass. Then he led the older animals to graze. Finally he let the most vigorous animals eat the harder grasses that were left, those that would have been difficult for the others to eat.

And once when a baby goat escaped from the flock, Moses followed it. He saw that it had stopped by a water hole to drink. "Poor kid," Moses said. "I didn't even know you were thirsty. You must be weary from all your running."

Moses lifted the baby goat over his shoulder and carried it back to the flock. During the many years that Moses tended Jethro's flocks, not one animal was attacked by wild beasts, and the flocks multiplied greatly.

Moses not only watched after his flock so that no harm would befall it, he also took care to make sure that they caused no injury to people. He always chose an open meadow for pasturing, so his sheep and goats would not graze on land belonging to others.

God does not raise a person to greatness unless God has tested that person in small things. And so God observed Moses with the sheep and the goats. "Moses has such kindness and compassion with his flocks," God said.

"He provides for each one what is best for it. Moses shall pasture My flock, the Children of Israel."

One day, while wandering through the desert, as was his custom, Moses reached Mount Horeb, the mountain of God. He was aware at once that this was a holy place. He noticed that birds flying by did not land on it. And it almost seemed to him that the mountain was moving toward him as if to meet him. It stopped moving as soon as he put his foot on it. Moses also saw a wonderful burning bush on the mountain, the upper part of it was a blazing flame. This flame did not burn up the bush, and did not prevent the bush from bearing blossoms!

Gazing at this thornbush, Moses thought of his people far away in Egypt, "My people are like this humble bush, small and unimportant. Will they ever be unburdened from their slavery and be freed?"

God spoke from the burning bush in Amram, Moses' father's voice. "If I speak in a loud voice, I will scare Moses, but if I speak in a soft voice, Moses will not treat My words with enough importance."

"Moses! Moses!" called the voice from the bush. Moses was overjoyed to hear his father speak, because he was assured that his father was still alive in Egypt far away.

"What is my father's wish?"

"I am not your father," said God. "I didn't want to frighten you and so I spoke with your father's voice. I am the God of your father, the God of Abraham, the God of Isaac, and the God of Jacob."

"Moses, you are humble and to reward you for you modesty, I will deliver the whole of the land of Egypt into your hands. I will also let you ascend to the throne of My glory and look upon the angels of the heavens."

Then, the angel Metatron came down to the lowly thorn bush and carried Moses up to the heavens with the sound of music and song accompanying them, and with thirty thousand angels to guard them on their way.

The angels led Moses through the wonder of the seven heavens. He saw a Temple with pillars made of red fire, staves of green fire, thresholds of white fire, boards and clasps of flaming fire, gates made of carbuncles and pinnacles of rubies. He saw the seraphim with their six wings exclaiming, "Holy, holy, holy is the Lord of hosts. The whole world is full of God's glory." And lastly Moses gazed on the throne of God.

"I do not want to leave these heavens," said Moses. "Unless You grant me a gift that I can take with me."

"I will give you the Torah as a gift," said God. "And the people shall call it after you, the Law of Moses."

AARON'S ROD

There was much grumbling against Moses while the Children of Israel wandered in the desert those forty years after the Exodus from Egypt.

"He takes too much power," said one.

"It is because of Moses that we suffer so in this desert," said another. "I would rather be back in the land of Egypt. At least there I had food to eat and water to drink."

"And now he says that his own brother Aaron is to be High Priest!"

"I think the High Priest should come from one of the other tribes."

"It is dangerous to place so much power into Moses and his brother's hands."

The complaining grew so much that something had to be done.

God called to Moses and told him to take a beam of wood and divide it into twelve rods. Then the prince of each of the twelve tribes of Israel was to take one of these rods and write his name on it.

"Place these twelve rods in the sanctuary for one night, and I will prove to all the people that Aaron is to be their High Priest," said God.

Word spread quickly throughout the camp that something important was about to take place near Moses' tent. Many people gathered and, by the time Moses picked up an ax to split a beam of wood into twelve pieces, he had many witnesses.

"Look," said one, "Moses is splitting the wood into pieces of the exact same size!"

"I wonder how this will prove who the High Priest should be?"

There was much excitement and speculation among the onlookers.

When Moses had twelve equal pieces, he called up the leaders of each tribe.

"Step forward," said Moses to Nahshon, leader of the tribe of Judah. "Take this quill and write your name on this rod."

And Nahshon did as Moses instructed.

"Elitzur of the tribe of Reuven," Moses called.

Elitzur also wrote his name on one of the pieces of wood.

"Eliav of the tribe of Zevulun," Moses called.

And so each of the leaders did the same until Moses called his own brother.

"Aaron of the tribe of Levi. Write your name on this twelfth rod."

"Now, come with me," Moses said. The twelve leaders of the twelve tribes carried their piece of wood with them, and followed Moses. All the people followed, too. Moses stopped in front of the sanctuary.

"You have all witnessed me cutting up the beam of wood. You have all witnessed each leader of each tribe as he wrote his name on a piece of wood, one exactly like the other."

"Yes, we have seen," agreed the people.

"Now the twelve leaders will place these rods in the sanctuary for the night. You are all free to wait here to see that no one enters the sanctuary after the rods are placed there. I will also order guards to watch to see that no one goes in or comes out. And I will wait here with them."

Many of the people waited outside the sanctuary through the night with the guards, and Moses, and the leaders of the tribes. It is easy to stay awake when one waits for a sign, a miracle. And these people had already witnessed other signs, in Egypt and in the desert.

When the morning light touched the sanctuary and the people waiting, Moses stood up as a signal. He and the twelve leaders of the tribes followed as the people went into the sanctuary. They walked to the altar where the rods had been placed.

Each rod looked exactly the same as it had the night before. Except for one. Aaron's rod had grown blossoms overnight, and almonds, and the name of God was written clearly on the wood in letters that blazed with fire.

"It is a sign!" cried all the people.

"God has spoken!" they said.

"We accept Aaron as our High Priest!"

Moses then placed Aaron's rod before the Holy Ark. It was this rod, which never lost its blossoms or almonds, that the Kings of Judea later used until the time of the destruction of the Temple. At that time, Aaron's rod disappeared. It is said that in some future time, Elijah the Prophet will come and fetch the rod from its hidden place to hand it to the Messiah.

THE FIELD OF BROTHERLY LOVE

hen it came time for King Solomon to build the Temple, he knew just the place that would befit such a holy site. It would be on Mount Moriah, on the threshing-floor of Ornan the Jebusite, because of what had happened there. His father David had told him the story.

Ornan the Jebusite had two sons, and when he died, he left his house and fields to them as an inheritance. They continued to live in the house together and work the fields together. Even after one brother married and had children, they did the same.

And after each harvest, when they bound their sheaves of wheat, they would divide the bundles equally into two parts. The part belonging to one brother was on one side of the threshing floor. The half belonging to the second brother was on the other side. It was the same, year after year.

Now there came a year when the harvest was not as full as it had been. The longed-for rains did not come and the crops suffered.

As the brothers bound the sheaves on the first day of this harvest, they noticed the difference. And each brother worried, though they did not say so to the other.

In the night, the unmarried brother awoke from a restless sleep. *I really do not need as much wheat as my brother*, he thought. *He has himself, a wife and three growing children to feed. I only have myself.*

And so he quietly rose out of bed, crossed to the threshing floor, and carried some of his bundles of wheat over to his brother's side. He felt much better then, and was able to fall back to sleep.

A little later that same night, the married brother awoke too from a troubled sleep. *My brother is all alone*, he thought. *I have my wife and children to help me now and in my old age. My brother has no one. He needs more wheat than I do.*

He talked to his wife and they agreed that he would go to the threshing floor and take from their share to add to the brother's.

In the morning, when the brothers went to the threshing floor, they saw that the amount of wheat in each one's portion was equal. They were puzzled, but they didn't say a word.

During the next night, one brother and then the other awoke to go to the threshing floor to readjust the portions once again.

One brother and then the other gathered the bundles in their arms to carry to the other's side. Except this night, they met in the middle of the threshing floor.

So surprised were they when they saw each other, that they did not know what to say. But then the smile of knowledge crossed each brother's face, and each knew how much the one cared for the other.

They dropped their sheaves and gave each other a warm embrace. And all their lives, they continued to live in the house and work the fields together, and share the harvest equally. From that time on they each knew that it did not really matter how much the one had on his side of the threshing floor, and how much the other had on his side of the threshing floor.

This is why David said to his son Solomon, "When you build the Temple, build it on the threshing floor of Ornan the Jebusite, where the two brothers met, their hands full of sheaves for the other. Truly this is a field of brotherly love, a befitting place for a Temple of holiness and peace."

KING DAVID AND THE FROG

ing David's harp hung on the wall over his bed, near a window. Every night at midnight, the wind blew through the window and played a tune gently on the harp strings so as to wake the King. David would rise and devote himself to studying Torah.

He also composed psalms, songs of praise to God. His songs would float out his bedroom window and into the night. It is said that some people living in Jerusalem would hear his music and say, "David, our King, is already awake and studying. We must begin to study also."

Some of David's songs were joyful and some sad. Some offered thanks to God and sang God's praises.

> I praise You, O Lord,
> For You have lifted me up.
> I cried out to You
> And you healed me.
> You are angry but for a moment.
> I might lie down weeping at nightfall,
> And at dawn awake with shouts of joy
> Because of You.
> You are my help.

I am more eager for You, God,
Than a watchman is for the morning.
O Lord, I will praise You forever.
(Psalm 130)

And some of David's psalms called out to God for help in times of need.
I turn my eyes to the mountains and ask
From where will my help come?
My help comes from the Creator
Who neither slumbers nor sleeps.
God will not let my foot give way
But will be my protection at my right hand.
God will guard me from all harm,
My going and coming,
Now and forever.
(Psalm 121)

And in many of the psalms, David talked of his desire to be close to God and to understand God's ways.

Oh, God, do not hide Your face from me,
You have ever been my help.
Do not forsake me.
Do not abandon me,
But deliver me.
One thing I ask of You,
Only that do I seek.
To live in the house of the Lord
All the days of my life,
And to frequent Your Temple, Your holy place.
I will look to You, God,
And be strong and of good courage.
(Psalm 27)

When David finished writing the psalms, he was so pleased with himself that he said, "Oh, God, is there anyone in Your creation who praises you with song better than I do?"

Almost as if in answer to his boast, David noticed the sound of frogs croaking in a pond underneath his window. The croaking grew louder and louder until suddenly, a large bullfrog jumped onto his window ledge, and then into his room. His croaking filled the King's bedroom.

"Do not think that you are the only one of God's creatures to fill the earth with song," croaked the bullfrog. "We frogs have been singing God's praises since long before you were born. And we do not wait until midnight to begin our songs. We are constantly singing of God's glory."

The bullfrog did not even wait for the King to reply. He jumped off the ledge and back into the night.

David thought about what this bullfrog had said and felt humbled by it. He understood that every living being sings its own beautiful song to God. Then he had to add just one more psalm to his collection.

Halleluyah!
Praise God in the heavens.
Praise God's greatness and mighty acts
With blasts of the horn
And harp and lyre,
Lute and pipe,
With timbrel and dance
And loud-clashing cymbals.
Let all that breathes praise the Lord.
Halleluyah!
(Psalm 150)

WHILE STANDING ON ONE FOOT

During the time of the Roman occupation of Jerusalem thousands of years ago, there were two great Rabbis, Hillel and Shammai. They each had their own students and their own schools where they taught their interpretations of the Torah and its laws. They also had very different styles of teaching. While Hillel was known for his patience, Shammai's reputation was for strictness.

Once a stranger who was not Jewish came to the door of Shammai's school and asked to talk to the great teacher. A student brought him to meet Shammai, who was in the middle of a giving lesson to a group of his disciples.

Interrupting his lesson, Shammai turned to the stranger and asked, "What is it you wish to ask me? Can't you see that I am explaining this passage in the Torah to my students?"

"This will not take long," answered the stranger, "because I do not have much time. Not like these students of yours who come every day to study with you. I am a merchant passing through Jerusalem with my goods. I have heard much about the brilliance of your teachings. My request is a simple one. I want you to teach me the Torah while I stand here on one foot. Then I will leave, happy with my new knowledge."

"Fool! How can you come in here and expect me to teach you the entire wisdom of the Torah while you balance for a few seconds on your leg? This is an impossible and rude request." And Shammai pushed the man toward the door of the room with his measuring stick.

Next the stranger went to Hillel's House of Study and knocked on his door. Much to the man's surprise, Hillel himself answered the door, and inquired what the man wanted of him.

"I am a merchant passing through your land and have heard what a wise teacher you are. So I have come to ask you to teach me the knowledge that is in your Torah. But since I do not stay in your city long, I ask that you do this while I stand here on one foot."

"In all my days as a teacher, I have never heard a request such as yours," answered Hillel. But he took a moment to think before he gave the stranger his answer. "You ask me a very difficult thing. To teach you in seconds what my students and I have spent a lifetime studying. Here is my answer to you."

So the stranger lifted one foot and balanced on the other, waiting to hear the Sage's words.

"What is hateful to you, do not do to your neighbor," said Hillel. "That is the whole Torah. The rest is commentary. Now I bid you go and learn it."

The stranger was so impressed with Hillel's patience and teaching, that he decided to continue to learn more, and he became a student of the great teacher.

* * *

Hillel's reputation for patience spread throughout Jerusalem, so much so that two men made a bet and decided to test the great sage's patience.

"I know I can provoke Hillel to anger," said one. "There is nobody on this earth who never loses patience, at least once. I will wager four hundred zuzim that I can make the scholar Hillel angry."

His friend agreed to the wager.

Just before the next Sabbath, when Jews all over the world were busy making preparations for the day of rest, the first man went to the house of Hillel and knocked on the door. Hillel was inside washing so as to be ready for the holy day.

"Is Hillel there? Is Hillel there?" called the man.

Hillel dressed hurriedly and opened the door.

"I have a question to ask," said the man.

"Yes, what is it?" said Hillel.

"Why are the heads of the Babylonians round?" the man asked.

"You may know that I am from Babylonia myself," said Hillel. "It is because the midwives there are not well trained and do not handle the babies' heads carefully enough."

"Thank you," said the man and left. But he did not go far. *I can think of many many questions to ask Hillel*, he thought. *I am only beginning.*

He turned around and went back to Hillel's house. He knocked on the door again.

"Is Hillel there? Is Hillel there?" he called.

Inside, Hillel had begun his washing for the second time, but interrupted it to dress quickly and answer the door.

"I remembered another question," said the man.

"Yes," said Hillel patiently.

"Why are the eyes of the Palmyrese always teary?"

"It is because they live among the sands and little particles get in their eyes and irritate them."

"I see," said the man and left.

But soon he was knocking again.

"Is Hillel there? Is Hillel there?"

For the third time, Hillel dressed quickly and answered his door.

"I have another question."

"Yes, what is it?" said Hillel.

"Why do the Phrygians have such broad feet?"

"It is because they live in a swampy land," answered Hillel. "With wide feet, they can walk around the marshy land more easily."

The man nodded and left. He was sure that with just one more interruption, Hillel would lose his well kept patience. So he went back to the Sage's house and knocked on the door confidently.

"Is Hillel there? Is Hillel there?" he shouted.

"I am here," Hillel answered, as he dressed quickly yet again and answered the door.

"What is your question?" he asked politely.

"Are you Hillel whom they call the Prince of Israel?"

"Yes, some people call me that," Hillel answered, as calmly as ever.

"Well, if you are he, let there be no others like you!" said the man, who was by now totally frustrated with this Hillel.

"Why do you say that, my son?" said Hillel, surprised.

"It is because of you I have lost four hundred zuzim. My friend and I made a bet. I was sure I could provoke you to anger by disturbing you with questions before the Sabbath."

"Better that you lose four hundred zuzim than that I lose my patience," said Hillel, who went back inside his house to finish preparing for the Sabbath.

RABBI YOCHANAN'S LESSON

Rabbi Yochanan ben Zakkai, a disciple of the famous sage Hillel, lived at the time of the destruction of the Second Temple by the Romans. It is said that before the destruction, he would sit outside the Temple all day long. He would teach those for whom there was no room in the already crowded sanctuary.

Rabbi Yochanan's teachings were devoted to peace, and he would not take part in the disputes about the political situation with Rome. After the Temple's destruction, he gathered with the scholars in the city of Javneh, and continued to study and teach the Torah and its laws.

There is a story about Rabbi Yochanan and five of his disciples in Pirkei Avot, the Ethics of Our Fathers. Of these five disciples, Rabbi Yochanan said, "Rabbi Eliezer is like a cemented well. When one teaches him, he loses not a drop of water. Rabbi Joshua's mother is a happy woman that she bore such a son as he. And Rabbi Yose is a pious soul. Rabbi Shimon fears doing evil and so does none. Rabbi Elazar is like a spring, flowing with everlasting strength."

One day, Rabbi Yochanan sent his five disciples out into the world.

"I want you to take a journey. Keep your eyes and ears open. Be watchful of how people act, what they say, how they go about their daily business.

"Then come back to me. Tell me what you think is the single most important thing that you can say about how we should behave in the world. What is one thing a person should cling to and remember as he or she goes about everyday life. This is what I charge you with today. I am eager to hear what you will say."

Each of his disciples went on a journey alone to watch and listen. They traveled in the countryside, and in towns and cities. They listened to people talk, and watched people act in marketplaces, and in inns on the road, in houses of study and in the fields. They saw the wealthy and the poor, men and women, young and old, the city dweller and the one who lives all alone in a hut in the forest. When each one thought they had watched and listened long enough, he returned to Javneh to tell Rabbi Yochanan what he thought was the most important thing he could tell another about living in this world.

"Yes, Rabbi Eliezer, my friend, " said Rabbi Yochanan. "To what piece of wisdom do you cling after all your travels?"

"One needs to have a good eye in this world. To observe carefully and clearly that which goes on around them in order to discern and not make leaps in judgment. To observe when another is suffering, perhaps in silence, and be generous with aid."

"And you, my friend Rabbi Joshua. What do you say?" asked Rabbi Yochanan.

"A good companion is to be treasured above all. Make a good friend and be a good friend for this is worth more than any valuable jewel," said Rabbi Joshua.

"Also a good answer," said Rabbi Yochanan. "What about you, Rabbi Yose? What do you say?"

"I think a good neighbor is truly important in life and is a blessing. One must also try to be a good neighbor. If each looks after the other in this way and helps each other, one is supported in life and one's burden's are eased."

"Yes, a good neighbor is important in life, too," said Rabbi Yochanan. "What have you learned, Rabbi Shimon?"

"It is important to look ahead at the consequences of your behavior before you act," said Rabbi Simon. "This is most important in life if one strives to be a truly good person. When we act in the world, our actions effect not only us, but those around us, and ripple throughout the universe in ways we might not even imagine."

"All four of you have observed well," said Rabbi Yochanan. "Now we must hear from Rabbi Elazar."

Rabbi Elazar said, "I think the most important thing in this life is to cultivate a good heart."

"I commend your words," said Rabbi Yochanan, "for a good heart includes all of what my other students have said."

THIS TOO
IS FOR THE BEST

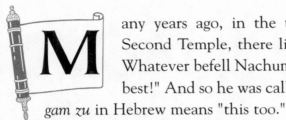any years ago, in the time after the destruction of the Second Temple, there lived a pious man named Nachum. Whatever befell Nachum, he would say, "This too is for the best!" And so he was called Rabbi Nachum of Gamzu, since *gam zu* in Hebrew means "this too."

It happened that the Jews in the Land of Israel wished to send a gift to the Roman Emperor as a peace offering. The sages worried about who would bring this gift to Rome and travel the long and dangerous road to get there. They decided that the person they would send was Rabbi Nachum because he had experienced many miracles. The sages filled a wooden box full of precious gems and pearls, and gave it to Rabbi Nachum.

First he had to travel on a ship for many days, and then he walked on foot for hours until he reached an inn where he could stay the night. After he ate and said his bedtime prayers, Rabbi Nachum fell asleep with the gift safely beside him, or so he thought.

In the night, though, the innkeeper came near to Rabbi Nachum. He had noticed the beautiful wooden box the Rabbi carried, and wanted to know what was inside. Very quietly, the innkeeper opened the lid. He stared with his mouth open at all the gems and pearls inside.

Why this must be worth a fortune! he thought. Never had he seen such valuables in all his life. The innkeeper gave in to temptation and took everything that was in the box. In their place, he put dirt and pebbles so that the Rabbi would feel an equal weight when he lifted the box.

In the morning, Rabbi Nachum took the box and continued on his way, suspecting nothing.

Finally, after many hours of walking, he reached Rome and the Emperor's palace. He waited for the Emperor to see him. "I have journeyed all this way and brought you a wonderful gift from the Jews in the Land of Israel," he told the Emperor.

The Emperor was very impressed with the exquisite wooden box and eager to see what was inside. This Emperor loved gifts. But when the Emperor lifted the lid of the box, he threw the gift on the floor, for he saw that the contents were only dirt and pebbles.

"Do the Jews of the Land of Israel mean to mock the mighty Emperor of Rome!" he cried out in anger. "I will make sure they suffer for this mockery. And you, too, messenger.

"Throw this man in prison!" he ordered the guards.

This too is for the best, Rabbi Nachum thought. He kept his faith and was not afraid when the guard came for him.

Rabbi Nachum did not know that at that moment, the Prophet Elijah was hidden among the court, dressed as one of the princes. Elijah went up to the Emperor and asked, "Why are you angry with this man, Your Majesty? Perhaps they have sent you magical earth such as their patriarch Abraham had. When he threw this earth at his enemy, it turned into swords, and when he threw the pebbles, they turned into arrows."

The Emperor was still for a moment. Then he called over the guard who was leading Rabbi Nachum to prison. "Bring this man to me!" he said. "I would see if there is any of this magic in his gift."

"Let us throw some of this dirt and pebbles into the air," said the prince who was really Elijah in disguise. When this prince took a small handful of the dirt and pebbles and threw them in the air, they did indeed turn into swords and arrows before the eyes of every onlooker!

The Emperor grew very excited for there was one province in his empire he had not been able to subdue. "Let us try this gift in a real battle," he suggested.

The Emperor himself, with all the princes of his court, and Rabbi Nachum of Gamzu, traveled to this province. The dirt and pebbles that the Rabbi had brought worked there too! When the soldiers threw the dirt into the air, each tiny particle miraculously turned into a sword, and every pebble into an arrow. The people of the province fled in terror at the sight of the miracle, leaving the emperor victorious and overjoyed!

"You must come back with me to the palace and I will reward you," said the Emperor. There they filled the wooden box with precious gold and silver, and gave the Rabbi rich robes to wear and a horse to ride. Rabbi Nachum journeyed back to his home with even more riches than he had brought.

Now on his return journey, the Rabbi decided to stay at the very same inn as before.

The curious innkeeper, who never expected to see this Rabbi alive again, let alone with such riches, asked him, "What did you give the king that he received your gift kindly?"

"I gave him only that which I brought from here," Rabbi Nachum said truthfully.

The innkeeper decided that he would do the same and be equally rewarded. And so he filled a wooden box with dirt and pebbles and went off to see the Emperor of Rome.

"The earth that Rabbi Nachum brought to you belonged to us. We have brought you more," the innkeeper said, expecting to be rewarded well. But when the earth he brought was thrown in the air, it just fell to the ground, nothing more.

"What trick do you try to play on me?" said the Emperor. "This is not the earth of the Jews' patriarch Abraham.

"Take this man away," he called to the guard. "He thinks the Emperor is a fool!"

And so the greedy innkeeper ended up in the Emperor's jail while Rabbi Nachum made his way safely back to the land of Israel still believing that "this too is for the best.".

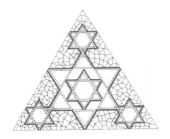

THE KING AND THE TWO GLASSES

O nce there was a wise king, but an old one. He had ruled for many years and now wanted to prepare his young son, the prince, to assume the kingship. He decided to send the prince on a journey.

"You are no longer a boy, my son. It is time you traveled and looked at other lands, at other kings and queens and how they rule. Then come back and tell me what you have seen," the king said.

So the prince left and journeyed for many months, traveling with the king's trusted advisors, some servants, and a guide.

He stayed in inns and listened to the people talk over their bread and wine. And he listened in the marketplace as they haggled over the price of chickens.

He saw lands that were prosperous, with people working hard. He saw other lands had beggars lining the streets, buildings in disrepair, people openly stealing from one another, and fear on the inhabitants' faces.

In some lands the people were friendly to him, helpful and kind. In others, people answered him rudely or hurried away.

The prince tried to make sense of all that he saw and heard. But he could not decide exactly what caused one land to be so different from another.

He returned to his home and told his father, the king, all he had seen. And he told him of his puzzlement as well.

"I am glad you have observed much, my son," said the king. "For wisdom begins there. And you have also seen how difficult it can be to make sense of it all."

The king then ordered that some glasses be brought before him and the prince, as well as a jar of very hot water, and a jar of cold.

Now the prince felt even more bewildered than before. "But father," he said, "what do these glasses and jars have to do with what I have just witnessed on my travels in the world?"

"I will explain. If we pour only hot water into these glasses, they will break. If we pour only very cold water into them, they will also break. We must be careful to mix the hot water and the cold so the glasses remain whole and do not shatter. It is so when you rule. You must with care mix the hot and the cold. You must mix justice with mercy and rule wisely.

"If you rule with only justice, and try to treat each person, as well as each incident in exactly the same way without weighing the circumstances, your land will be an unforgiving one and hardships will abound within its borders.

"If you rule with only mercy, forgiving each crime with no consequences for any wrong the person may commit, then there will be no law at all in your land, and no regard for the law. There will be hardships for different reasons. The strong, the bully, the greedy, the misguided will step over the weak, the humble and the innocent. And there will be no one to protect them.

"You have seen lands with much poverty, with beggars on the streets, and thieving one from another, corrupt business dealings, where greediness and selfishness abound. These are the lands ruled without any regard for justice.

"You have seen lands with no beggars, but where the people are unfriendly and stone faced, not helpful to the stranger, and afraid to move one foot in front of the other. These are the lands ruled without any mercy.

"What you want for your kingdom is a land where the people work hard and are prosperous; where they are friendly and helpful to the stranger.

"Just as God made the heavens and the earth, God created mercy and justice for us to mix and use wisely. Listen to your people, my son, and act with these empty glasses and pitchers of hot and cold water in mind."

THE WITCHES OF ASHKELON

A long time ago, eighty witches lived near the city of Ashkelon in ancient Israel. Every day, they made mischief and caused much grief for the people living there. There was the day the cows gave no milk, and another when giant drops of ice rained from the sky to fall on the ripe fruit of the fields. Birds sang the songs of frogs and babies sounded like sheep.

These eighty witches lived in a cave outside the city, and the people never knew when they would come or what they would do.

One day, a learned student of the city had a dream in which his teacher, who had recently passed from this world, appeared to him. "You must go to Rabbi Shimon ben Shetach, head of the Sanhedrin—the highest rabbinical court—and give him this message from the Other World," his teacher said. "He once made a promise that he would rid Ashkelon of the eighty witches, but all this time he has failed to do this. He must act on this pledge."

"But why would Rabbi Shimon believe me? I am just a student!"

"He will believe you. You will see."

So the very next morning, the student reluctantly knocked on the door of the great Rabbi Shimon's house, and told him of the message he had received in the night.

"Don't worry. I believe you," said Rabbi Shimon. "For no one ever heard that pledge. I said it in my heart, but never brought it to my lips."

Rabbi Shimon heeded the message from this student's dream. When the first stormy day came, for witches are powerless when wet, Rabbi Shimon called together eighty of his students.

"You must come with me and listen to what I say," he told them. "I will give you each a robe and a clay jar to put it in to keep it dry. We will go quietly to the cave of the eighty witches. I will enter the cave alone and you must wait outside for me. When I whistle once, you are to put on your dry robes. When you hear me whistle for the second time, you must all rush inside the cave. Each of you is to grab a witch and carry her high in the air. A witch can do no harm if her feet do not touch the ground. And do not forget to keep the clay pots with you. You will need them."

The students and Rabbi Shimon walked to the cave, the pots with the robes in them upside down on their heads to keep the robes and themselves as dry as possible.

At the entrance to the cave, his students hid themselves while Rabbi Shimon called out, "Open for me. I am one of you."

The witches opened the great wooden door that sealed the entrance to their cave. "How is it that you appear dry in this storm?" they asked.

"I walked between the raindrops since I am a great magician."

"And what do you want?" they asked of him.

"I come to learn and to teach. Let us show each other our skills and tricks."

The witches thought this a good idea for they loved to show off all their tricks.

"You may come in," they told him.

They allowed Rabbi Shimon to step just inside the cave door but no more.

Then one of them pronounced a magic formula, and loaves of freshly baked bread appeared in the cave.

Another said a different spell, and bowls filled with all kinds of delicious smelling roasts of beef and lamb appeared on the table next to the bread.

A third witch chanted her incantation. Instantly bottles of clear red wine flew into the cave, and landed safely on the table.

"Now show us what you can do, magician," said one of the witches. "Can you do anything greater than these tricks we have just showed you?"

"Even though it is raining outside, I can conjure up eighty dry and handsome men who will magically appear. They will dance with you, and eat and drink with you, and provide you with all kinds of entertainment!"

The witches liked Rabbi Shimon's idea very much. Eighty handsome young men! "Yes, we would like that," they agreed. "And if you can do this even in this rain, we will admit that you are a superior magican!"

So Rabbi Shimon whistled once. Outside the eighty young men took the dry robes out of the clay jars and put them on.

Then Rabbi Shimon whistled for a second time. All eighty of his students rushed inside the cave. Each grabbed one of the witches who were delighted to see these dry young men.

The students lifted the giggling, happy witches high in the air so their feet couldn't touch the ground. They held onto the eighty witches very tightly. But by the time they carried them out of the cave, into the rain, the witches were no longer giggling and laughing. Now the witches knew Rabbi Shimon had played a trick on them, and they grew angrier and angrier. They kicked at the men, and shouted spells out into the storm. But they had no power since their feet could not touch the ground. And with each raindrop that fell on them, they grew smaller and smaller. By the time Rabbi Shimon and his students reached the top of a very high mountain near Ashkelon, they could fit the now tiny witches into the clay pots they still had with them.

The students sealed the pots very tightly, and hid them in a secret cave in the mountain. To this day, the people of Ashkelon have not seen a one of those eighty witches. Nor have they had to put up with any of their tricks!

FROM THE KABBALAH AND HASIDIM

THE ARI AND THE HIDDEN SAINT

R abbi Abaye says in the Talmud, "There are in the world not less than thirty-six righteous persons in every generation upon whom the Shekhina, God's radiant presence, rests." These Lamed-Vav-Tzaddikim or Lamedvovniks often hide behind an exterior façade of modesty, poverty, and sometimes even ignorance or rudeness. They live humbly, and follow the example of the sages of the Talmud by earning their bread as tailors, woodchoppers and blacksmiths. The people around them never suspect that they are really hidden saints. If they should happen to suspect it and ask, of course the lamedvovnik loudly denies such a thing. However, if a genuine need aris-es, the lamedvovnik comes out of hiding and, by using kabbalistic powers, averts the misfortune. Then once again the secret saint lives in hiding, but somewhere else this time, where no one knows his or her true identity.

Once in the city of Safed in the Holy Land in the 1500s, there lived one of these thirty-six hidden saints. He was very poor, but shared whatever he had with those who had even less than he. One week, as the Sabbath approached, the hidden saint grew sick and could no longer work. His wife and children were hungry, and there was no money for food, or candles, or wine for the Sabbath table. No one knew how poor the family was, because they would never ask for help.

"Have faith in God," said the hidden saint. "God raises up the fallen!"

No one knew of the family's troubles in Safed except for one person, Rabbi Isaac Luria. He was called "The Holy Lion," the Ari, and was master of the secrets of the mystical teachings of the Kabbalah. Before the Sabbath began, the Ari took off his white robes, which he wore to welcome the Sabbath Queen, and dressed in some dusty old clothes. He wanted to look like a poor traveler. He even carried a knapsack and a staff.

The Ari stood in front of the door of the hidden saint's house until he was noticed.

"Shalom aleichem," said the traveler.

"Aleichem shalom," said the saint. "Do you need directions?"

"I have no where to go for the Sabbath and was standing here, wondering what to do."

"I am sorry to say that I do not have any food to offer you, but you can certainly stay with us," answered the saint.

The traveler seemed very grateful, and gave the saint some coins. "Here is enough for the Sabbath."

"But who are you?" asked the saint.

"They call me Rabbi Nissim," the traveler answered.

So the saint and his family prepared for the Sabbath, using the traveler's coins to buy what they needed at the market. When it was time, they sat at the table set so beautifully for the Sabbath with candles and wine and loaves of twisted bread called challah.

They waited for the traveler who had not yet returned from praying at the synagogue. They waited and waited. Rabbi Nissim seemed to have disappeared. The saint went out and looked for the traveler up and down the streets. He did not want to start the Sabbath meal without Rabbi Nissim. Then suddenly, the stranger's identity became clear to the saint. Of course! He had been an angel from Heaven sent to help the poor family! Wasn't his name Nissim, which means miracles?

Neither the saint nor anyone else ever found out that Rabbi Nissim had been none other than the Holy Lion, the Ari himself.

THE KABBALAH

J ewish mysticism began at least two thousand years ago and sought to uncover the mysteries of God and the universe through a system of symbols rather than through only intellectual, literal study of the holy texts. Early mystical literature revolved around visions of the Holy Chariot mentioned in the first chapter of Ezekiel, and in descriptions of the heavens and the dangers of trying to ascend there. The book called *Sefer Yetzira*, written around the third to sixth centuries C.E., talks about the mysteries around the creation.

During the eleventh century, mysticism became a way of life for some people, and not just a path of study. These mystics aimed for a high standard of religious observance and moral conduct. They meditated, and plumbed the mysteries of prayer and text in order to come closer to the Source of All. By this time, Jewish mysticism had spread to countries like Spain, France and Germany.

One of the most famous Jewish mystical texts, the *Zohar*, is said to have been written by the second century Palestinian Rabbi, Shimon bar Yohai. Many scholars believe it was actually written by Moses de Leon in the 1200s. Instead of looking at the world as rational and logical, the *Zohar* approaches the world with the understanding that it is composed of layers of meaning, some easily seen, and some hidden.

By the middle of the 1500s, the center of Jewish mysticism was the city of Safed in the Land of Israel. The Ari, Rabbi Isaac Luria Ashkenazi, who lived in Safed at this time, had a tremendous impact on Jewish mysticism and kabbalah. He taught that God had to withdraw in order to create the universe; God had to make room for it. The Ari called this withdrawal *tsimtsum*. After this withdrawal, God filled vessels with Divine light and placed them in the universe so that the light could pour out into the emptiness. But something happened. The Divine light was so great that the vessels shattered, and the sparks of light scattered everywhere, becoming trapped in the broken pieces of the vessels that once held them. In order to repair this brokenness, people must search for these broken pieces and lift them up, back to the Divine Source, by observing the commandments, the *mitzvot*, and by living righteously.

Kabbalah and Jewish mysticism became very popular throughout the Jewish world. Then, in 1665, Shabtai Zvi, a Turkish student of the Kabbalah, announced that he was the Messiah and created a whole movement around himself. Many people became his followers and believed in his visions. When the Turkish sultan ordered Shabtai Zvi to become a Muslim or die, though, Shabtai Zvi converted. Eventually the Shabtai Zvi movement died down, but what had happened with this false Messiah had a great impact, especially on the Jews of Eastern Europe. Many rabbis felt the study of kabbalah could be dangerous, and could lead to other movements of this kind. They encouraged only older and very learned people to study the mystical Jewish teachings.

Then, in the 1700s, Israel ben Eliezer, the Ba'al Shem Tov, began what is called Hasidism in Eastern Europe. Hasidism revived interest in Jewish mysticism and the Ari's vision that if one performs the commandments with holy intent and awareness, then one can find and liberate the Divine sparks that are trapped in the universe. In this way, order can be restored to the world. Therefore everyday life gives a person the opportunity to come closer to God if one realizes that every action one performs can bring a person closer to the Divine Source, and so to a state of inner peace and joy.

THE PRINCE WHO THOUGHT HE WAS A ROOSTER

Once in a distant kingdom, there was a prince who decided he was a really a rooster. He took off all his clothes, crept under the great table where the royal family dined, and stayed there day in and day out. He would only eat seeds and crumbs such as was fed to the chickens and roosters on the farms of the kingdom. And he would only make sounds such as a rooster makes.

Now the king and the queen tried every means they could think of to make their son come out from under the table and act like the prince he was. They tried being kind to him, saying words of encouragement and understanding. They tried offering him what had once been the prince's favorite foods, roast beef and custard puddings. They spoke sternly to him, even threatening him, saying he would no longer be heir to the throne. They asked their physicians and advisors, wizards and soothsayers to work their wisdom and magic and potions on the prince. But nothing the king or the queen, the physicians and advisors, wizards and soothsayers did convinced the prince to come out from under the table and be a prince.

The king and queen grew more and more desperate. Even though they feared what would be said about the prince if they let it be known in the kingdom that their son now thought he was a rooster, they were forced to look outside the palace for a cure. The royal couple let it be known far and wide that they offered a great reward to the person who could convince their son that he wasn't a rooster.

One day, a sage from another land came to the palace. "I think I can help the prince but you will have to let me do it in my own way."

The king and queen agreed. To their surprise and the astonishment of the entire court though, the sage took off all his clothes and joined the prince under the table, crowing like another rooster.

"Oh, no," the king groaned.

"Now we have two roosters," said the queen.

But neither interfered in the ways of the sage. They were that desperate.

The sage continued to crow.

The prince eyed him with suspicion. "Who are you and what are you doing here?" he asked the sage.

"Who are you and what are you doing here?" said the sage.

"I am a rooster," said the prince.

"I, too, am a rooster," said the sage. "Can't you see?"

For days the two of them lived under the table, crowing and eating seeds and crumbs together. They became friends.

Meanwhile the king and queen and the court, unable even to attend to the affairs of the kingdom, watched these two "roosters" under the table.

Finally, on the fifth day, the sage motioned to the king. "Bring me two shirts and two pants," he said.

The king sent for shirts and pants and the sage put one of each on.

"What do you think you are doing?" said the prince. "I thought you told me you were a rooster just like I am. Are you suddenly a man?"

"You must not believe that just because a rooster dresses like a man he stops being a rooster," said the sage in a kindly voice.

The prince had to agree. The next day both the sage and the prince wore their shirts and pants under the table. But they continued to peck at their seeds and crumbs and crow like roosters.

Next the sage asked the king for some dishes and foods from the palace kitchens.

"What are you doing now?" said the prince. "Are you going to eat like them, too?"

"You musn't think that just because you eat food off plates like a man, you stop being the rooster you are," said his friend the sage.

The next day, the sage took another step. He got out from under the table and sat at a chair.

"Are you crazy?" said the prince. "First you put on clothes like a man, then you eat food like a man, and now you sit at a table like a man."

"You should never believe," said the sage, "that just because you wear clothes like a man, and eat like a man, and sit at a table like a man, you stop being what you are, a rooster, and become a man. Just behaving like a man doesn't automatically make you a man."

With this, the prince came out from under the table and sat next to his friend, the sage. They sat next to each other for many days, eating and talking in this way until finally, the prince was doing everything that a prince usually does. And one morning, to the delight of the king and the queen and the entire court, he woke up and realized he wasn't a rooster after all.

THE TREASURE

Once there was a poor widow by the name of Sarah who lived in the city of Cracow and made her living by selling eggs in the marketplace. Now this Sarah was a sensible person, with a good head on her shoulders, and dependable, too.

But one night, she had a dream. It was about a bridge in the faraway city of Prague. And under this bridge, Sarah dreamt she was digging, digging, digging until her shovel struck something hard, a chest. When she opened this chest in the dream, she saw it was filled with gold coins. She felt happy, so happy, and then she woke up.

Now Sarah had this exact dream the next night. And the next. Sarah began to wonder about the dream. A great desire rose in her to go to Prague and dig under this bridge that she saw in her dreams, to see if indeed there was a treasure buried beneath it.

But at the same time, Sarah knew she could not do this. What a crazy idea to travel all that way to dig under a bridge one saw in one's dream. And anyway, what money would she use to buy a shovel and travel to such a place?

So Sarah tried to put this dream out of her head. But she couldn't. She even thought of it as she was calling out in the marketplace, "Fresh eggs for sale. Right from under the chicken. Still warm."

Thoughts about this dream would not leave Sarah alone. Finally, she traded all she had, even her dishes and her winter coat, for a shovel and round trip passage on a wagon bound for the city of Prague.

Once in Prague, she walked the streets looking for the very bridge that she saw in her dream, all the while thinking what a crazy fool she was. But then she found it. The very same stone bridge she had seen in her dream. Then she noticed the guardsmen marching over it, back and forth. Very quietly so as not to be seen, she snuck under the bridge and looked all around for the exact spot where she saw the treasure in her dream. When she spotted it, she took her shovel and began to dig.

So absorbed was she in her digging that she did not hear the guardsman approaching.

"Halt!" he cried. "What do you think you are doing under the king's bridge?"

"I mean no harm," said Sarah frightened. "It is just this dream I have night after night."

"I'm talking about digging, not dreams," said the guardsman. "Perhaps a trip to the jail is in order for one who digs on the king's property without permission." And he grabbed Sarah's arm.

"The dream was about digging." Sarah spoke quickly now, trying to explain. "I dreamt about this exact bridge and a treasure buried under it."

"You foolish woman," said the guardsman, laughing and letting go of Sarah. "Who follows their dreams? Why, if I paid any attention to my dreams, I would be miles away in Cracow digging under the stove of Sarah the eggseller. I've never even been to Cracow and I certainly don't know any Sarah the eggseller. What an act of folly it would be for me to follow that dream, don't you think?"

Sarah tried not to show her surprise at the guardman's words.

"Certainly," she replied. "If you let me go, I promise I will not dig here anymore, but will return to my home on the same wagon by which I came."

So the king's guardsman let Sarah go.

Sarah's trip home seemed to take much longer than her trip to Prague. She couldn't wait to see her own little house. And her own little stove!

Finally, the wagon reached Cracow. Sarah jumped off, still holding onto the shovel. She ran down her street, through her door, and into her house. She took the shovel and started digging right under her very own stove.

"What? Am I crazy?" she muttered to herself as she dug. "First I follow my dream and then I follow a strange guardsman's dream."

But she would not stop and finally, just as in her dream, she struck something hard and brown. A wooden chest. Filled with gold coins.

"I had to travel all the way to Prague only to learn of a treasure that was all this time buried right here beneath my very own feet," murmured a very grateful Sarah, now wealthy even beyond her very own dreams.

ONLY THE STORY

T here are many stories told about Rabbi Israel of Rizhin. These are but two of them.

When disaster threatened his community, when someone was sick, when any kind of prayer was needed, the holy Ba'al Shem Tov would go to a certain place in the forest near his home. There in the middle of the woods in his special place, the Ba'al Shem would light a fire, and say a long prayer, and always a miracle would occur. The disaster would be averted. The sick person would be well. The childless woman would become with child.

When disaster threatened his community or when someone was sick, or some kind of prayer was needed, the Great Maggid of Mezritch, a disciple of the Ba'al Shem Tov, would say, "I do not know how to light the fire, but I know the place in the woods and I can say the prayer."

And he would go to the same place in the woods as his teacher the Ba'al Shem Tov did before him. He would say the very same prayer, and a miracle would occur.

When Rabbi Moshe Leib of Sasov, a disciple of the Maggid, needed to call on divine help, he would go to the very same place in the forest, and say, "God, I do not know how to light the fire, or say the prayer, but I do know the place and that must be enough." And it was.

Now when Rabbi Israel of Rizhin, grandson of the Maggid, needed to call on the Divine, he would say, "I no longer know the place in the woods, nor do I know the prayer or how to light the fire, but I can tell the story and this must be enough."

And it was.

This story is also told about Rabbi Israel.

Rabbi Israel of Rizhin said to his disciples, "When the holy Ba'al Shem Tov felt his final hour approaching, all his students gathered at his bedside. He promised them that as soon as he arrived in heaven, he would do everything he could to hasten the coming of the Messiah, who would bring the days of peace on earth."

When the Ba'al Shem Tov's soul reached heaven, he told of his wish to meet the Messiah. And of course his wish was granted. After all, he was the holy Ba'al Shem Tov. One refused him nothing. But when he met this descendant of King David, the Messiah, he reached such heights of ecstasy, that he forgot his promise.

The Ba'al Shem Tov's disciple, the Maggid of Mezritch, knew of this, and was determined that the same thing would not happen to him. Before he left this world, the Maggid said, "I know what I will do to avoid what happened to my teacher. I will not ask to see the Messiah. I will see everyone but him. Then he will go down to earth and all evil will be banished forever."

But when the Maggid passed from this world, he was made into an angel so that he would forget what he had promised the people below.

"I will not let this happen to me," Rabbi Levi-Yitzhak of Berditchev would promise his disciples. "I will refuse to enter Paradise. I will stand at the Gates and remind God of God's duties to all of the children on earth. I will speak and shout."

And Rabbi Levi-Yitzhak did speak and shout and make much noise at the Heavenly Gates. Much to their surprise, for they had never had to do so before, the angels had to actually push Levi-Yitzhak into Paradise.

"Do not worry that this will happen to me," Rabbi Israel of Rizhin said to his students. "When I pass into the Other World, I will resist longer and better than my teachers, and I will not forget. I will stand at the Heavenly Gates and shout about you and your troubles. I will stand firm and hold onto those gates and the angels will not be able to push me into Paradise until they have listened to me. Even if this takes two hundred years!"

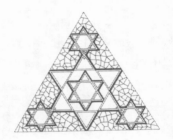

THE WINDOW
AND THE MIRROR

nce Rabbi Eisig of Ziditzov was caught in a terrible downpour near a small village and was forced to seek shelter. Dovid, a poor shoemaker, took the rabbi in and was honored to have such a great guest. Dovid made Rabbi Eisig as comfortable as he could. Yet, all the while he readied the rabbi's meal and bed, he sighed.

"Why do you sigh?" asked Rabbi Eisig. "Is there something wrong?"

"It is only because I wish I could offer you more in the way of hospitality than I am able," answered Dovid. He spoke so sincerely that the rabbi was very moved.

The rabbi asked for a blessing for poor Dovid, that he might be able to care for the needy in the future in the way he so wished.

And the rabbi's blessing came true. Dovid's little shoe shop prospered more and more each day. More and more orders for shoes and repairs, better and better buys on leather came his way. Dovid's reputation for fine work spread from one village to the next, so that he was able to hire workers and turn his small shoe shop into a factory.

Dovid was so successful that he was able to buy a fine house and hire servants to care for it. Now a wealthy man, he was interested only in his growing fortune, and did not enjoy the simpler deeds and pleasures he had thought important when he was poor. He no longer bothered to greet those who came to his door, but hired a butler to turn them each away.

Soon word spread from village to village, not only about Dovid's reputation as a fine shoemaker, but also of his reputation as a wealthy and selfish man.

Rabbi Eisig was greatly dismayed to hear this news about his old friend Dovid. It is time for another visit, thought the rabbi, and a lesson.

When the rabbi knocked on the door of Dovid's fine new house, he was met by the butler. In a gruff voice, the butler asked, "Who are you? What do you want with my master?"

"Tell your master that the man who asked for his blessings is here," answered the rabbi.

After a few minutes, Dovid himself came to the door and ushered Rabbi Eisig into the front room.

"Welcome, Rabbi," said Dovid hurriedly. "I was just about to go to my factory. Here, take a seat for a minute. It has been a long time since you were here, and so much has happened."

"I've heard," said the rabbi who, instead of sitting down, walked over to the window.

"Look out Dovid, and tell me what you see," said the rabbi.

"I see Basya carrying her eggs to market, and Haim peddling his books from one door to the next," said Dovid, with an impatient little laugh. "And there's Itzchak, the orphan boy, running errands for Mendel the fish seller. See, that package he's carrying probably has some fresh fish in it for one of Mendel's regular customers."

"Good," said the rabbi. "Now I want you to come here, where I am, and look in this mirror. Tell me. What do you see?"

"Why, I see myself," said Dovid, bewildered at the rabbi's game, and impatient too.

"I want to ask you this," said the rabbi. "If both the window and the mirror are made of glass, why do you see others through the window, but only yourself through the mirror?"

Dovid wasn't sure of the answer so he looked all over the mirror as if he had never seen it before, trying to puzzle out the rabbi's question. Finally he said, "It must be because of this layer of silver painted on the back of the mirror," and he pointed to the back of the large ornamental mirror.

"Then," said the rabbi, "perhaps it is time to scratch off the layer of silver on your mirror, Dovid, and in your life. So you will be able to see others as well as yourself, as you once did when you were poor."

Dovid looked from the mirror to the window and back again. His face colored and he lowered his head. "I understand what you are saying, Rabbi, and I am ashamed of myself."

Then he went to his desk and took a sackful of coins from one of the drawers.

"I will start by giving these out myself to the poor who come to my door when I am home," he said. "And I will instruct my butler to do the same."

Dovid walked over to the mirror again. With his finger he scratched away the silver from one of its corners.

"This will be a little window in my mirror, a reminder of your visit, Rabbi," said Dovid.

Rabbi Eisig smiled at Dovid. And when he left Dovid's house, he knew that soon different news would be spreading from one village to the next—news of the shoemaker's reputation not only as a wealthy man, but a kind and generous one as well.

A GAME OF
HIDE AND SEEK

 ne day, Rabbi Baruch's grandson Yechiel was playing with his friend Noam. Since it was raining outdoors, they were in the house. And since Rabbi Baruch was studying, they had to pick a quiet game. They chose one of their favorites, hide and seek and played in whispers.

First Yechiel counted to ten and Noam hid. Yechiel searched everywhere. Under beds, behind the wood pile by the stove and the sack of flour in the pantry. Finally, he spotted his friend inside the cupboard where his grandmother stored the bedding.

"I almost fell asleep, you took so long," said Noam. He was proud of himself for finding such a good place.

"You're lucky you're small and skinny," said Yechiel. "And can squeeze into such a spot."

"Now it's your turn to hide," said Noam.

While Noam counted, Yechiel looked around the little house. This time he wanted to find a place they had never thought of to hide.

And then he remembered. The pickle barrel! It was empty! They had finished the last of Grandmother's wonderful sour pickles just yesterday and she had washed out the barrel, thinking of the new batch to be made. Noam will never think to look in there for me!

So Yechiel hid and waited. At first, he could hear Noam, far away, clos-

er, far away again. He smiled to himself, thinking of how long it was taking Noam to discover his special hiding place.

After a while, he could hear no sounds in the house. No footsteps, no
opening and closing of doors and drawers, none of Noam's "Yechiel, I'm
coming closer" or his "I know just where you are" taunts.

Where was that Noam? Maybe sitting in Grandpa Baruch's big chair by
the stove just waiting for Yechiel to give up and come out from hiding.

Well, I won't come out, thought Yechiel. *I can stay here forever. Even
though it does smell of pickles and is making me want to sneeze.*

So Yechiel waited some more.

Finally, he had had enough of the pickle barrel. And enough of the
waiting.

I know, he thought. *I'll sneak out. I won't show myself. I'll surprise Noam
in that chair.*

So quietly, as quietly as one can climb out of a big pickle barrel, Yechiel
left his hiding place, and peeked around the pantry door. There was
Grandfather Baruch's big chair by the stove, but there wasno Noam sitting
in it. Noam wasn't standing or sitting waiting for him anywhere. Now
Yechiel knew that Noam had given up searching for him long ago and gone
home, leaving Yechiel to sit all alone in that pickle barrel.

It's not fair, Yechiel thought. *I kept looking when it was my turn.*

And suddenly, Yechiel started to cry.

He ran into his Grandfather's study and told him the whole story.

His grandfather wiped Yechiel's tears with his handkerchief and patted
his back. "Yes, yes, my little Yechiella. I know just how you feel. And so
does God. For think of it. God says the very same thing that you just told
to me. God says, 'I hide. But no one wants to find me.'

"Some look a little here or there," continued his Grandfather. "But just
as God hears them coming closer, they give up looking for God just like
your friend Noam gave up looking for you."

THE HOLY GOAT

After the famous Rabbi Menachem Mendel of Kotzk went into seclusion, one of the rare visitors he would receive was Rabbi Yitchak of Worke. One time when Rabbi Yitzhak came to see the Kotzker, he said, "Peace upon you, Rebbe." Immediately the Kotzker said, "Don't call me Rebbe! I am something else. You want to know what? Well, I'll tell you. I'm a goat. A holy goat!"

Of course, Rabbi Yitchak didn't know what to say and stood there speechless. His teacher a goat! What could this mean?

"You don't believe me," continued the Kotzker. "I can tell. Then listen to my story about the holy goat and you will see what I mean. It is the story of an offering, a sacrifice.

"Once there was a poor man, a Jew, who lost his snuffbox. It was a small snuffbox that his father before him had used to store his tobacco. Whenever he opened the snuffbox, the strong smell would remind him of his father. So the snuffbox meant a lot to him. He searched everywhere for it, but couldn't find it.

"The poor man started to cry. He cried as he looked everywhere, in the marketplace, the House of Study, the bathhouse. After a while, he did not even know where he was going, and found himself in the middle of a forest that surrounded the village on one side. He wandered, lost, until an unusual creature, one he never knew existed, came up to him. It was a goat, a holy goat, that wandered time and space, waiting for night. It was at night that the goat touched the heavens with his amazingly long black horns. He woke up the stars with his touch, and they sang of the glories of the universe.

"When he saw the poor man, the goat asked him, 'Why are you so sad?'

"'I lost the snuffbox that belonged to my father. He is gone now and it was all I had to remind me of him.'

"'I can help you,' the holy goat said. 'I can give you a snuffbox that would equal your father's in its worth for it would be made of my horn that touches the sky and makes the stars sing. My horns are so long that if you cut off just one piece, it will not prevent me from reaching the stars and making them sing.'

"The holy goat bent down so the man could cut off a piece of his great horn.

"When the man returned to his village and went to the House of Study, he offered people there a pinch of his tobacco. They all marveled at its wonderful smell.

"'It has the smell of paradise!' one said.

"And the others agreed.

"'You must tell us where we can buy this fine tobacco,' they begged.

"Everywhere he went, people came up to him wanting to smell his tobacco, asking where he bought it, plying him with questions. He did not want to tell them of the holy goat who had been so generous to him in the forest. But, in the end, he did. He told them the whole story.

"Of course, before the last word was out of his mouth, everyone in the village was running toward the forest, their knives in their hands. And they did find the holy goat still wandering through time and space, waiting for night so he could touch the heavens and make the stars sing of the glory of God.

"Each person begged the goat for just a little piece of his horn so they could make a snuffbox too.

"'Your horns are so long it won't make a bit of difference. You will still be able to reach the stars,' they said.

"And for each person, the goat bent down, a little more reluctantly each time, and let them cut a piece of his horns to make a snuffbox that would smell like paradise. The holy goat's horns got smaller and smaller until finally, he had no horns left at all.

"Though the holy goat still wandered through time and space waiting for the stars to come out in the heavens, he could not reach them and make them sing. He could only look longingly at them from far away.

"And that, my friend," the Kotzker said to Rabbi Yitchak, "is why I call myself the holy goat."

HANNAH RACHEL WERBERMACHER

annah Rachel Werbermacher was the most famous of the female Hasidic leaders. She was born in 1805 in Ludomir, Poland, and was also known as the Maid of Ludomir.

Hannah had a strong desire to learn. Her father, though a shopkeeper, enjoyed studying Talmud and Midrash, the rabbinical commentaries on the Torah, the Five Books of Moses. Most girls of her time did not study these holy texts, unless they were related to the famous Hasidic rabbis. But Hannah convinced her parents to allow her to study with her father because of her perseverance and interest. They really did not have much choice.

She was a serious child who learned quickly and soon could discuss the holy books like an adult. She preferred study to play with other children, and had very few friends. The fact that she was such a loner and hardly laughed worried her parents very much.

When Hannah was about nine years old, her mother died. Her father continued to worry about his only child and was uncertain about how to guide her, especially with her mother gone. He even took her on a journey to seek advice from the great Rabbi Mordecai of Chernobyl. Rabbi

Mordecai had a daughter, also named Hannah, who was very learned and studied the holy texts. Maybe he could help.

The rabbi's advice to her father was to find Hannah a man of like mind for her to marry and share her life with. At one point this seemed about to happen, and Hannah became engaged, but Hannah decided she wasn't ready to marry, and told her betrothed this. Not long after this, Hannah's father died and she was alone. He left her their little green house and enough money to live on.

One day when she was visiting her mother's grave, as she often did, Hannah had a spiritual experience of visiting the Heavenly Court that was to affect her for the rest of her life. After this experience, she wore the ritual fringes, and prayed wearing a prayer shawl and tefillin, leather prayer boxes, all usually worn by men.

Soon after Hanna's mystical experience at her mother's grave, the people of her town began to realize how much this young woman knew, and how helpful her advice was. More and more people began to come to her for counsel.

On the Sabbath, Hannah preached sermons from her apartment which was next to the synagogue that had been built for her by the community. She also received the sick and did healings. Some Jews found it difficult to accept that a woman like Hannah, who was not the daughter of a famous rebbe, would have so many followers. Some also did not agree with what she preached, that Jews should take action in partnership with Heaven, and look for a way to live that was not so oppressive as was living under the Czar. Some people even threw stones through her window and fought with her followers on the streets. But this conflict only made her more famous.

Hannah was not judgmental with the people who came to her for help. Her teachings centered around accepting yourself and the gift of God that is within you. She said that this would then lead to the acceptance of others.

There was a lull in the conflict around Hannah, and during this period she flourished. Now many scholars and rabbis also came to hear her speak and filled her Green Shul along with the people in her own community. Some rabbis, in order to be able to accept Hannah, said that the spirit of a great male rabbi lived in her. As time went on, Hannah became more and more confident in herself and her role as rebbe, no matter what was said about her.

The peaceful lull did not last forever, and once again turmoil surrounded Hannah and her unusual position. There were those who had thought that if they left matters alone, Hanna and her followers would just fade away. With time, they saw that this was not happening, and again controversy surrounded her. It fell on Rabbi Mordecai's son, Rabbi Aaron, to do something. In 1855, a committee of rabbis came to Chernobyl to discuss the Maid of Ludomir.

After much heated debate, one member of the committee remembered that Hannah had agreed to marry when she had visited Rabbi Mordecai many years before. The rabbis hoped she would finally keep her promise, and that this would make her appear more respectable to the larger Jewish community. If she was married, she might also begin to lead a more conventional life for a woman.

It might also protect Hannah from slander, reasoned Rabbi Aaron, as it did his own learned sister and other Hasidic women who had become spiritual leaders. Of course, these women also had the advantage of being born into families of famous Hasidic rabbis, whereas Hannah was the daughter of a shopkeeper.

And so Hannah, at age forty, agreed to marry a man who had been her father's business partner, and had become a close personal friend and helper. Only two weeks later, the marriage was annulled at Hannah's insistence, however. In the years that followed, Hannah's followers diminished in number. Whether this was due to her quick marriage and annulment, the controversy around her, or the fact that life was slightly easier under the new Czar, Hannah did not know. She later resolved to emigrate to Palestine, where, at first, she worked in a bakery in Jerusalem and often visited the nearby Western Wall.

She soon joined with a few other people to till the land outside the walls of Jerusalem. More people, both Jews and Arabs, worked with them in their efforts to reclaim the land. Hannah found healing in the Holy Land, and once the settlement was well underway, she moved to Safed, the city of mystics, of Shimon bar Yohai and Isaac Luria. People again began to come to Hannah for blessings and healings and teachings. There she studied the Kabbalah and joined others in prayers to bring the Messiah. She died in 1892 in Jerusalem.

In his book *Shosha*, Isaac B. Singer used Hannah's life as the basis for the play *The Ludmir Maiden*.

THE WEALTHY MAN AND THE MUD

O nce Rabbi Israel of Riszhyn, the Riszhner, and some of his students were traveling on a cold winter's night when they came to a town. Since it was so late, they decided to try to find a place to stay for the night, but the town was so small, it didn't even have an inn. One of his students told the rabbi that a wealthy man named Reb Aharon lived in this town, but he would only invite other wealthy people or great rabbis into his house, never poor ordinary folk.

"Maybe if you ask him, Rabbi Israel, he will invite us to stay," said the student. "He will know who you are."

So Rabbi Israel and his students went to this Reb Aharon's house. Just to see if this story was true, Rabbi Israel stayed in the background while one of his students knocked on the door. Sure enough, this student knocked and knocked and no one came to open the door, though, for a moment, they could see someone's face in the window.

Then Rabbi Israel stepped forward and knocked on the door himself. This time, a servant answered the door and invited the rabbi inside. Reb Aharon welcomed him and insisted he stay the night.

"I have my students traveling with me," Rabbi Israel said and asked that they be invited to stay the night as well.

Reb Aharon looked out the window at the group of students standing in front of his house. "But how can I invite them in, Rabbi?" he said."Look at all the mud on their feet from their journey. My whole house will be covered with mud."

"I want you to listen to a story, Reb Aharon," said the Riszhner. "It is about a rich man who was also stingy. He did not allow anyone in his house. Once on a journey, he happened to pass a family that stood helplessly beside their wagon. The wagon had gotten stuck in the mud and turned over on its side. They were all trying to push the wagon out of the mud, the mother and father and their three little ones. Taking pity on the family, this rich man invited them into his wagon and brought them to their destination. He even paid to have their wagon fixed.

Years later, when the rich man died and went up to the Heavenly Court, the angels began counting his good and bad deeds. The deeds were placed on a scale. Good deeds were weighed on one side of the scale and bad ones on the other. All the times the man had refused to invite a needy person into his house and help them were counted on the side of the evil deeds. That side was tipping the scales heavily, and the rich man was getting more and more nervous about the outcome.

Then one of the angels said, "Wait!" She disappeared and soon came back with a whole family, the family whose wagon had turned over in the mud.

The angel put this family on the side of the scales that represented the rich man's good deeds. She told the Heavenly Court the whole story of what had happened all those years ago. Even with the weight of this whole family, however, the scales still tipped in the direction of the rich man's evil deeds. After all, there had been many many times he had turned away a poor traveler or beggar who knocked on his door.

"Give me a little more time," begged the angel. And she disappeared once again. When she returned this time, she carried a very heavy box of mud. She placed all the mud on the side of the scale with the family.

"This is the mud that the family carried into the wagon when they were rescued," she explained to the Heavenly Court.

And this mud made all the difference. The scale now tipped in the direction of the man's good deeds.

"Let him have another chance," said a second angel. "Send him back down to earth and see how he acts this time. Then we will see if he should enter Paradise or not."

After the Rishner finished his tale, Reb Aharon could barely move. He knew exactly why the Rizhner had told it to him.

But then he came to life and practically ran to the door, throwing it wide open. "Come in, come in!" he called to all the students outside. "And please, bring all your mud in with you!"

A Match Made
in Heaven

ou know I have a daughter," said one rabbi, the Amdinover, as he sat eating the wonderful food at a wedding party.

"Yes, I have heard. A treasure! A beauty!" said the other, the Brezhinover.

"And you have a son," said the Amdinover.

"I do. A fine scholar. A good son."

The rabbis continued to talk, interested in making a match between their son and daughter, between the offspring of two of the greatest Hasidic houses in all of Europe.

They were making progress. It was a delicate matter, this matchmaking. One wrong slip of the tongue, and one rabbi might decide the other's offspring wasn't good enough, or had a character flaw, or the dowry expected might be too high.

On the other hand, the food and drink was plentiful and filling, the surroundings merry with music and dancing.

Time passed, and it was now growing late. The match would have to be agreed upon soon or never.

The Amdinover did not hesitate. "My daughter Rachel is just the right age for a match, and eager," he said. "What do you think of your Chaim and my Rachel as a match?"

The Brezhinover agreed. "My son is a beautiful soul and would be a good husband to your Rachel. Just remember the saying, look not upon the container but upon what is within."

"Of course," said the Amdinover, though he found what the Brezhinover said a bit unsettling.

During the long journey home, the Amdinover forgot this remark, and began making plans in his head. He couldn't wait to tell his wife and daughter the good news. Imagine a match with the son of one of the other great Hasidic houses!

His wife and daughter were very pleased! Why wouldn't they be? It was a match made in heaven! News spread about the match throughout all the towns around. A large wedding was planned, and everyone in the Hasidic world was invited!

Of course it was arranged that the bride and groom would meet before the wedding. But because the distance between their two towns was so great, a separate meeting was not planned. So as to make just one long journey and not two, the groom and his family planned to arrive in Amdinov two weeks before the date of the wedding, giving plenty of time for the prospective bride and groom to meet.

Both households were busy during the next few months. There was much to do—wedding clothes to be made, food and drink to be planned for, places for those traveling to stay, a new household to be outfitted.

What actually happened, however, was very different from what either family had planned. The groom and his family left in plenty of time for their journey, but their train hit an obstruction on the rails and went off the tracks. Fortunately no one was hurt, but the groom and his family had to wait for three days until the train could continue on its way. And then the coachman who was to meet them at the train and carry them on the last leg of their journey was nowhere to be found.

After searching for a way to get to Amdinov, the groom and his family ended up hiring a driver with a rickety old wagon. They would not arrive in the style they had hoped for, but they knew if they did not get there soon, there would be no time for the bride and groom to meet each other. Custom did not allow them to meet during the seven days prior to the ceremony.

It turned out that the poor excuse for a wagon broke down on the road, and by the time it was fixed, they had no hope of reaching Amdinov in time for the bride and groom to meet. Not only that, the groom and his family arrived just minutes before the ceremony was to begin.

A large crowd of guests was already assembled and waiting as they pulled up in the dilapidated wagon. Everyone was eager to begin. Everyone that is, except for Rachel, the bride-to-be. When she heard all the commotion outside her window, and realized the groom and his family had finally come, she couldn't help but peek out to get a glimpse of her future husband. She burst into tears at what she saw, and locked herself in her room. She refused to marry the Brezhinover's son.

Her mother tried to talk to her through the door. So did various aunts and cousins. But they weren't even sure Rachel heard them through her sobbing. What could be done? All these people gathered and no wedding?

At last, her father went up to her room. At the sound of her father's voice, Rachel unlocked her door. But she stood there resolutely. "I am not marrying him, father. And I can't believe you would do this to me!"

"Do what? Isn't he a fine scholar, destined to be a great rabbi some day? Everyone praises him, his kindness, his understanding."

"But father. He is a cripple!"

And so her father went downstairs to tell the families that even he could not convince his daughter to go through with the wedding.

"Allow me to talk to her myself," said Chaim.

"That's impossible!"

"Never heard of!"

For the bride and groom to meet minutes before the wedding was almost as disastrous as canceling the wedding itself! But under the circumstances, the rabbis decided to grant Chaim permission to talk to Rachel.

Chaim went upstairs and knocked on Rachel's door. She opened it thinking it was her father coming up to tell her that the groom and his family were leaving.

Instead she was horrified and ashamed to see Chaim standing before her.

"I have something very important to tell you," Chaim said.

Rachel felt worse than ever. To be confronted by the groom-to-be himself after she rejected him! How could this be happening to her?

"You know that matches are not made here on earth but in Heaven," said Chaim.

Rachel nodded, but continued to hold her head down. She could not look Chaim in the eyes.

"It says in the Talmud that forty days before the creation of a child, a Heavenly voice declares whom this being will marry," Chaim continued.

"Forty days before the woman I was to marry was born, I saw her in a vision. She was a beautiful woman from a fine family, intelligent, full of faith, and warm hearted. But her physical being was flawed. She would be lame."

Rachel looked up at Chaim, surprised by his words. For a moment, she happened to gaze past him, to the mirror hanging on the wall. In it she could see her reflection, a beautiful young woman in a bride's dress. But one thing was different. This Rachel in the mirror had only one normal leg and one very shriveled one.

Rachel couldn't help but gasp at this reflection.

"I prayed that it would be me who would be crippled and not my bride," Chaim continued, thinking Rachel's gasp was only her response to his story.

When Rachel glanced again at the mirror, the woman looking back at her had two perfectly normal legs. But Rachel had seen enough to know that what Chaim spoke was true.

She agreed to the marriage to the great relief and joy of both the Amdinover and Brezhinover families, and all their honored guests. And Chaim proved to be as understanding, kind and wise a husband as she could have ever wished for.

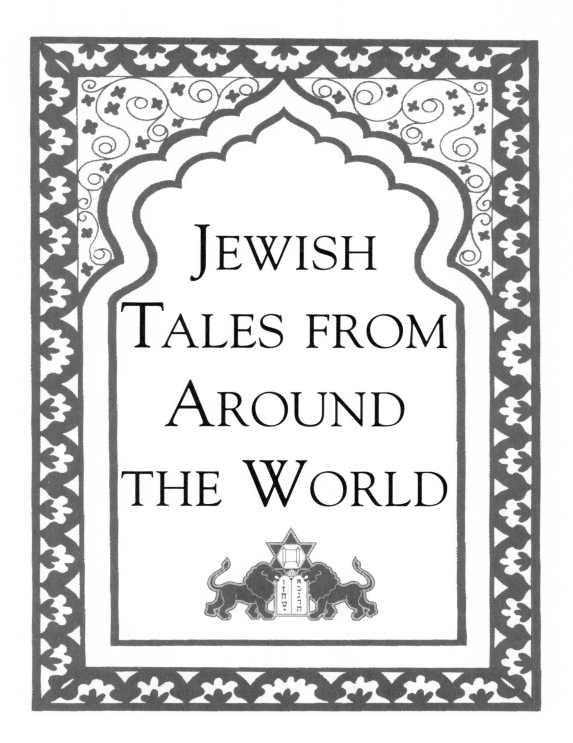

JEWISH
TALES FROM
AROUND
THE WORLD

SOLOMON AND THE WHITE EAGLE

Palestine

When Solomon was still young, but sat upon the throne, he had a dream and God came to him in the dream. "Ask me for anything you wish," said God. "I will grant your request."

"I am so young. How am I able to judge the people of Israel? Grant me an understanding heart that I may know good from evil."

And God answered, "You have not asked for long life or riches for yourself, as you could have, but for the gift of wisdom to benefit the people Israel. And so I have done as you ask. You have the gift of understanding the speech of animals, of the trees and grasses, the corn in the field and the blossoms on the tree. You shall have dominion over the demons and spirits and they shall obey you. And you shall exceed every person on the earth in wisdom and understanding."

When Solomon woke up, he walked to the window, wondering if what he remembered in his dream was reality. He heard all the noises of his garden, the birds, butterflies, peacocks, parrots, hoopoes and hawks welcoming the sun. While he was gazing in this way, he saw a blue winged bird come flying out of a bush and chirrup to the other birds, "Have you not heard, sisters, that King Solomon shall reign over us, and that he has been given the gift of understanding our speech?"

"Nonsense," said another bird whose wings were flecked with silver. "Who ever heard of a king being lower than his subjects. When we fly in the air, we are higher than Solomon, so he cannot be ruler over us. The eagle is our king. He lives in the highest places of all!"

Solomon understood every chirp of this bird talk, so he knew that his dream was true. He summoned every winged creature to gather in his garden. "Peace to you," he said to them when they had gathered from every garden and field, forest and jungle on earth. "Know that God has appointed me king over all the earth and over you also. Fear not, though, for I wish only peace and safety for all who take refuge in my shadow. You gladden my heart with your song. But the small bird spoke wisely. How can a king dwell below, and his servants fly higher than he? Such a thing cannot be.

"Therefore, this is what I want you to do, small bird with wings flecked with silver. Since you are so wise, I want you to fly to the realm of the eagles and summon the great White Eagle to Jerusalem to speak with me."

The poor little bird with wings flecked with silver shivered with fright.

"But King, I am such a little bird. I cannot summon the eagle! He will kill me for such impudence!"

"I will attach a letter around your neck, and you will carry it to the wilderness of Palmyra, to the tops of the high rocks where the great eagles live. You will fly to the highest peak where the greatest eagle, the White Eagle, lives. As soon as the White Eagle sees the letter around your neck, it will come down obediently to fly to me."

So the little bird with silver flecks flew into King Solomon's chamber, and perched on the golden footstool. The King placed a letter around its neck with the royal seal, bidding the White Eagle to come to him.

After five days passed, while King Solomon and all his court were sitting in the garden of the palace, there came one great blast of wind after another, each stronger than the last. The King lifted his eyes, and saw a white eagle soaring through the skies, coming down from the clouds, flapping its great wings. Its head pointed to the place where King Solomon sat on his throne.

"Do not worry," the King told his court, who would have fled into the palace the very next moment. "There is nothing to fear."

Within seconds, the eagle landed right in front of Solomon and bowed. Between its wings was the little bird with wings flecked with silver. Solomon took the letter from the bird's neck, and let her go, but he kept the eagle with him. And that very same day, after taking some food for the journey from his kitchens, the King mounted the eagle and flew to the wilderness of Palmyra on the giant bird. The next day all could see the King return from his journey, sitting on the eagle while it soared through the skies bringing him back to his palace.

"You must come before me once each month," Solomon told the eagle. "So that I may ride on your back wherever I wish."

And it was in this way that all the winged creatures of the earth knew that Solomon did rule over them, and that, indeed, Solomon often soared above all of them on the back of the mightiest of all airborne creatures, the White Eagle itself.

KING SOLOMON AND THE BEE

Palestine

One day King Solomon lay in his garden under a fig tree for an afternoon nap. Barely had he closed his eyes, when a bee came buzzing by. It landed on the King's nose and stung it. Solomon leapt up. The pain in his nose was sharp, and in moments his nose had swelled and turned as red as an apple.

He looked around for the culprit, but she had already fled from him. In his anger and pain, he summoned every bee and wasp, mosquito, all insects that bite to gather before him. Soon the garden was filled with these creatures. Each queen bee came with her workers. There were swarms of gnats, clouds of mosquitoes, companies of yellow jackets. The buzzing grew louder and louder as they tried to find out from the others why the King had called them all.

"What is thissssss?" they buzzed.

Finally, the King cried out, "Silence!" He pointed to his nose. It was now bigger than a grapefruit. "Who has done this to me?" he asked in a stern and pained voice

A murmur rose among the insects. "Who could have done thisssssss to the king?" they buzzed.

Suddenly a little bee left her swarm and flew toward Solomon. "I am the culprit," she admitted.

"You dared to sting the King!" Solomon roared like a lion.

"I am a young bee," said the bee. "And I cannot always tell the difference between a flower and a nose. I'm truly sorry, oh King. You have such a beautiful nose! As sweet as honey!"

"And your tongue is as sweet as honey," said Solomon, slightly amused at the tiny bee's use of flattery in her defense.

"May my sin be as small in your eyes, oh, King, as my understanding is small. Forgive me, oh Sire, and I promise you that if ever the day comes when I can be of service to my King, I will be there, tiny and insignificant as I am."

The King was amused by the bee's impudence. "How could a little bee such as yourself ever be of service to me, the King?" Solomon said. "But I admire your courage, little creature, and because of that you may go free."

Before the King could utter another syllable, the bee had disappeared.

"Imagine, such as that one being of help to the King!" Solomon was so amused by the little bee that he let all the other insects leave in peace, too. In a few days' time, the King's nose had resumed its normal shape, and he forgot all about the brave little bee and her promise.

Many many days passed. Now there was great excitement in King Solomon's court because the Queen of Sheba was coming for a visit. She had heard tales of the King's wisdom, and was making the long journey of seven years from her kingdom to his so that she could test his wisdom. She came prepared with the most difficult riddles for this test, as well as with many servants and even more gifts.

The Queen of Sheba was as intelligent as she was beautiful, and her riddles sorely tested Solomon's wisdom. So far he had been able to answer every one. For this last riddle, she had gathered all her youths and maidens before the King in rows. Each one was holding a bouquet of flowers. All of these bouquets but one were hand crafted in her kingdom, and so well crafted that they appeared very real. There was only one bouquet that was real. The Queen's test was that Solomon must identify that one bouquet from where he stood.

Solomon gazed out over all these youths and maidens, and all their bouquets. He was worried. How am I going to pick the right bouquet? They all appear so real, especially at this distance.

Solomon was very distressed by this last puzzle. He was afraid the clever Queen had finally outsmarted him.

Then the King became aware of a loud buzzing by his ear. He turned to look and suddenly his face brightened. It was his friend, the brave little bee, making good on her promise all those months ago.

"Do not worry, oh King. Follow me and see where I land," said the little bee.

With a confidence he had not felt before, the King said to the Queen of Sheba, "You have presented me with a very difficult riddle, oh Queen. But of course I can show you which is the real bouquet of flowers."

And much to the surprise of the Queen and her court, Solomon walked down the rows of her youths and maidens until he stopped before one youth in particular.

"This is the real bouquet," he said, pointing to the one on which his friend the bee had landed.

And so the little brave bee repaid her debt to the King, and the Queen of Sheba was forced to agree that King Solomon was the wisest ruler in all the world. And indeed he wasssssss.

IF IT PLEASES GOD

Palestine

Reb Moshe, a wealthy land owner, stuffed his coin purse full and went off down the road to the marketplace to buy two of the strongest, finest oxen to plow his land.

He walked briskly, in a hurry to reach the market early and get his business done.

On his way, he was stopped by an old beggar with a cane and a bundle.

"Good day," said the old man. "And where are you going?"

"To buy some oxen," answered Reb Moshe quickly. He had no time for old beggars today.

"If it pleases God," added the beggar.

"I shall buy the oxen whether it pleases God or not," said Reb Moshe. "See. I have the money right here," and he patted the purse by his side as he made his way past the beggar.

"But you will not have good fortune," said the old man.

Unconcerned with the beggar's words, Reb Moshe continued on his way.

He could hear the noises of the market, even before he saw it. And smell it too. He went to one merchant's stall and then another until he found exactly the two oxen he wanted. Well fed but not too fat. Young but not too young. Strong with good color, no signs of disease and with good temper.

"I will take these two," he told Reb Yaacov, the owner of the oxen. He had dealt with Reb Yaacov before and trusted him.

The two bickered over the price, as is the custom of marketplaces everywhere, until they settled on a price fair to both.

Then Reb Moshe reached into his purse to pay Yaacov, but to his surprise and dismay, found it completely empty. Immediately he thought of the old beggar he had met on the road, but he dismissed the thought.

"This purse must have a hole in it," he told Reb Yaacov. "Hold these two oxen for me. I will go home and bring you the money."

"I want to sell the oxen, not hold them," answered Reb Yaakov. "But I will wait this once because everyone knows that Reb Moshe certainly has the money to purchase two oxen."

Reb Moshe then hurried home, filled his purse, a different purse this time, and was making his way back to the marketplace when he met a peddler carrying his wares on his back.

"Good day," said the peddler. "And where are you going?"

"If you must know, I am going to the market to buy some oxen," answered Reb Moshe gruffly. "As a matter of fact, Reb Yaakov is holding them for me right now."

"If it pleases God," said the peddler.

"What does my buying oxen have to do with God?" said Reb Moshe, and he quickly pushed his way past this second stranger.

When he approached the marketplace this second time and reached for his coin purse, not only were the coins missing, but the purse was too. He felt like such a fool. A confused fool.

"Truly I don't know what happened, but I assure you I will return promptly with the money," he told Yaacov. "Double if you will hold the oxen for me."

"I have had two other offers, good ones," said Reb Yaacov. "But for you, Reb Moshe, I will wait."

Reb Moshe hurried home once again. This time, however, he chose a different path to the marketplace. It was longer, but he did not want to meet yet a third stanger.

Much relieved, he was almost to the marketplace, close enough so he could hear the bellowing and clucking and shouting, when it happened again. He met another stranger on the road. This time, the stranger was a poor musician, a fiddler who wore a soiled top hat and patched great-coat.

"Good day," said the fiddler. "And where are you going?"

"To buy some oxen," said Reb Moshe. He hesitated for a moment then added, having finally learned his lesson, "That is, if it pleases God."

The fiddler smiled. "Yes," he said. "And may you have much success."

"Thank you," said Reb Moshe. He nodded politely at the fiddler then practically ran the rest of the way to Reb Yaacov's stall, happy to see the two oxen still there and his purse with its coins still by his side.

"Such a shame you had to run back and forth, back and forth," Reb Yaacov greeted him. "For look what I found in your absence." He held up Reb Moshe's coin purse and all the missing coins. "You must have dropped them and we didn't even notice."

"Yes, that is what must have happened," agreed Reb Moshe. But he knew better.

THE SLAVE

Palestine

T here was once a poor man named Avram who could find no way to feed his wife and children. In his desperation, he prayed to God.

"Oh God, I have no one to tell my tale of woe to but You. No brother or cousin or friend. I can no longer bear to see my little children cry from hunger. Please, in Your mercy, look out for us."

As Avram stood praying and weeping with all his heart, he was suddenly startled to see a stranger simply appear before him.

"What troubles you so?" asked the stranger.

Avram poured out his whole tale of woe to the stranger—all about his poverty and the suffering of his family.

"All I can do now is pray," said Avram.

"No, there is something else you can do," said the stranger. "Take me to the marketplace and sell me as a slave. I only ask that you give me one of the coins from the profit."

"How can I do that?" protested Avram. "No matter how poor we are."

"You must," the stranger said. "Then you will be able to take care of your own needs and the needs of your family."

"But what about you?" Avram asked.

"You musn't worry about me," said the stranger. "I can take care of myself. You will see. I promise you this."

So a still reluctant Avram and the stranger walked to the marketplace where Avram was able to sell the stranger to a rich prince for a fine sum of money. As the stranger had requested, Avram gave him one coin from the profit. Surprisingly, the stranger gave the coin back to Avram with a blessing.

"May you be blessed with riches," said the stranger, who was no other than Elijah the Prophet himself. "Now go. Buy flour and oil, a fish, some dried fruits and have a fine meal with your family. Let that be the first of many."

With relief and joy, Avram left the Prophet, hurrying off to do his bidding.

The prince who had purchased Elijah told him of the palace he was planning to build and was delighted when Elijah said he was a builder.

"I will give you your freedom," the prince said, "if by six months time you can have my palace completed."

"Within six months, you will have your palace," Elijah agreed.

After nightfall of the same day, while the prince and all around him slept, Elijah noiselessly offered a prayer and a magnificent palace stood completed on the site of the prince's choosing.

When the prince awoke the next morning, he was astonished by the sight. His palace, inside and outside, in every detail, matched the description he had given his new slave, the builder. And then some.

The prince looked everywhere for the slave, to thank him and give him his freedom as he had promised. But the slave had disappeared.

This was no ordinary slave, the prince realized, but a messenger of God's.

While the prince was admiring his new palace, Elijah appeared once again before Avram, to tell him not to worry. That now he was free and the prince had his fine new palace, and that Avram should be sure to thank God for the mercy God had shown him.

As far as the latter, Elijah need not have been concerned, for Avram was thankful always for the blessings he had received, especially the smiles on his wife and children's faces.

THE POWER OF PRAYERS

Palestine

It was the Prophet Elijah's custom to descend each day from the heavens to attend the academy of the famous Rabbi, Judah ha-Nasi. One day, a day of the New Moon, the Rabbi waited for the Prophet, but he did not come.

"Why were you not here yesterday?" the Rabbi asked Elijah the next day, when the Prophet arrived at his usual time.

"It is because each day I must awaken the three Patriarchs, Abraham, Isaac, and Jacob one by one," Elijah explained. "First, I wash Abraham's hands so he might offer his prayers. Then when he is done, I lead him back to his resting place, and do the same with Isaac. Then with Jacob. Because of the special prayers for the New Moon yesterday, my duties took even longer."

"But why not awaken and serve the Patriarchs all at the same time?" asked the Rabbi.

"That is not allowed," said Elijah. "For if the Patriarchs were to pray together, the force of their combined prayers might be so powerful as to bring the Messiah before the proper time."

Rabbi Judah was thoughtful. Then he asked, "Are there any here on earth so pious that their prayers would have the same effect as the Patriarchs'?"

Elijah hesitated for a moment but went on. "The same power exists in the prayers of Rabbi Hiyyah and his two sons, if they pray together."

Rabbi Judah was filled with hope. He and all the other Jews of his time yearned daily for the coming of the Messiah, the descendant of King David who would bring the age of peace to the earth and reign over Israel to the end of time.

The Rabbi acted quickly. He ordered a day of prayer and fasting among the people.

Then he summoned Rabbi Hiyyah and his two grown sons to lead the prayers.

As the three prayed, a white light filled the academy, and a warmth and joyousness could be felt by each congregant.

Then they came to the Amidah, the Standing Prayer.

When they chanted the word for wind, a great storm arose around the synagogue, howling and shaking the very foundations of the building.

When the three chanted the prayer for rain, rains came in a downpour, so suddenly and so fiercely that people and animals were caught unprepared and ran for shelter.

And when Rabbi Hiyyah and his sons began the passage of prayer for the revival of the dead, the entire universe trembled, causing a disturbance even in the heavens.

"Who has revealed our secret to the world?" The question reverberated throughout the upper worlds.

"It was Elijah," came the answer.

The Prophet Elijah was called to appear before the Heavenly Throne and reprimanded for giving away the secrets of the Heavens to those on earth.

"It is not yet time for the Messiah to come. You must undo what you have done." These words surrounded Elijah, coming from here and there, above and below.

And so the Prophet once again descended to Rabbi Judah's academy. Since Elijah could assume the appearance of any kind of being, human or animal, he chose this time to appear as a ferocious bear. When he lumbered into the midst of the praying congregation, he so frightened the people that they ran in all directions.

In this way, the power of Rabbi Hiyyah and his sons' prayers was broken, and the day of the coming of the Messiah was delayed.

THE HORSEMAN

Iraq

In the country now called Iraq, there were once two villages near the tomb of Ezekiel, the great prophet. For hundreds of years after Ezekiel's death, it was the responsibility of the people of the village nearest his tomb to guard it.

Though they lived close by one another, the members of the one village would have nothing to do with the members of the other village—all due to an old feud.

That is, almost nothing—until a young man from one village named Hasan fell in love with a young woman named Shamah from the other village, the one that guarded the tomb.

Hasan saw Shamah for the first time one day when he was riding near Ezekiel's tomb. She walked so straight and tall, with a large bundle balanced on her head, going to the market, that Hasan gazed mesmerized at her graceful, rhythmic movements, at the kindly expression on her face. The silver bracelets that jangled on her ankles filled the air with delicate music. Catching his gaze, the young woman shyly looked down.

After that, Hasan rode near the tomb often in the hopes of seeing her again. And he did. With each glimpse, her sweetness and grace grew in his eyes. How often it is that what one cannot have is what one deeply desires. So it was with Hasan.

This love grew not only from one side. Before she lowered her eyes,

Shamah had time to look over this young man. Hasan was a strong, fine featured youth, who looked even stronger, more powerful and beautiful mounted on his black horse with robes and head covering swirling about him. Yet despite his fierceness, there was warmth and goodness in his face.

Soon Shamah dared to meet his gaze, though not to stop or speak with him. In this time and in this place, a gaze could sometimes say much more.

Being able to think of nothing else except this young woman, Hasan learned her name and her family's name, and one day, he went to her father.

There was much whispering in the village as Hasan approached his love's tent.

"Who is he?" one man murmured.

"Is he mad?" said another. "No one has dared come here from his village since before my father's time."

Of course Shamah's father would not accept Hasan as a bridegroom for his daughter. He shook his fist at Hasan when the young man tried to tell him of his good standing in his village, and what a fine husband he would make.

"Be gone!" was the answer.

Hasan had no choice but to turn around and leave. He saw no sign of Shamah, and rode in despair back to his own village.

In the days that followed, Hasan was not himself, and his family and friends worried about him. Their words were no comfort to him.

Hasan was inconsolable.

Thus, when he came up with his plan, his friends agreed to help him. So desperate were they to see Hasan recover, they were willing to risk their own lives to help him.

They rode one night together and in secret toward Shamah's village.

"We'll stay here with the horses and keep them still," promised his friends when they neared the village. "Hurry."

Hasan crept in among the houses of the village. Outside Shamah's tent, he whispered her name just once and waited. Then he whispered her name again as loudly as he dared.

Shamah's face, even lovelier up close in the moonlight, appeared in a doorway. She gasped, but showed no fear. Only longing and gladness. Following Hasan, she crept away from the tent. When they reached his group of friends, she and Hasan leapt onto his horse and rode away.

The next day when Shamah's family awoke, they could not find her and searched everywhere.

"She has never gone so early to market before," said her mother, her face tight with worry.

"I do not think she has gone to market," said her father, reaching for his sword. "I think it is that Hasan. He came for her in the night. Look." And he pointed to two sets of footprints on the ground outside their tent.

Her mother gasped and lay her head in her hands.

Shamah's father gathered the villagers. They mounted their horses and rode in force to recapture her.

They circled Hasan's village and demanded that Shamah be brought to them. But the tents were empty and she was nowhere to be found. So they rode right into the nearby market, scattering eggplants and flat breads and cucumbers, and sending goats and sheep in all directions.

They attacked any villagers who could not scramble under their market stalls in time.

"We'll be back for her," they shouted. "And you will all be punished for stealing her."

The anger of one village against the other was loosed.

"They cannot ride in here, destroy everything, and scare and injure our people," cried those from Hasan's village, who mounted their horses in turn.

The people of Shamah's village were expecting them. They all gathered inside the walls that surrounded Ezekiel's tomb for protection.

Those of Hasan's village began their work at once. They dug deeper and deeper by the walls of date and palm trunks so that those very walls would soon topple.

Surrounded by their old enemy, Shamah's people grew desolate and lost all hope, until one reminded the others, "Are we not guardians of the Prophet's tomb? Have we not watched over him all these hundreds of years? Perhaps he will hear us."

With great fear and hope and devotion, they prayed to the Prophet Ezekiel.

Suddenly there was a tremendous noise outside the walls. Shamah's people could not see what caused it, but those who were outside the walls could.

"Look! A horseman!" those from Hasan's village shouted.

From nowhere and everywhere the strange horseman came towards them riding a gigantic mount. The man's eyes burned with fire, and, as his horse's hooves hit the earth, sparks flew upward in all directions. The day grew dark, except for a circle of light about the horseman, like a halo around the moon. In this halo he rode, holding a fiery sword high.

He neared the frightened villagers and threw his sword down so that the earth swallowed it.

"This is what you must do," the horseman said. "Forget all that has gone on between your people. It is time. You must all join together at the wedding of the one called Hasan to the one called Shamah. From this day on, I name their children the guardians of my tomb, forever."

Hasan's people crouched and stared in awe, realizing who the strange horseman was.

"Agreed?" came the Prophet's voice again.

"Agreed," they whispered.

"And you, behind the wall, do you hear me?"

"Yes, we hear you," came the voices of Shamah's people.

When those from Shamah's village pushed open the gates, the horseman was gone. But his words had been enough.

The people from Hasan's village hugged and kissed those of the other, and together they planned the greatest wedding feast of all time, a true feast of reconciliation, where the brave Hasan married his chosen one, Shamah, before all their friends and family.

And every year, on the day that is the anniversary of Ezekiel's reappearance on earth, Hasan and Shamah's descendants leave gifts at the Prophet's tomb, giving thanks for the miracle that brought them peace.

The Midwife and the Cat

Kurdistan

Many years ago, there was a midwife named Miriam, an older woman who supported herself by delivering the babies of Zakho, her town. At the end of one particular day, a day which had been very busy with births, Miriam got right into bed. She was just about to drift off into sleep when she saw a red-haired cat at the foot of her bed. The cat was obviously pregnant.

I wonder how the cat got inside? It's really a beauty, Miriam thought. *I wish I could deliver its kittens.*

And because she was so tired and didn't have the energy to get up out of bed, she let the cat go on its way and fell asleep. She had not been asleep long, when she was awakened by a loud knocking on the door.

"Oh, not another baby who wants to come into the world in the middle of the night," murmured Miriam, pulling herself out of the warm bed to answer.

There was a man she did not recognize at the door. "Can you come with me and help with a birth?" he asked.

"Of course," Miriam answered. "Wait here while I dress."

The man led Miriam to a carriage pulled by two goats. Miriam and the stranger traveled through the streets of the town and out into the country, down the familiar road. They traveled for a long time until they came to a stone bridge Miriam had never seen before. On the other side was a field filled with men and women dancing around one very beautiful woman who looked ready to give birth.

The man who had brought her seated Miriam next to the woman "This is the woman you are to assist," said the man. "But be careful not eat or drink anything these demons offer you or you will become one of them."

Demons! So that was it! That explained the strange journey and this celebration in the field, Miriam realized.

"But why have you chosen to bring me here?" whispered Miriam. "Surely, demons do not usually call on a human midwife?"

"No, but you requested to be present at this birth."

"I did?" said Miriam. Then she looked closely at the pregnant woman, at her silky reddish hair, the way she moved her body, the shape of her face.

Oh, my, thought Miriam. *This woman resembles that cat I saw just before I fell asleep!*

"I have never before seen a demon," said Miriam. "Have you told me all I must know? Only that I shouldn't eat any of their food or drink anything?"

"Yes," answered the man. "And you will be safe."

So Miriam began to make preparations for the delivery all the while listening to the sounds of the dancers. They were chanting these words, "If it is a healthy baby, we will give her great gifts, but if it is not, it will be her end."

Suddenly Miriam realized the dancers were talking about her! She knew she was a good midwife, but whether a baby was born healthy or not? That was in God's hands.

And so was she! Miriam tried to concentrate on her preparations. If she let her thoughts wander, she would not be able to do her best.

Luckily, she did not have to wait long. The demon woman gave birth soon, and to a healthy little boy!

What merriment there was among the demons! They ate and drank, laughed and danced around. They offered Miriam food and drink, but though she was there for many hours, she was careful not to taste one morsel of food or one drop of drink.

In order not to offend the demons, Miriam told them she could only eat food she prepared herself because she kept the laws of kashrut.

When the dancing and merriment came to an end, Miriam took her leave of the demon mother and baby, and asked to be taken back to Zakho.

"First you must tell us what gift you would like," said her hosts.

"I performed a good deed," said Miriam. "That is a gift in itself."

"No! No!" they insisted. "You must take a gift!"

"Well, then, give me that bunch of garlic I see near your fire," she said.

So the demons gathered up the garlic and gave all of it to her. Miriam got into the carriage pulled by two goats with the same stranger who had brought her.

When she reached her home, she was so tired, she just tossed the garlic by the woodpile, intending to get rid of it in the morning. She knew could not eat it. The strange man had warned her of that. And she went to bed.

In the morning, one of her grandchildren woke her up. "Grandma, where did you get all the gold?" she asked.

"What gold are you talking about, child?" asked Miriam. "Show me."

The child led Miriam by the hand outside the house to the woodpile. There, to Miriam's great surprise, she saw that the child was right! The garlic had changed into gold! Miriam took the golden garlic and divided it up among her children and grandchildren. And from that day to this, Miriam's descendants have been blessed with good health and fortune.

WHICH IS THE SWEETEST MELODY?

Afghanistan

There was a shah in Persia named Shah Abbas who was very bright and enjoyed a good sense of humor. He also liked to speak in parables, letting the stories themselves convey his message. While most of his court were still pondering the Shah's story, one of his ministers, a Jew named Merza Zaki, would smile, already understanding the Shah's intent.

One day, in the midst of discussion about many things with his ministers, the Shah asked them this question. "What is the sweetest melody of all?"

"It is the sound of the flute," said one. "Especially when it is the only voice in the night air played by a shepherd watching his sheep on a lonely hillside."

"I think the sweetest melody comes from the harp," said another minister. "It can lull one to sleep and into the land of wonderful dreams with its uplifting yet soothing songs."

"The sound of the violin is the sweetest," said a third minister. "And its sounds can be sweet in happy, lively ways, as well as sad and haunting ones. Most definitely the answer is the violin."

Not one of the ministers agreed with another. The sound of bickering filled the throne room.

Only Merza Zaki among all the ministers was silent. He did not suggest what he thought was the sweetest melody.

Days later, when everyone had forgotten about the argument over which melody was the sweetest, Merza Zaki invited Shah Abbas and all his ministers to a banquet in their honor. When everyone was seated at the great table, musicians entered the hall to entertain them. There were harp players, violin and flute players, and drummers. The music filled the air with its beautiful sounds. But the guests couldn't help wondering, for there was no food on the table, not a morsel.

Perhaps, they thought, servants would bring the food into the banquet hall on platters, and so they waited patiently, enjoying the music. But no servants came bearing trays of food, and the guests' hunger grew. This was most unlike Merza Zaki, who was famous for the usually generous and abundant portions of food he offered those lucky enough to be invited to his house. Usually the table was laden with all kinds of delicacies as soon as the guests sat down. And then, when they had eaten their fill, yet more food was brought to the loaded tables, copper vessels of rice and meat dishes, pitchers of wine, and trays of sweet honey and nut pastries.

This time, the guests were too embarrassed to say anything. They just sat there, listening to the music with less and less attention. Most of their attention was now on their stomachs and the empty table! This went on for hours, until midnight! They had no idea why Merza Zaki had invited them to a banquet if he wasn't going to serve them even one spoonful of rice! A few of the guests began to complain in quiet tones to their neighbors. Many wished they could get up and leave, but that would be an insult to their host, who was such an important minister.

Finally, after all these hours had passed, Merza Zaki motioned to a servant. The servant left the room and then re-entered, carrying a large pot of cooked food. The spicy smell filled the air, and a look of relief passed over every guest's face.

Then Merza Zaki took a silver spoon and beat on the pot lid. Clink! Clink!

The servants began to put food before the guests, who ate as if they had never seen meat and rice before.

Only Shah Abbas had not begun to eat. He was looking at his host and smiling. "Ah," he said. "It was not until a few moments ago that I understood why our friend Merza Zaki had not fed us all these hours, and had us sit here listening to all these talented musicians play their instruments.

"It was to show us which is the sweetest of all melodies! To the ear of one who is very hungry, the clink of a spoon on a pot lid is clearly the sweetest of all melodies!"

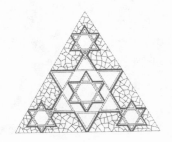

THE BEWITCHED DONKEY

Tunisia

Once there was a poor man named Ezra who, though he had very little money, would always try hard to observe the Sabbath and holidays. He would scrape together his coins to buy the food, wine, candles, and whatever else he needed. But here it was only one week until Passover and he had no coins to scrape together. His pockets were empty. How was he going to buy the matzot and wine, the greens and bitter herbs? He was very worried until he thought of an idea. It was only because he was so desperate that he decided to try it.

He sought out a wealthy man named Yehuda who lived in his town. Ezra knew that this Yehuda grew tired of being asked for money and would often answer no. But Ezra wasn't going to ask for money, not this time!

"Good day, sir," Ezra said. "I am here not to ask you for money, but merely for the loan of one of your fine donkeys until tomorrow."

Since this good deed would cost him nothing, Yehuda agreed. "I will expect to see you and the donkey tomorrow," he said.

That day was the last market day before Passover was to begin. Ezra brought Yehuda's fine donkey to the market, and put it up for sale at such a reasonable price that it was practically a bargain. A Bedawi came to look over the donkey. Seeing that it was a healthy and strong animal, he bought the donkey and led him away.

Ezra followed them at a distance until they reached the village where this

Bedawi lived. Ezra hid out of sight while the Bedawi hitched the donkey to a post and went inside. Then Ezra waited. When all was dark and silent, Ezra crept into the Bedawi's courtyard and stole the donkey.

He brought it all the way back to Yehuda's house.

"Here is your donkey, no harm done," said Ezra.

Then Ezra left Yehuda's house and ran all the way back to the Bedawi's courtyard. He hitched himself up where the donkey had been and waited again.

In the morning when the Bedawi woke up and came out to look at his new donkey, he was stunned. Where his donkey had been standing only the night before, there stood a man hitched to the post! The Bedawi was so shocked that he did not recognize Ezra.

"I am really a man," explained Ezra. "But the demons decided to have fun with me and turned me into a donkey. During the night I changed back into a man."

The Bedawi was very frightened. "You'd better go," he told Ezra. "I don't want to have anything to do with demons or donkeys who transform into men."

Ezra left as the Bedawi had asked, pleased that his plan had worked. He ran all the way back to his village to buy what he needed for Passover with the money the Bedawi had paid him for Yehuda's donkey.

Then, after Passover, it happened that the wealthy Yehuda decided to sell the donkey and brought it to the marketplace. The Bedawi, who still had no donkey and needed one, also went to the market. This Bedawi immediately recognized the donkey and went up to it. He leaned forward to whisper something into the donkey's ear.

"You poor soul," he said. "Those demons have been playing around with you again. This time I will let someone else buy you. I'm too clever to lose my money and buy a bewitched donkey such as you are two times in a row!"

RABBI HAIM AND THE KING

Morocco

Rabbi Haim ben Atar was a skilled tailor as well as a Torah scholar. His custom was to sew clothes for one or two days. After he had earned enough money, he would stop working and learn with his students in the Yeshiva, the school. When he had no more money, only then would he go out and look for more jobs.

Now the daughter of the king was getting married, and the king wanted to find a tailor who could make the kaftans for her dowry. A kaftan was a particular style of dress worn by the children of kings. He called the chief tailor and told him exactly what he wanted for his daughter's dowry. And he wanted these things immediately! The chief tailor knew whom to ask—Rabbi Haim, for Rabbi Haim was the only tailor who could sew such a kaftan.

The chief tailor went looking for Rabbi Haim. He looked everywhere in the marketplace but couldn't find him. Then he asked for directions to the Rabbi's house and inquired there.

"He is in the Yeshiva studying with his students," the Rabbi's wife told him.

The chief tailor went to the Yeshiva and found Rabbi Haim there.

Rabbi Haim was reading out of one of the holy books with his students all around him, listening intently.

"I've looked for you everywhere," he told the Rabbi. "The king needs a tailor to sew for his daughter's dowry, and you are the only one who knows how to make such fine kaftans. You will be well paid for your work."

"I will not be sewing until next week," answered the Rabbi.

"What?" said the chief tailor.

"You heard me," said Rabbi Haim. And he continued to study and teach.

Since the Rabbi continued to ignore the chief tailor, he had no option but to leave.

Soon the King called his chief tailor to him, because he wanted to see the kaftans.

"What am I to do?" said the chief tailor. "The rabbi who can sew the kaftans will not work."

"I will have this Rabbi Haim brought to me," said the King. "I must question him myself."

So Rabbi Haim was brought before the king.

"Why didn't you sew the clothes for me?" he asked.

"I never do any sewing until I have no money left," said Rabbi Haim. "As long as I have some money, I study the Torah and teach my students. Then when I have no money, I work again. Right now I have enough money for the rest of the week, and so I can continue my studies, thank God."

"You dare say this to the King?"

The king was so angry that he called a guard and sentenced Rabbi Haim to the pit where he would be thrown in with lions, tigers, and other wild beasts.

"I will need to take my books with me," Rabbi Haim said. And he put his books of Jewish law, his prayer shawl, and his prayer boxes, his tefillin, into a sack. "First throw the sack into the pit and then me," he told the guards.

The guards did this and left for the night.

The next morning, when the guards came back to the pit, they were expecting to find very little left of the poor old Rabbi who dared to defy the king. But what they saw utterly astounded them. There was Rabbi Haim, untouched. He was wrapped in his prayer shawl, wearing his leather prayer boxes on his forehead and arm. He was reading aloud from the holy book in front of him to the lions and tigers and other wild creatures. They listened to the Rabbi's chanting just as his students in the Yeshivah did.

The guards ran to tell the king.

"I do not believe this could happen!" the King said.

"Then come and see," the guards told him.

The King went to the pit and peered down. He, too, saw Rabbi Haim standing there, reading aloud from the holy books with the wild animals all around him, listening.

"This man must be a saint! We must pull him back up and release him!" said the King.

"Pull up my things first," Rabbi Haim called, "And then me."

The guards did just as the Rabbi instructed.

Rabbi Haim was allowed to go back to his Yeshivah, and study and learn with his students. The King's tailor was told never to bother him there. If the King needed him to sew something, the chief tailor was ordered to wait until such time as the Rabbi appeared in the marketplace looking for work. Then he could ask him. Such was the miracle that happened to Rabbi Haim Ben Atar.

CATS AND MICE

Ethiopia

nce, a long long time ago, a handsome young cat fell in love with a pretty little gray mouse.

"Would you marry me?" asked the cat. "For I truly love you."

"I would," answered the mouse. "I love you, too."

The cat told his family that he and mouse wanted to be married. The mouse told her family. The two families agreed to the marriage, and planned a date for the wedding ceremony. It was to be held in the field where the bride's family lived.

But a few weeks before the wedding was to take place, some of the cats, who belonged to the bridegroom's family, came up with an awful plan. They would go with the groom and the rest of the family to the wedding. But as they neared the mouse's family, they would pounce on the mice without warning and eat every one. They thought a whole family of mice would make a tasty treat indeed, one not to be missed, wedding or not.

The mice, however, were not unprepared. Before the wedding ceremony, a few of the little gray mouse's family got together.

"We must protect ourselves," one said. "We trust our little one's groom, but we do not know if we can trust the rest of his family. Cats, after all, are hunters of little creatures like us."

"You are right," said another mouse. "It would be smart to prepare. But what can we do?"

"Let's dig some holes," said the first mouse. "Lots of holes all over our field. We can jump into them if there is any danger."

"A good plan!" said the second mouse. "And easy enough."

Every day of the next few weeks, the mice were busy digging deep holes all over their field. And they practiced jumping into them. Of course, they all hoped they would not need these holes, and that the wedding would be a fine affair.

The day of the wedding came. The pretty little gray mouse and the handsome young cat were very excited. They did not know of the worries or plots of their respective families. And they were so busy with their own plans that they had not noticed any unusual behavior in those around them.

All of the groom's family gathered together to accompany him to the wedding ceremony. The groom looked more handsome than ever with his sleek clean fur and attractive whiskers. The cats carried their tasty dishes for the fine feast that would follow the wedding, dishes of fish and bird and succulent herbs.

The mice awaited their guests. They had their tasty dishes prepared with berries and nuts and spices. And they assembled their little band of a drum, a banjo and a fiddle to play music at the festivities. They were playing when the cat's family arrived as a way to welcome them. But every mouse was careful to be playing and dancing close to one of the deep holes they had dug. Just in case their fears proved true.

Soon after their arrival, and much to the horror of the pretty little gray mouse and the handsome young cat, one of the groom's family went over to a little mouse as if to greet it. But it pounced on the mouse instead! The mouse saw the cat coming and quickly danced right into the nearest hole, out of range of the cat's deadly paw.

Other members of the groom's family jumped on nearby mice, but they gracefully danced away and escaped, too!

What a wedding this was! The marriage had to be called off! The cats, who had not even caught one single mouse, returned home very angry that they had been bested by the tiny little mice.

The mice stayed in their little holes until night, when there was absolutely no smell of cat in the air, before they would dare come out of their holes. But for weeks they could talk of nothing else! They had out-witted the much bigger and stronger cats with their plan!

And this is why, from that day to this, cats continue to hate mice, while mice are very wary of cats.

DONA GRACIA NASI

Portugal and Turkey

Dona Gracia Nasi was born in 1510, thirteen years after the expulsion of all practicing Jews from Portugal. Her family had chosen to stay in Portugal, and many members of her family practiced Judaism in secret. If they tried to practice it in the open, they risked death at the hands of the Inquisition for being unfaithful to the Church.

Dona Gracia's husband was wealthy from his banking business, and from trading in gems and spices. After his death when she was twenty six years old, she decided to leave Portugal for Antwerp with her daughter, her sister, and her brother's son Joao. Her husband's brother lived there, and administered a branch of her husband's business. In Antwerp, she and her brother-in-law ran the business together until he died, and Dona Gracia had to take over the whole enterprise herself.

Once she was out of Portugal, Dona Gracia set up a fund to try to halt the activities of the Inquisition in Spain and Portugal. She also established a secret organization to get Jews out of these countries. This organization was much like the Underground Railroad in the United States in the pre-Civil War days. Her business agents in different cities provided the secret stations that helped Jews flee the Inquisition.

Dona Gracia decided to leave Antwerp, which was a city allied with Spain, and so not safe for a secret Jew such as herself. In addition, a

Catholic nobleman there proposed marriage to her daughter Reyna. Dona Gracia worried that if they refused the offer there would be serious consequences. So one night, she and her family left without telling anyone. They took only their money and some jewelry.

They went to Venice and then Ferrara, Italy where she felt safe enough for the first time to live openly as a Jew. Once she could be open about being Jewish, she could do even more to help her people. She eventually moved to Constantinople, Turkey in 1552 at the invitation of the sultan. There she built a business of wool, spices, shipbuilding, shipping, and international banking. She was generous in her support of Jewish life in the Ottoman Empire, of hospitals, schools, scholars and synagogues. She also continued her activities on behalf of persecuted Jews the world over.

For instance, in 1555, she learned that Pope Paul IV had imprisoned one hundred secret Jews from Ancona, Italy, and had already burned twenty-five of them at the stake. She used her influence with the sultan to have him seize and take into custody all ships from Ancona that were docked in Turkish ports. She also persuaded the sultan to write the pope urging him to release the remaining crypto-Jews. Lastly, she organized a boycott of the Ancona port by Jewish merchants. Although not totally successful, hers was the first attempt in history by a Jew to use international economic pressure against persons who were persecuting Jews.

Dona Gracia also worked for the establishment of a safe haven for Jews in the land of Israel. Through an arrangement with the sultan, the city of Tiberias and seven surrounding villages in Israel were rebuilt as places where Jews could live. Houses, schools, and even a silk manufacturing business were built there. Dona Gracia died in 1569, however, before she could move to, or even visit, Tiberias. She had achieved well-deserved fame, fortune and power, and was appreciated by her people for all her support and help, but above all, for her good heart.

RABBI LOEW AND THE GOLEM OF PRAGUE

PART ONE

Eastern Europe

R abbi Loew, the Maharal, lived in the city of Prague in the 1600s. It was a hard time for the Jews then. Because they were different from their neighbors, and observed a different religion, they were forced to live in certain sections of the city called ghettoes. Whenever anything bad happened, they were always the first to be blamed. Sometimes they were even physically attacked for no reason or for a false reason.

In his desire to help his people, Rabbi Loew wrote down a dream-question, as he had learned to do from the Kabbalists. He slept with it under his pillow at night. In his question, he asked God what kind of power he could use in order to protect the Jews of Prague.

Before too long, he received an answer. "Create a Golem, a man of clay, to protect your people against their enemies." Rabbi Loew understood the mystical message embedded in the words of his dream message.

He called his son-in-law, Yitzchak ben Shimshon haKohen, and his trusted disciple, Yaacov ben Hayyim, and swore them to secrecy.

"You will be my helpers," he told them. "I cannot do this myself. For the creation of this Golem, we will need to call on the powers of the four elements—fire, wind, water, and dust. I was born with the power of the wind element, and you, Yitzchak, were born with the power of the fire element. Yaacov was born with the power of the water element. Therefore, it will take all three of us to create this Golem."

Then Rabbi Loew told them which prayers they must meditate on and which rituals they would need to do for the next seven days to prepare themselves.

When the three men had completed their seven days of preparation, they gathered at midnight on the banks of the Moldau River. There they worked with the mud and clay to form the figure of a man six feet long. They shaped its face and arms and feet until the clay took the form of a man lying on his back.

The Maharal placed a slip of paper on the clay man's tongue on which was written the unutterable name of God. On his forehead he wrote the Hebrew word for truth, *emet.*

Then all three of them stood at the feet of this clay figure, looking at his face. The Maharal told his son-in-law Yitzchak to walk seven times around the Golem, beginning on the right side and going around his head, and then to his feet on the left side. He gave Yaacov the combinations of letters to chant as he walked.

When Yitzchak did these seven circles around the clay figure, the Golem's body began to glow like burning coals.

Then the Maharal ordered his disciple Yaacov to do the same seven trips around the clay figure, except he gave him different combinations of Hebrew letters to recite as he walked. When Yaacov completed his seven circuits around the clay body, the glowing fire of the Golem was extinguished because of the water that had entered the clay. And now mists began to rise from the Golem. Nails appeared on his fingers and hair grew from his head.

Then the Maharal himself completed the last of the seven circuits around the Golem. At the end of his seventh one, all three men said a verse from the book of Genesis aloud.

"And God breathed into his nostrils the breath of life, and the man became a living soul."

Just as the verse ended, the Golem opened his eyes, and looked at the three men with a puzzled expression. The Maharal ordered the Golem, "Stand up on your feet!" And the Golem stood.

They dressed him in the shoes and clothes which they had brought with them. Now the Golem looked like an ordinary man. He could see, hear and understand, but he could not speak.

The Maharal told him, "You must know that we created you out of the dust of the earth so that you can protect the Jews from any evil that may rise up against them. Your name will be Josef because in you is the spirit of Josef Sheda, who was named in the holy book, the Talmud. He was half man and half demon, and saved the sages of the Talmud many times from great calamities.

"You will live with me," continued the Maharal. "During the day you will stay in my court of law and help me as a servant of my court. You must carry out all that I ask of you, even if it means you must walk through fire, or cross mighty rivers, or jump down from high towers in order to do it.

"For even if you enter the fire, or cross the mighty river, or jump from the high tower, you will not be harmed. Fire cannot burn you, nor water drown you, nor swords kill you.

"I will tell the people that I went out very early this morning to the ritual bath. On the way I met this poor stranger wandering the streets who couldn't talk. I took pity on him, and brought him back to live with me. Now do you understand all that I say?"

And the Golem nodded to indicate that he understood all the Maharal's words. Then, just before dawn, four men left the banks of the Moldau River where three had gone before.

RABBI LOEW AND THE GOLEM OF PRAGUE

PART TWO

Eastern Europe

When Rabbi Loew, Yitzchak ben Shimshon haKohen, Yaacov ben Hayyim, and the Golem reached Prague, the Rabbi told everyone how he had found this stranger wandering the streets and taken pity on him.

"He cannot speak," he said. "And he will live with me and serve me in the court of law. His name is Joseph. And no one must give him orders except for me."

Rabbi Loew was especially careful to tell the members of his own household that only he would give Joseph directions.

"Do not ask Joseph to help in menial tasks," Rabbi Loew told his wife Pearl. "He must be ready for any emergency that comes."

Soon after the Golem's arrival in Prague, his first Sabbath approached. He sat in the Rabbi's house because the law court was closed. And Pearl bustled about him getting ready for the coming Sabbath.

"I have so much to do," she said to Joseph. "And you are just sitting there. What could it hurt for you to help me with one little task."

She gave him two buckets, and took him out to the well. "Bring the water to the house for me," she told him.

Pearl was so pleased when Joseph returned almost immediately with the brimming buckets of water.

"Good, Joseph," Pearl praised the Golem.

Pearl expected Joseph to resume his seat in the kitchen, perhaps until she would need him again. But Joseph grabbed the two empty buckets and went back to the well.

Back and forth, back and forth, Joseph went with the buckets. From the house with the empty buckets to the well. From the well with the full buckets to the house. When all the sinks in the house were full of water, Joseph poured the water on the floor. Soon there was a flood on the kitchen floor, then a flood through the whole house! Pearl shouted at Joseph to stop, the children shouted, even the neighbors came, but no one knew how to stop the Golem. Finally, Rabbi Loew came home and stopped Joseph with his order. Pearl had learned her lesson. She never asked the Golem to do any other task!

Within a matter of weeks, Joseph the Golem became a familiar figure in the ghetto. He sat in a corner in the law court, his head resting in his hands. He never spoke, but waited for the Rabbi's orders.

Rabbi Loew always gave the Golem orders in secret, whenever trouble arose in the city and the Jews were in danger. For some of his missions, Rabbi Loew gave the Golem an amulet to wear around his neck so that he would be invisible. There were many nights when the Rabbi told the Golem to wear his amulet and walk the streets of the Jewish ghetto, guarding it against any disaster. Many times, the Golem captured a thief or murderer or person bent on one sort of mischief or another.

Though he could not speak, all his other senses were very sharp, and the Golem was very successful in averting troubles. He was ever careful to watch over the children as the Rabbi had instructed him. And he was very cautious around the time of Passover, when those who did not know the

Jewish customs of the holiday accused the Jews of using Christian blood to make their unleavened bread, their matzah.

Once, in the middle of the night, as he walked the streets unnoticed, the Golem spotted a man with the carcass of a cow in the back of his wagon. The dead cow was covered with a cloth, but the Golem, with his keen sense of smell, could smell it. Immediately the Golem was on the alert. He followed the wagon until it stopped in front of a butcher's home where all were fast asleep. He watched as the wagon's driver crept off the wagon seat, around the wagon, and pulled this cloth-covered carcass off. The Golem recognized this man. Rabbi Loew had pointed him out to the Golem and told him that this man was one of the city council members, the one most responsible for all the hatred against the Jews. What was he up to this night?

As the Golem watched, the man took off the cloth, dragged the carcass to the steps of the little house, and left it there. Then he made his way back to the wagon. The Golem could clearly see that there was something inside this cow, the lifeless body of a child.

Now the Golem knew what this city councilor was plotting. He wanted to blame this innocent butcher for a murder he did not commit, and so stir up trouble and anger in the rest of Prague against the poor Jews of the ghetto.

The Golem moved into action. He grabbed the man and, with a rope that was in the wagon, tied the city councilor to the carcass so tightly that the man could not move. Then he dragged both to Rabbi Loew who went with them to stand in the front of the city hall until day when the other city councilors would arrive. They exposed the evil plot to the whole of Prague. It became clear to all that the Jews had not been guilty of murdering innocents all these years. This hateful man had been planting dead bodies around the ghetto to lay blame and incite anger.

In time, under the watchful care of Joseph the Golem, the Jews of Prague were able to breathe more easily, and were even able to drink the wine on Passover, and eat the matzah, and open the door for Elijah without worrying that an angry mob would be there instead of the great Prophet.

Months passed without incident. The next Passover came and went peacefully. And Rabbi Loew knew that the Golem's job was done. He feared if he kept the Golem alive, someone might discover his secret and misuse his powers. After all, look what had happened to his own wife and family when they had just instructed him to fetch water!

So Rabbi Loew called the Golem to him one evening, and sent him to sleep in the Great Synagogue of Prague, instead of to his usual place by the stove in the law court.

"Sleep there, in the attic, among the prayer books and prayer shawls, " the Rabbi said.

Then, hours later, Rabbi Loew called his son-in-law Yitzchak ben Shimshon haKohen, and his trusted disciple Yaacov ben Hayyim to him, and they went up the steps to the attic of the Great Synagogue where the Golem was already asleep. The Rabbi gave permission to the old caretaker, the beadle, of the synagogue, Reb Abraham to follow them up the stairs so he could hold two burning candles in his hands and give them light. He ordered Reb Abraham to stand at a distance, and to keep secret all that he would witness this night.

The other three men took their places at the Golem's head. They reversed all they had done at the time of the creation of the Golem. They stood facing his feet and each took his turn walking around the Golem. They each walked seven times around the Golem as they had before, but this time in the opposite direction. And each recited the combinations of letters they had said before except in the reverse, as the Rabbi instructed them. The Rabbi then removed the piece of paper from the Golem's tongue that had the unutterable name of God written on it. And from the word for truth that he had written on the Golem's forehead, Rabbi Loew removed the first letter. So the Hebrew word for truth, emet, was changed to the word for death, met.

Then Rabbi Loew called Abraham the beadle closer, and took the candles from him so his son-in-law and his disciple could see. They wrapped the Golem in the old prayer shawls that were in the synagogue attic. Then they took the Golem, who was now only clay in the shape of a man, and hid him under a pile of old books. The four men left the attic, washed their hands in water, and went to sleep.

When morning came, Rabbi Loew told everyone that the Golem had run away in the night, and no one knew where he was. So as not to arouse suspicion, the Rabbi waited one week to make his announcement that no one was to go up into the attic of the Great Synagogue, and that no more old books or prayer shawls should be put there. The old attic was too much of a fire hazard to store anything more. But those close to Rabbi Loew knew the real reason, that Joseph the Golem was resting there.

IT COULD ALWAYS BE WORSE

Eastern Europe

Once there was a poor farmer who lived in a hut with his wife, his mother-in-law, and his seven children. It was so crowded and noisy in his little hut that sometimes the farmer thought he would pull out every hair on his head. His wife sang, his mother-in-law whined, the baby cried, and his other six children chased each other so that there wasn't a safe place to put his feet down.

Now it was winter and they couldn't even go outside. The farmer quarreled with his wife, his mother-in-law picked on everyone, and the children kicked and grabbed at each other.

"I can't stand this for one more minute!" shouted the farmer.

"What are you going to do then?" asked his wife.

"I'm going to see the Rabbi," said the farmer. "He'll know what to do." And he put on his winter coat and boots, and went to the House of Study to find the rabbi.

The rabbi was studying one of the holy books when the farmer walked in.

"I have a problem," said the farmer, and he told the rabbi all about his little hut, and the whining and grabbing and chasing and singing. "If you don't help me, Rabbi, I think I will lose my mind."

The rabbi thought for a while, and then smiled. "I know just the thing!" he said.

The farmer let out a sigh of relief.

"Tell me, do you have any chickens?" asked the rabbi.

"Yes, Rabbi," said the farmer, wondering what his chickens had to do with this. "I have half a dozen chickens, and one rooster."

"Then this is what you must do," said the rabbi. "Go back home, and bring all your chickens, and the rooster into the house, every one."

"But Rabbi, this makes no sense. I told you. We all live in a tiny hut. Besides, I've fixed up a nice little chicken coop for the chickens."

"Don't worry. My plan will work. Trust me."

"Of course, I trust you, Rabbi," said the farmer. "I will do what you say."

The farmer went home and, much to the surprise of his wife, his mother-in-law and his seven children, he carried the chickens and the rooster into the house.

Now his wife sang, his mother-in-law whined, the baby cried, his six other children chased each other around the house, the chickens clucked, and the rooster cocka doodle dooed.

And do you think he got a wink of sleep? The noise was worse than before!

Early the next morning, the farmer went straight to the rabbi.

"Now not only is it noisy, and my children chase each other, but the chickens chase them, and I step in their eggs, and one of these days, that rooster is going to peck out my eye!"

The rabbi looked thoughtful.

"Do you have a goat?"

"Yes, I have a goat," said the farmer.

"Then I want you to bring the goat into the house," said the rabbi. "And don't ask me any questions!"

So the farmer went home and, grumbling every step of the way, dragged the goat into the hut.

Now there was his wife's singing, his mother-in-law's whining, his baby's crying, his children's chasing, the chickens' clucking, the rooster's crowing, and the goat's bleating.

This time, the farmer tried not to run so fast to the rabbi. Things were only getting worse! Who knew what the rabbi would ask him to do next! But after a week, the goat had eaten half their clothes and terrified the chickens!

The farmer went back to the rabbi.

"Do you have a cow, by any chance?" said the rabbi.

The farmer groaned. "Of course, I have a cow, Rabbi."

"Well, you must go home and bring this cow into the house."

"Rabbi, you must be joking." But the farmer went back home and did as the rabbi said. What choice did he have? He went to the shed, and led his big brown milk cow into the house.

"Just think," he told his shocked wife, "you won't have to go outside in the cold to milk it!"

Now the house was filled with the sounds of his wife singing, his mother-in-law whining, the baby crying, the children chasing, the chickens clacking, the rooster crowing, the goat bleating, and the cow bellowing. The poor farmer felt like he was caught in one of his own bad dreams. A nightmare really!

He stood it for as long as he could, and went back to the rabbi to complain.

"Now Rabbi, it is worse than ever. And no, I don't have a horse, so don't even ask."

The rabbi chuckled. "Now," he said. "Go back to your hut and take the cow, the goat, the rooster and the chickens out of your house."

The farmer ran all the way home to do as the rabbi said. He led the cow and the goat back to the barn, and the chickens and rooster to their coop.

With all the animals out of the hut, it seemed so nice and quiet, so spacious. Why there were no chickens and their eggs to step on. There was no goat that butted him, no rooster that pecked at him, no cow taking up half the hut, knocking into all the furniture.

There was no bellowing, no bleating, no crowing and no clucking. There were only the sweet sounds of his wife singing, his children playing and cooing and his mother-in-law doling out her sage advice. Why, their little hut seemed like paradise now instead of a bad dream. And the poor farmer never had to run to the rabbi again to complain. About anything!

THE COACHMAN WHO WAS A RABBI

Eastern Europe

 akob Kranz of Dubno was a *maggid*, a preacher who traveled from town to town in Eastern Europe in the 1700s. Wherever he traveled, he was always received enthusiastically, and showered with the greatest of honors by the townspeople. His coachman Efraim watched all this, and was very impressed.

One day, Efraim asked the Dubner Maggid, "I have a favor to ask you, Rabbi. I know I am an ignorant coachman, and know nothing of the laws as you do. But I wonder if, just for one day, we could trade places. We would exchange clothes, and you would sit up here driving the coach as I do, and I would sit inside as you do. Then all the people would think I was the Dubner Maggid, and they would give me all the honors and attention. Only for this one day. Then I would really know what it feels like to be so respected, and to be showered with such attention."

Now the Dubner Maggid understood the troubles of everyday folk and had a good sense of humor besides. But he did not want his good coachman to suffer any embarrassment either.

"But what will you do, Efraim," said the Maggid, "if the local scholars ask you a question about the laws in the holy books, and you do not know the answer? You know that clothes don't make a rabbi."

"I'm willing to take that chance," answered Efraim.

"Then, here. Take my clothes," said the Maggid, and he stood up and gave Efraim everything but his underwear.

Efraim did the same.

The Maggid, who was now the coachman, drove them to the next town. Everyone came out to welcome the great preacher, who was really Efraim. Then they led him to the House of Study, while the coachman, who was really the Maggid, followed at a discreet distance.

Efraim loved all the attention. Sitting in the seat of honor, he said to himself, "So this is what it feels like to be the Maggid!" Meanwhile the real Maggid, who sat in a corner, was feeling quite amused by the whole escapade.

Efraim however, was soon startled out of his revery by one of the local scholars. "Rabbi," this scholar said, "I have been waiting all these weeks for you to come because I have been troubled by a particular question. I knew you would be able to answer it for me." The scholar opened up one of the holy books, and read the passage to Efraim.

"Now he's sunk," the Maggid said to himself, and chuckled. He was familiar with the passage, and it was a difficult one.

With his brows knitted together, Efraim peered at the holy text as if he could read every word. But really, he did not know one letter from the next. Everyone in the room was silent because no one wanted to disturb the Maggid while he was reading and thinking.

Then, with an impatient gesture, Efraim pushed the text away. "A fine lot of scholars you are," he said. "Is this the most difficult question you could find to ask me? Why this passage is so easy, even my coachman could explain it to you!"

And with that he called on the real Dubner Maggid. "Please Coachman," he said. "Come here for a minute and explain this passage to these so-called scholars!"

THE GOLDEN SHOES

Chelm, Eastern Europe

Now there are fools everywhere, we all know that. But try to imagine a whole town of them! That would be the town of Chelm.

One day the Council of Sages met in Chelm. They had to bring boxes full of provisions, of salamis and prunes, radishes and gefilte fish, for who knew how long it would take them to discuss the weighty matters of the day. The first issue on the agenda was the problem of identification in the bathhouse. Since everybody knows that it is your clothes that identify you, what happens when you take them off to bathe yourself? How will you still know who you are? How will you know you are Shmuel the tailor and not Berel the baker? This was such a difficult question that it was tabled for the next council meeting.

Next issue. With so many problems creeping up that needed solutions every day, Yonkel the scholar suggested electing a Chief Sage that everyone would listen to. How much easier this would make everything in Chelm!

And next thing he knew, Yonkel was elected to the position. He was jubilant! Thrilled! He strutted around Chelm, proud of his new title. But he wasn't strutting for long, for no one paid any attention to him.

Yonkel knew it was because he looked like any other citizen of Chelm, no different.

So it was decided at the next meeting that the council would buy Yonkel a new pair of shoes, a golden pair, and then everyone would treat him as the Chief Sage of Chelm should be treated. With respect!

But as luck would have it, it rained all that night. On the very first day that Yonkel went out into the streets of Chelm wearing the golden shoes, he ended up walking up to his ankles in mud. In no time at all, his golden shoes were covered. No one knew he was the Chief Sage. And no one paid him any attention.

Yonkel went back to the council to complain. "No one listens to me, the Chief Sage! I'm going to resign if something isn't done!"

"Don't worry," said Basya, the chicken plucker. "We'll think of something." And they did. They had Shmerel the shoemaker make Yonkel a fine pair of leather shoes to wear over the golden shoes so the golden ones wouldn't get muddy.

Yonkel was very pleased with his new leather shoes, but when he put them over the golden ones, and walked in the streets of Chelm, still not one person noticed him. He was treated just like any other ordinary citizen.

So back to the city council Yonkel went.

"These leather shoes are very nice," and he nodded toward Shmerel the shoemaker. "But I get no more respect than I did before. What good is it being Chief Sage! I want to quit!"

"No, we need a Chief Sage! Chelm must have a Chief Sage!" said Berel the baker. Let's put our heads together and come up with a solution."

So all the council members put their heads together.

And as usual, it worked.

"I know what the problem is!" said Shliemiel the water carrier. "The leather shoes are nice, very nice." He nodded toward Shmerel the shoemaker. "But no one can see the golden shoes under them. There's a simple solution to this."

"Tell us!" everyone encouraged Shliemiel.

"So simple! We ask Shmerel to make the Chief Sage another pair. This time he should make the shoes with holes in them so that every citizen of Chelm can see the golden shoes that are underneath!"

"Brilliant!" cried all the other Chelmites.

So Shmerel the shoemaker made Yonkel another leather pair to protect the golden shoes. This pair, though, had holes in it so every citizen of Chelm could see the gold shining through and recognize the Chief Sage.

Unfortunately, as Yonkel went through the town, still no one paid the least bit of attention to him. And when he looked down at his shoes, he saw that the mud had crept in through the holes in the leather shoes. No gold shone through at all. There was just mud all over.

Back to the town council Yonkel went. "I have had enough. Enough of muddy shoes and enough of no respect."

"No, no!" all the council members cried out. "This is Chelm and in Chelm we are all wise. We will come up with another solution."

Once again they put their heads together.

"Straw!" Yente the Gossip suddenly cried out. "If we stuff the holes in the leather shoes with straw, the golden shoes will not get muddy!"

"A genius of an idea!" agreed all the other council members.

So they stuffed straw into all the holes in Yonkel's leather shoes, and once again he walked about the streets. But this did not work either. Still no one could see the golden shoes through the holes in the leather ones. The straw covered them up.

"There is no solution to this problem," said Yonkel to the council. "I give up. You can elect someone else to be your Chief Sage."

"Nonsense. There is always a solution in Chelm," said Yente.

And indeed there was, though only a Chelmite could have thought of it! For at the last minute, when all was lost, and Chelm was about to go without a Chief Sage to solve their most pressing problems, Shmelke spoke up. "Who says Yonkel has to wear the golden shoes on his feet? He can wear them on his hands. That way they won't get muddy. Everyone will see them. Everyone will know he is the Chief Sage."

And to this day, if you go to Chelm, you will see a man who walks the streets with one golden shoe on his right hand and another golden shoe on his left hand. This is the wisest man in all of Chelm, the Chief Sage himself! And now everyone certainly notices him!

COUNT YOUR BLESSINGS

Chelm, Eastern Europe

O nce, in the town of Dubno, there lived a very wealthy man named Reuben. He had a magnificent mansion with many servants, and a room just to store his treasures. He and his wife and children dressed only in the finest clothes from head to toe, and rode in a gilded carriage pulled by the two most handsome horses the people of Dubno had ever seen.

But no one knows in this life how that wheel of fortune will turn, or on which number it will land. It so happened that with one very important business deal, Reuben lost almost all of his wealth, including his magnificent mansion. All that was left to him and his family was a cottage with a small but very pretty garden.

To earn his livelihood, Reuben rented a stall in the marketplace where he sold yards of material, thread and needles, and made enough to support himself and his family in their little house. Though they had food, and good food, on the table every day, clothes to wear, and a roof over their heads, Reuben yearned for the days when they had lived in the fine mansion, waited on by servants, and rode in their gilded carriage pulled by the most handsome of horses.

"Gone are those happy years when I wore silks and velvets. Now I can't even afford to sell them," Reuben bemoaned to all who would listen.

"Gone are those days when our cook Ruchel made delicious meals for us. Potato kugels and gefilte fish, carrot tsimmes and sweet honey cakes. And she made the most beautiful braided breads for the Sabbath! Soft on the inside, crusty on the outside. Now my poor wife Tsiporah has to do all the cooking by herself. And, I shouldn't say this, but she could take a few lessons from old Ruchel."

Several years passed in this way, and then that mysterious wheel of fortune turned again for poor Reuben. A fire broke out in his cottage. No one knew how it started, but in a few hours, it consumed everything he owned, every bit of clothing and all the materials he sold at market, every piece of furniture, every plank of wood – all to the ground. There were not enough buckets of water in all of Dubno to put it out.

Reuben had to sell his small piece of land with the garden so he could buy a horse and wagon. He became a carter, carrying bricks and stones one day, sacks of flour and sugar the next. He had to work very hard to feed his family, himself, and his horse. He worked so hard that he no longer moaned and groaned about his fine mansion and all the servants who waited on him. No, now, his tune had changed. He missed his little cottage with its garden patch and the fresh cucumbers that Tsiporah, though she might not have been the best cook, could still make into delicious sour pickles.

"How well we ate in those days with our garden," Reuben would say. "Such an abundance of fresh tomatoes and peppers and onions! Enough and more than enough. And the eggs we could trade for, the rich milk and cheeses! What a good life we had with that little cottage and its garden patch. Now look at me. A poor carter with a skinny horse and loads of troubles!"

For a few years, Reuben and his family lived this way, squashed into two rooms they rented in an old neighbor's house, struggling to put bread in their mouths, not to mention their horse's.

But this was not the end of it. For the wheel of fortune was still turning. This time Reuben's horse took sick and died. What use is a wagon without a horse? Since Yaakov did not have the money to buy another, he became a porter. He grew shorter and shorter with the heavy loads he carried on his back.

One day as Reuben labored through Dubno under yet another heavy burden, he came upon an old friend. His friend had not seen him for a long time, and remembered him from years before when he'd had the fine mansion and the golden carriage.

"Reuben," his old friend said, "Is that you? What's happened? What awful luck! What's become of your great wealth, your magnificent mansion, that carriage and horses the like of which no one in Dubno had ever seen?"

"Don't bother me with such nonsense," snapped Reuben. "Who remembers that fine mansion? Or that golden carriage and horses? What I long for now are those wonderful days when I owned a horse and wagon and was a carter!"

Yonkel's Visit to Warsaw

Chelm, Eastern Europe

onkel was the Chief Sage of Chelm. He had been born in Chelm, grew up in Chelm, and had never been further from Chelm than Lubomle across the river. Certainly he had never been to the big city of Warsaw like Leybush the milkman. And Leybush wasn't even the Chief Sage!

Ever since he had been to Warsaw, Leybush would talk of nothing else. Why, Chelm wasn't good enough for Leybush anymore. There were buildings so tall in Warsaw, Leybush said, that to see the tops you had to bend so far back that you practically fell over from the looking. The marketplace sold such wonders, Leybush didn't even know the names of half the things, but his mouth watered just the same. And the important people he saw and, well, you get the picture.

So, of course, this Leybush put a bug into Yonkel's ear. And this bug bit him but good. The bite itched and itched until Yonkel was scratching it all day, every day. Finally, he told his wife Rivka not to expect him for supper that day or the next because he, Yonkel, was just about to set off down the road to Warsaw, on foot of course. Yonkel might be the Chief Sage of Chelm, but that didn't mean he had enough pennies to ride out of town in style.

But before he could get out the door, Rivka said, "You're going to walk all the way in those shoes, Yonkel?"

"Of course," said Yonkel. "Should I walk in my cap? My trousers you want me to walk in?"

"You'll wear them out walking all the way to Warsaw," warned Rivka.

So Yonkel reconsidered, sage that he was, and started down the road to Warsaw in his stocking feet, carrying his shoes in one hand so he wouldn't wear them out. In his other he carried the sack of food his good wife Rivka had packed for his journey, a roll and cheese, and an onion. Yonkel didn't mind walking barefoot, so happy was he to at last be on his way to see the great city of Warsaw.

Yonkel walked a mile, maybe two, maybe three, and he was hungry. So he sat down under a tree at a fork in the road, took out his roll and cheese and onion and ate. Then he felt sleepy. He decided to take a little nap. But he was worried that when he woke up, he might forget which way was the way he was going and which way was the way he had come. So, being the Chief Sage of Chelm, and used to working out problems, he came up with a solution. He would put his shoes down by the side of the road so they faced in the direction he was going, to Warsaw, of course. Then he fell asleep under the shade of the tree.

While he was sleeping the sleep of a baby, pure and sweet, a peddler came by and spotted the shoes by the side of the road.

What luck! I need a new pair of shoes, thought the peddler. *Someone must have accidentally dropped them.*

But when he picked them up and saw all the holes in the bottoms, he just as quickly let them go. "Uch. No wonder someone left these here." And he went on his way.

The problem was that when the peddler dropped Yonkel's shoes, they fell pointing in the opposite direction, not to Warsaw, but back to Chelm. Of course, Yonkel didn't know this.

After a while, Yonkel woke up from his nap, picked up his shoes and continued on his journey. How clever of me to leave my shoes pointing in the direction of Warsaw, he thought. Now I know I can't make a mistake and take the wrong road.

It didn't take Yonkel long to reach the outskirts of a city.

"I'm surprised," he said to himself. "I thought Warsaw was much further. Leybush must have been exaggerating."

As Yonkel kept walking, he marveled at how much Warsaw looked like his own Chelm. The houses, the streets, the people all looked like those he had left at home.

Soon he passed the bathhouse. The man sitting at the door looked just like Yekl, the man who worked at the bathhouse in Chelm. The man waved at Yonkel and Yonkel waved back. They not only look like the people in Chelm, but they're just as friendly, thought Yonkel.

Next he came to the synagogue. He couldn't believe his eyes. "Why this is exactly like the synagogue in Chelm!" As he watched the people coming out, his amazement grew. Every person looked just like a person at home! There was Berel the baker and Yente and even Leybush. Yonkel laughed to himself. Could this Leybush exaggerate as much as the Leybush back home? Tall buildings my foot. These buildings were no taller than the ones in Chelm!

Yonkel was so busy thinking about that storyteller Leybush that he wasn't paying attention to where he was going. When he looked up, he realized he was walking down a familiar street, just like his own in Chelm.

This is so like my own street! he marveled. *And Warsaw is so like Chelm. One shouldn't bother traveling at all. One city is just like another. One street is just like another. One house is just like another. I might as well have stayed in Chelm!*

He stopped in front of a house that looked just like his own. And a woman who looked just like his own Rivka stepped out. Some children who looked just like his very own Malka and Mottel came out behind her.

"Yonkel," called the woman who looked just like Rivka. "Back so soon? And what are you doing standing there staring like someone just dropped a rock on your head?"

Now Yonkel could not believe his ears as well as his eyes! Why this woman not only looked like his Rivka but she sounded like her too! I'd better go inside this house and see what this is all about, Yonkel thought. Why, this stranger who looks like a twin to my own Rivka even knew my name.

So Yonkel stepped into the house that looked just like his house, and pretended he was this woman's Yonkel.

The inside of this house looked just like the inside of his house. Every piece of furniture was exactly the same. *This is so strange*, thought Yonkel. *I certainly never expected this! Warsaw is exactly like Chelm, to the very last detail. But I know perfectly well that this isn't Chelm, and this isn't my house, and this isn't my Rivka, and these aren't my children, Malka and Mottel. They just look like them.*

So Yonkel sat at this Yonkel's table, and began to feel very homesick for his very own Chelm, and his very own home and family. He began to wonder, too, if the Warsaw Yonkel who lived in this house looked exactly like him, just like this Warsaw Rivka looked like his Chelm Rivka. And where was this Warsaw Yonkel anyway?

To this very day, our Yonkel is still asking himself these questions, waiting for the Warsaw Yonkel to come home so this mystery of mysteries can be solved. And as for that itch to travel and see bigger places, "Why bother," says Yonkel. "Every place looks like Chelm anyway? That Leybush was not only a storyteller but an out and out liar to boot!"

HERSHEL FROM OSTROPOL

Eastern Europe

Hershel was a jester, always a smile on his lips and a joke from his mouth. He made a living from his joking, if you can call that a living. Once Haim hired him to cheer him up when his son went off to America to pick some gold up off the streets, and Leeba did, too, after her tenth child was born and the dirty laundry filled every room in the house from top to bottom. Why, even the rabbi hired Hershel when all the problems of the town began to weigh on him like a sack of potatoes.

But a doctor or a tailor or a butcher Hershel wasn't and the money he made from his jokes hardly provided food for himself, his wife and his children. One day his wife came to him saying, "I need money. How do you expect me to feed the children without a penny?"

"I have no money," said Hershel.

"And I don't have a piece of bread to give the children," she answered.

Hershel thought for a moment. Then he sent his little Yonkele to the neighbor's to borrow a whip.

What is this Hershel up to now with a whip? his wife worried.

But Hershel meant no harm. As soon as Yonkele brought him the whip, he went off to the marketplace with it. He stood in the center of the market and cracked the whip loudly, once, twice, three times shouting, "I'll take you to Letitshev for half fare!"

Of course, several people ran over to Hershel. Half fare! What a bargain!

Hershel collected their money and gave it to Yonkele. "Give this to your mother," he told him. "I'm going to Letitshev."

Hershel started walking down the road to Letitshev with his passengers following him.

"But where is your wagon and horses?" they asked.

"Don't worry and come along," Hershel answered. "I'll take you right to Letitshev."

Hershel and his passengers walked out of town and down the road. "He's probably picking up the wagon and horses at the bridge. See over there, by the river where that little barn is," one said to the other.

But Hershel walked right by the barn and over the bridge and so did his passengers without stopping to pick up even one horse let alone a wagon.

By now they were halfway to Letitshev and the passengers said one to the other, "This man swindled us out of our money, but what good does it do to turn back now?" So they all walked together until they reached the town of Letitshev.

Once there, the passengers turned on Hershel and demanded their money back, every penny.

"Why should I give you your money back?" said Hershel. "I promised to take you to Letitshev and we are here, are we not?"

"Yes, we are here, but we had to walk every step of the way. We thought you had a wagon and horses to carry us in."

"Did I ever say a word about a wagon and horses?"

The passengers looked at each other stunned. What could they say to this? All they could do was grumble loudly and go their own ways.

When Hershel got home, his wife met him at the door with a smile on her face instead of a frown.

"Yonkele brought the money to me and we ate such a nice meal of bread and soup. Of course, I saved some for you. But explain to me Hershel. I know you had a whip. But where did you get the horses to take those people to Letitshev?"

"Don't ask such foolish questions!" Hershel said. "Who needs horses? If you crack a whip, you can always find some horses."

HERSHEL'S NEW COAT

Eastern Europe

N ow you know who Hershel from Ostropol is, and you can see from the last story about the whip and the trip to Letitshev that our Hershel could talk his way in and out of almost any situation. Well, this time, Hershel desperately wanted a new coat. His was falling to pieces and he was ashamed to show himself in public. But what could he do? He didn't have a penny. Ah, but he knew his wife Razel did. She was saving a little pile of pennies in case of an emergency and she kept it hidden, of course. She didn't want Hershel to get his hands on it.

Hershel thought every day about that secret pile of pennies and of what a handsome coat he could buy with it. Why, with that new coat, he reasoned, he could get more work and make more pennies in a week than Razel could hide in a year! After all, who wanted to hire someone to cheer them up with his jokes if he walked around in torn and tatters! They'd more likely cry than laugh.

"If only I could figure out a way to get Razel to give me that money," Hershel said to himself.

And figure out a way our Hershel did. One day not long after, Hershel climbed the ladder to the attic loft. His wife was below, sweeping the floor. Imagine her surprise when she all of a sudden heard Hershel shouting angrily to someone up in the loft.

"Who are you yelling at, Hershel?" she called up to him.

"Who do you think?" Hershel called back. "At Poverty, that's who."

"How did he get up there?"

"He says he got so tired of our tiny, dark rooms downstairs, that he came up here for a change."

"What does he want?"

"Can you believe he wants us to buy him a new coat! And he of all people knows how poor we are! But he says if we get him this new coat, he'll leave us altogether and never visit us again."

When Hershel came down from the attic, his wife said, "I think it would pay to buy a coat for Poverty, Hershel. Then we would be rid of him forever!"

"And how could we do that? Have you seen a money tree growing in front of the house?"

"Well, to tell you the truth Hershel, I've saved a few pennies here and there." With that Razel disappeared under the bed and came out with a purse full of coins.

"Here, Hershel, take these and buy that Poverty a coat."

Hershel couldn't get out of the house fast enough to run to the tailors with the money.

"Wait a minute," said his wife, pulling Hershel back into the house by his collar. "You forgot to take Poverty's measurements!"

"Oh, such a smart wife I have!" said Hershel. "Of course!"

And Hershel climbed up the rickety stairs into the loft again.

As fast as he climbed up, he climbed down. "It turns out I don't have to take his measurements," he told Razel. "Poverty and I are exactly the same size. We could be twins."

Then Hershel did run to the tailor's who measured him for his new coat. When the coat was finished, Hershel put it on and felt like a new man.

What a difference this coat would make! No more torn and tatters for our Hershel.

But when he came home, Razel wanted him to take that coat right off. "If Poverty sees you wearing his coat, he might never leave this house. Go up there right now and give it to him!"

"You're absolutely right," said Hershel. He took the coat off and climbed up to the loft.

A little while later he climbed back down still carrying the coat.

"Hershel, why didn't you give Poverty his coat?" demanded Razel.

"I don't believe it," said Hershel. "The coat doesn't fit him anymore."

"What do you mean? You said he was exactly the same size as you. Like twins!"

"That was true," answered Hershel. "But that was before we spent the money on the coat. Now we are poorer and Poverty has grown bigger! He can't fit into it anymore."

KETSELE'S GIFT

United States

*randpa will love this*, Iris thought as she carefully copied the Hebrew letters into her notebook. She smiled when she pictured how surprised Grandpa would be at all her hard work. He would probably hug her tightly to him, or maybe even throw her into the air as he had done when she was little.

If only Grandpa knew English better, she thought. *I could tell him all about my new school and my new friends . . .*

Iris heard footsteps. They couldn't be Grandpa's. Not yet. She turned around.

"Doing homework?" Mama asked.

"No. I'm copying words out of this Hebrew dictionary to show Grandpa how much I'm learning in Hebrew school. I hope he'll like it."

"He's very proud of you, Iris." Mama gave her a little squeeze. "But come downstairs soon. We have to get dinner ready."

When Iris walked into the kitchen, she smelled Grandpa's favorite dinner: brisket of beef, boiled potatoes and tsimmes, a sweet carrot dish simmering on the stove.

She was chopping mushrooms and onions when the doorbell rang.

"Grandpa's here!" Iris raced out of the kitchen and opened the front door.

"Grandpa!" she shouted, throwing her arms around him. He was so tall, she barely came up to his chest.

"My shayna madala, my pretty one," Grandpa said affectionately, lifting Iris in his big strong arms. He kissed both her cheeks. Big, juicy kisses. "Oh, so zaftig you are. So big."

When he put her down, Iris snuggled against his gray woolen vest. He smelled like hair cream and mothballs.

"Guess what, Grandpa! I have a surprise for you."

"Maybe I have a surprise for you, too," he said. "Come, shayna madala. Help me unpack."

Iris followed Grandpa to the guest room. He handed her a big package of games.

"Some new ones! Thanks, Grandpa," said Iris as she opened her present. Grandpa always had more time to play games with her than Mama or Papa. "I'll get you my surprise, now."

"Go, ketsele." That was Grandpa's special name for Iris. Mama said it meant little kitten.

Iris ran to her room for the notebook. When she returned, she handed it to Grandpa and waited to hear what he would say.

Grandpa flipped through the neatly lettered pages. "Very nice, ketsele. All by yourself?"

Iris nodded.

"Very nice," he said again and kissed her cheek. Then he set the notebook aside and sniffed the air. "Do I smell my favorite dinner?"

"Uh-huh. Brisket and tsimmes." Iris tried not to sound disappointed. She thought Grandpa would get all excited when he saw the notebook. Maybe he's just hungry. He'll probably make a big deal about it after dinner.

Everyone enjoyed Mama's cooking that evening. Especially Grandpa.

"Such gut brisket, Chana," he said to Mama. "Such gut potatoes. Such gut tsimmes." To Grandpa everything Mama made was good.

After dinner Grandpa sat on the couch reading a newspaper from the city. Iris sat next to him, waiting for him to say something about her note-book. But he didn't. *I bet he will after he rests a little*, she thought.

Iris looked at the newspaper. It's all in Hebrew, she thought at first. But as she looked more carefully, she realized that the printing was a little different. The letters were the same, but there weren't any dots near them and the words were really long. She couldn't find any that she knew.

"Where are the dots, Grandpa?"

"Nu, dots you want?" he said and kept on reading.

Iris slipped off Grandpa's lap and went into the kitchen where Mama and Papa were washing dishes.

"Mama, what kind of newspaper is Grandpa reading?"

"His Yiddish paper," she answered.

"Is that the same as Hebrew?"

"No. Yiddish is different even though it uses Hebrew letters and has some of the same words. It's the language Grandpa spoke when he lived in the old country, in Russia."

"But Grandpa sings from the Hebrew prayer book in synagogue."

"He does. But he doesn't know what the words mean."

"I didn't know that," said Iris. *Maybe that's why he wasn't excited when I gave him the notebook*, she thought.

Iris went up to the guest room and grabbed the notebook and a pen. She scooted downstairs and climbed onto Grandpa's lap.

"Oof," he cried. "Such a big madala. And such an old zayde."

Iris laughed. "Grandpa, would you show me how to write ketsele? And maybe shayna madala, too? And zayde and tsimmes. . . ." Iris was surprised at all Grandpa's words she remembered.

"Hold on a minute. Where's the horse race?" Grandpa joked. But Iris could see he was happy by the way his neck and face got all red and his eyes danced.

"You want to learn Yiddish? An American girl doesn't need Yiddish in this new, wonderful country."

"But I want to, Grandpa. I do."

Grandpa opened the notebook to a blank page and wrote something. "That says madala, little girl," he explained.

Iris copied quickly, and soon she and Grandpa had filled three pages with Yiddish words. She even learned some new words such as vance for bedbug.

"That's if someone is, how you say, a nag," Grandpa said. "Call him a vance."

Great. A new word I can use on my brothers, she thought.

"Enough for the first lesson. You want to do it every day when I'm here, ketsele?"

"Every day," Iris said. "That way I can learn to talk to you in Yiddish, Grandpa. And maybe even read your newspaper."

"Ah, some good stories in here, ketsele." Grandpa patted Iris's hair with his great big hands. "My Yiddishe ketsele."

ISRAEL STORIES

ELIEZER BEN YEHUDA

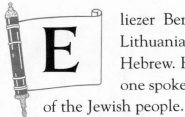liezer Ben Yehuda was born Eliezer Yizhak Perelman in Lithuania in 1858 and is considered the father of modern Hebrew. His dream was of a Jewish homeland where everyone spoke the same language, Hebrew, the ancient language of the Jewish people.

As a child, Eliezer was raised in a Hasidic household in Lithuania. His father died when he was five years old. When he was thirteen years old, he was sent to live with his uncle and study at a school, a yeshivah. The head of this yeshivah introduced Eliezer to famous worldy, as well as Jewish, literature. To save Eliezer from this exposure to the outside world, his uncle sent him to study in another city. It was here that Eliezer met Samuel Jonas, who was also a hasid, and was writing for Hebrew magazines. Jonas and his family taught Eliezer Russian, and persuaded him to study at a Russian secondary school.

The Russo-Turkish War broke out just as Eliezer was finishing his secondary school education. The struggle of the Balkan countries for their freedom inspired Eliezer with the hope that the Jewish people could also live freely in their own homeland, which was then called Palestine. He felt that what the Jewish people needed was a national movement to bring them back to their land, and restore their historic language, Hebrew.

Eliezer wanted to move to the land of Israel, but decided that he needed a profession first, in order to support himself there. So he went to Paris to study. At this time, Eliezer was also writing about the idea of a Jewish homeland under the pen name of E. Ben Yehuda. He wrote about how so many of the European peoples were fighting for their freedom. He felt that the Jewish people should too, and if the Jewish people settled in the land of Israel, this land could become a center for the Jews who were scattered all over the world, even for those who never moved there. At least they would know that there was a Jewish land with its own language and culture.

In Paris, Eliezer met a Jewish journalist who told him that the Hebrew language was not dead, and that while traveling, he had spoken it with Jews in Asia and Africa. He also met Joseph Halevy who, as early as the 1860s, had proposed inventing new Hebrew words for things that did not exist in Biblical times. Another person who influenced Eliezer in these early years was a scholar who spoke Hebrew to him with a Sephardic pronunciation, and told him there were Jews in Jerusalem who were already speaking to each other in Sephardic Hebrew. By this time, Eliezer thought that all the Jewish children in the land of Israel should be instructed in schools using the Hebrew language, instead of in the many different languages of the lands they had come from.

In 1881, Eliezer left for Palestine, and was joined by a childhood friend Deborah Jonas, whom he married. When the couple arrived in the city of Jaffa, he told Deborah that they would speak only Hebrew in their new home. Thus, theirs was the first home to speak modern Hebrew in Palestine. When their son Itamar Ben-Avi was born, he became the first modern Hebrew speaking child.

In Palestine, Eliezer taught in schools where he used only Hebrew, and founded a newspaper written only in Hebrew. Some people Eliezer met did not want to use Hebrew for their daily speech, and were very much against his ideas. Even though Hebrew had been spoken in everyday life in Biblical times, many people had become accustomed to only speaking Hebrew in prayers and religious study. Jews spoke the languages of the countries in which they lived for their daily lives. But Eliezer Ben Yehuda believed very strongly in the importance of using Hebrew once again as a national language, and worked very hard to bring his vision to life despite some opposition.

He invented new words in Hebrew because there were so many things and ideas for which there were no words in Biblical Hebrew, things like electricity, ice cream, railroads, bicycle, umbrella. Some words were made from parts of old Hebrew words, while others were taken from different languages and given the sounds of Hebrew letters. Eliezer formed a committee of people who helped him build up the vocabulary of modern Hebrew from the Biblical Hebrew, which only had seven thousand seven hundred and four words.

Eliezer also wrote the *Complete Dictionary of Ancient and Modern Hebrew*. He hung a sign where he worked which said, "The time is short, the task is great." Work on this dictionary was continued after Eliezer's death in 1922 by his second wife Hemdah and his son Ehud. It was published in 1959 in seventeen volumes with an additional introductory volume. This dictionary contained more than fifty thousand Hebrew words, much much more than the 7,704 words Eliezer had to start with.

Eliezer Ben Yehuda lived to see his dream come true, a land where the Hebrew language was once again spoken after more than two thousand years. And he helped to unite the people and the land with his hard work, perseverance and vision.

THEODOR HERZL

T heodor Herzl was born in Budapest, Hungary in 1860. He went with his father to services at the Liberal Temple near the house where he was born, and became a bar mitzvah there. His mother, though, was more interested in raising him in the spirit of the enlightened German-Jewish ideas of the time, rather than in a religious or Zionist environment. From early on, Theodor showed promise as a writer and had a desire for greatness. When he was ten, for instance, he said he wanted to be the builder of the Panama Canal!

When Theodor was eighteen years old, he studied law in Vienna, Austria, and joined a German students' society there. He left the society in 1883 when his fraternity brothers said that Jews could no longer join the society, though those who were already members could stay.

He practiced law for a short time, and then devoted himself to his passion of writing full time. He wrote stories and plays. From 1891 to 1895, he was the Paris correspondent for the *New Free Press* of Vienna. In Paris, he witnessed a growing anti-Semitic sentiment. At first, he thought Jews should convert and assimilate, and become members of the socialist movement. But it was not long before he decided against this solution to the problems of discrimination against Jews. He began to write publicly about the issue in the hopes that people, Jews and non-Jews alike, would discuss anti-Semitism openly with mutual respect and reach some solutions.

However, in 1894 an event occurred which was to profoundly effect Theodor Herzl's thinking. It was the Dreyfus Case. Alfred Dreyfus was a French army officer who was accused of selling secrets to the Germans. There was very little evidence against him, and he had no reason to betray France. He proclaimed his innocence. It was clear from the trial that his only sin was that he was Jewish. The court found him guilty and imprisoned him for life on Devil's Island, off the coast of South America. His brother and others pressed for further investigation, and discovered that the real traitor was a Major Esterhazy, but government officials did not want to admit that the army had made a mistake. So new "evidence" against Dreyfus was forged and Esterhazy was declared innocent. When a writer named Emile Zola, who was not Jewish, wrote a book beginning with the words, "I accuse" and attacked Esterhazy's acquittal, Zola was accused of slander. He was forced to leave France or be imprisoned himself. Crowds of people in France picked on Jews, destroyed their stores, and demanded that the Jews be expelled from France. Eventually, the people who believed in Dreyfus's innocence and worked hard to clear his name succeeded. In 1906, twelve years after the case had begun, Dreyfus was declared innocent of all crimes.

Theodor witnessed all of this, and it was to change his thinking. Instead of hoping that mankind would gradually move toward tolerance, he began to search for a way that would make Jews safe from this kind of anti-Semitism. He focused on the idea of moving the Jews from where they now lived, scattered all over the world, to a land and government all their own, and he began to work toward this goal. In 1896 he published a small book named *The Jewish State* that called for an independent country for the Jews. "The Maccabeans will rise again," he said.

Theodor Herzl's preference for the location of the Jewish state was the

Land of Israel. He also believed that before mass settlement could occur anywhere, whether it be the Land of Israel or Argentina or wherever the Jews preferred, there would have to be a preconceived plan. He hoped that the financial backing for this plan would come from the Jewish banking families like the Rothschilds, but if this did not happen then he would turn to the common people.

There was quite a reaction to his book after it was published. His was not the very first book on this subject, but it came at the right time, and many people read it and talked about it. Numerous people rejected his plan, thinking it too extreme. They called Theodor Herzl a dreamer. But others responded with enthusiasm and wanted him to assume the leadership of this cause. Theodor did this and became the leader of the Zionist Movement, a movement whose goal was the creation of a Jewish State in the Land of Israel, Zion, the ancient homeland of the Jewish people.

Herzl began to meet with leaders all over the world. He was a dignified and handsome man who commanded respect wherever he went. He spoke with the German Kaiser William II, the grand vizier and the sultan in Constantinople, the Pope in Rome, and Jews all over the world. He founded a weekly newspaper to publicize and clarify the idea of a Jewish homeland. He succeeded in organizing the First Zionist Congress held in Basel, Switzerland in August of 1897, the first official, worldwide gathering of Jews ever. Almost 200 Jewish leaders attended. They were from Western and Eastern Europe, England, Algeria and America. They were of all ages, of different Jewish religious denominations, and represented different political-economic groups, from capitalist to socialist.

This Congress set up a World Zionist Organization to create "for the Jewish people a home in Palestine secured by public law." Plans were made at this congress and later ones for a national bank and a national fund to buy land. People were asked to join Zionist groups where they lived and to raise money to buy land and support the settlements in Palestine. A national anthem called "Hatikvah," the Hope, was sung, and a national flag displayed. It had two blue stripes like the ones on a prayer shawl, and a six-pointed star, the Star of David.

Until his death from heart disease and pneumonia in 1904 at the age of forty-four, Theodor Herzl worked tirelessly to realize his dream of a place Jews could live where they would not have to experience the discrimination and anti-Semitism he had witnessed. It had been only about nine and a half years since Theodor had covered the Dreyfus case for the Vienna newspaper. And it would be only another 45 years until Theodor Herzl, who had asked in his will to be buried in the Jewish state, would be brought to Jerusalem and reburied in a hill overlooking the ancient city.

As Herzl himself once said, "If you will it, it is no dream."

JOSEPH TRUMPELDOR

Born in 1880 in the Caucasus region of Russia, Joseph Trumpeldor attended a religious school and then a Russian municipal school as a child. Since he could not attend high school because he was Jewish, he studied dentistry.

Near his home in Russia, a group of people formed and lived in a collective community modeled after one described by the famous Russian writer Tolstoy. Both Tolstoy's ideas and this nearby community influenced Joseph who combined the idea of agricultural collective communities with Zionism, the establishment of a Jewish homeland in the Land of Israel.

Joseph was drafted into the Russian army in 1902. He often volunteered for dangerous missions and distinguished himself in the Russo-Japanese War of 1904. In that war, he was badly wounded, so much so that his left arm was amputated. Even though he could have returned home after this injury, he asked to be sent back to the front lines.

After surrendering at the battle of Port Arthur, he and his fellow prisoners were sent to a prisoner-of-war camp in Japan. At this camp he worked hard for the benefit of his fellow prisoners. He also organized a Zionist group, as well as a group of Jewish soldiers whose goal was to settle in the Land of Israel and establish an agricultural community there.

In 1906, the Japanese returned Joseph to Russia, where he was made an

officer and awarded a medal for bravery. He was the very first Jewish officer in the history of the Russian army.

During the next few years, Joseph formed a group that he hoped would
eventually establish a collective settlement in the Land of Israel. The aim
of his organization was to free the Jewish people from oppression and discrimination by creating an independent life in the Land of Israel. He went
to Palestine with some of his friends and worked at a farm there. While he
was in Palestine, Joseph also helped defend the Jewish settlements in the
Lower Galilee.

Because he would not take Ottomon citizenship when World War I
began, he was taken out of Palestine by the Turkish authorities and
brought to Egypt. There he accepted the British Army's proposal to create
the Zion Mule Corps. Joseph looked at this as the first step toward forming
a Jewish military force that would eventually free the Land of Israel.

He was deputy commander of the Zion Mule Corps, and took part in
the major British battles with the Turks where he was known for his bravery and willingness to do the most difficult of tasks. The members of the
Zion Mule Corps were the first Jews to ever serve as a unit within an army
of a modern country. They wore the Star of David on their shoulders while
they risked their lives bringing supplies to the front lines, and their reputation traveled quickly throughout the Zionist world.

After the war ended, Joseph traveled to both London and then Russia,
and made efforts to create Jewish legions in both places. He had hoped that
he could form a Jewish regiment that would fight against the horrible
attacks on Jews called pogroms that were taking place in Russia. But the
Russian government outlawed the Jewish defense organization that
Trumpeldor worked hard to create.

He continued his work to organize young Jews who would travel to the

Land of Israel and form farming communities there. In 1919, he returned to the Land of Israel where he tried to convince the British military authorities to bring thousands of Jewish soldiers from Russia and form a Jewish legion. He thought this would be essential for Jewish national existence in Palestine. His idea was rejected by the British.

When danger faced the Jewish settlements in the Upper Galilee because of armed skirmishes between French authorities and Arabs, Trumpeldor was asked to help. He went to the northern tip of Israel and, together with the settlers and other volunteers, worked on fortifying the settlements.

Two months after he arrived there, while he was eating breakfast one morning, word came that Arabs were attacking the nearby settlement of Tel Hai. Joseph took his gun and dodged the Arab bullets with others from the settlement to reach the people in Tel Hai. Joseph saw that in the rush to get there, someone had left the village gate open. When he ran to close it, he was shot in the stomach. The battle went on all day until the Arabs were forced to retreat. Toward evening, Joseph and others who were injured were taken to a nearby settlement for medical help, but Joseph died along the way. His last words were, "Never mind. It is good to die for our country."

He was buried along with five of his comrades in the nearby settlement, but their remains were later moved to a new cemetery closer to Tel Hai. In 1934 a memorial sculpture was placed there, with a great roaring lion on its top. Joseph's life and death became a symbol for Jewish pioneers from all over the world who came to the Land of Israel. Many songs, stories and poems were written about the hero of this Jewish brigade of men and women who fought to defend their settlement. Joseph, his courage, initiative, hard work, and love for his land became an inspiration for many.

GOLDA MEIR

Golda Meir was born in Kiev, Russia in 1898. She and her family emigrated to the United States when she was 8 years old because of the poverty in Russia and the discrimination against the Jews there. They settled in Milwaukee, and after she graduated high school, she studied to be a teacher. Golda never forgot the terrible pogrom that she experienced as a little girl in Russia. Her home and the homes of other Jewish people were attacked, and some of the people were killed for no other reason except that they were Jewish. Golda felt that the Jewish people must have their own homeland so that other Jewish children would not have to experience what she did. In 1921, she and her husband decided to settle in Palestine, and she quickly became involved in political activities there.

Golda was an excellent speaker and a hard worker, and she became active in the labor movement that David Ben-Gurion had helped to organize. One of her most dangerous jobs was in 1948. She disguised herself as an Arab woman and drove across the Transjordan border with an Arabic-speaking Israeli who carried false identification papers. She wanted to speak secretly with King Abdullah, hoping to convince him not to join the attack with the other Arab states on the about-to-be-declared new State of Israel. She and her driver were stopped many times by Transjordanian soldiers, but luckily they never spoke to Golda. If they had, they would have discovered she could not speak Arabic, and her mission would have been over.

Golda did reach the King and did talk to him. Unfortunately, he would not promise peace, and so Golda and her driver made their way back to Israel knowing that along with their other Arab neighbors, Transjordan would also fight the newly established State of Israel.

After the establishment of Israel and the war that followed, Golda was appointed minister to Moscow. Because of her presence there, many Jews attended High Holiday services at the Moscow Great Synagogue. This was something that had not happened for a long time in the Soviet Union, a country that tried to suppress all religious practices among its citizens.

In 1956, Golda became foreign minister of Israel. Because she was one of the few women to hold such a high position in a government, she became famous worldwide. She was very effective in her abilities to convince statesmen and representatives of other governments of Israel's needs and interests. She was very active in the United Nations, and her speeches there drew a lot of attention.

Golda Meir became the fourth prime minister of Israel in 1969. She saw Israel as a center of a united Jewish people all around the world, and spoke often about the Israeli government's solidarity with the Jews of the Soviet Union. At that time, the Jews of the Soviet Union were openly struggling to gain the right to settle in Israel, but were not allowed to leave the Soviet Union.

When Israel's Arab neighbors launched a surprise attack on Israel in 1973, the country was almost cut in half before the army was able to turn the attack around. Many young Israelies died in the fighting. Because her government was caught by surprise, Golda left her position as prime minister in disgrace. Would there always be war she wondered.

Toward the end of her life, Golda's hope grew again. The president of

Egypt, Anwar al-Sadat, who had been Israel's enemy, came to Israel to talk about peace. When Golda shook his hand, she said to him, "What took you so long?"

When Abba Eban, an Israeli statesman and contemporary of Golda Meir's, describes Golda, he says that as a political leader, she was much like a grandmother who likes to protect her grandchildren against being bullied by the tough kids in the neighborhood. She had the ability to give those around her a sense of security even in the most explosive situations.

Golda Meir died in 1978. She was a remarkable and courageous woman who acted on her convictions and gave of herself tirelessly in her work for her country and people.

NEVE SHALOM/WAHAT al-SALAM

There is a small community in one of the hills leading up to Jerusalem called Neve Shalom/Wahat al-Salam. This means Oasis of Peace in Hebrew and Arabic. It is a cooperative village where Jews, Muslims and Christians of Israeli citizenship live. The people who live here keep their own religious, national and cultural identities within this community which is based on mutual acceptance, cooperation and respect.

As one resident said, "We didn't come here to lose our identities. I came here with my anger, my hope and my willingness to make compromises. We came here, Jews and Palestinians, not to say we would forget, but to prove that there is a better way. It's hard to visualize that things can be different. It's our role to help that vision."

On the road to the village, one passes old tanks and armored cars that were destroyed in the war of 1948, and soldiers. These are reminders that peace does not come easily in this part of the world.

Over twenty five years ago, this village was founded by the Rev. Bruno Hussar, and the land for the village was donated by the nearby Trappist monastery. This piece of land had not been inhabited since the 11th century and had no water or trees. The first structure was an old bus Hussar and some helpers tugged up the hill in 1972. He built his own residence later, a plywood packing crate large enough to hold a bed and a table. Finally, in the late 1970's, a few families became interested in joining Hussar on this hilltop. Though some people told him he was crazy, Rev. Hussar wanted to prove that ancient enemies could overcome their differences and live together in peace. "This is a dream of faith," Hussar said. "I won't say religion, because in this part of the world, religion divides people, but faith unites."

Rev. Hussar, a Dominican monk, was born in Egypt to a non-observant Jewish family who had come there from Hungary. He grew up unaware of any religious tradition. While he was living and studying in France, he converted to Catholicism, and later he became an Israeli citizen. He decided to devote his life to promoting understanding among Christians, Muslims and Jews. Rev. Hussar was one of the people who was instrumental in writing the document for the Vatican Council that declared there was no theological basis for Christians to blame Jews for the death of Jesus.

The village runs its own nursery, kindergarten and primary school that also accepts students from nearby towns and cities. Here, students speak both Arabic and Hebrew, and learn about each other's religion, history, and culture. In the rest of Israel, most Arab and Jewish children live in their own villages and go to their own schools. They usually do not learn to speak both Hebrew and Arabic like the children of Neve Shalom/Wahat al-Salam.

When children first come to this school from nearby villages, they have to speak to each other through translators. And they are tutored in the language they do not know. The children who grow up in Neve Shalom/Wahat al-Salam already know how to speak Arabic and Hebrew. The children in this school are encouraged to talk about their fears and what has led to violence between their peoples. This school is one of the very few where Jewish students learn about Arabs, and Arab students learn about Jews. In this school, friendships form between Arab and Jewish students who spend their days learning and playing together, and often visit each other's families outside of the school day. In this atmosphere, understanding grows.

Neve Shalom/Wahat al-Salam also operates a School for Peace that conducts workshops for Arab and Jewish youth, students, teachers, lawyers, business people, and others from all over Israel as well as the Palestinian Authority. The workshops give people a chance to meet and discuss issues that tend to divide them. It provides opportunities for constructive dialogue and conflict resolution for Jews and Palestinian youth and adults. Often the sessions in these workshops are painful, but people respect each other for telling the truth. People at Neve Shalom/Wahat al-Salam believe it is valuable to discover what others feel, even if it is not comfortable to hear it.

The village does not have a political charter and is not connected with any political party. Its purpose is educational and it stands as a living example that coexistence is possible.

HOLIDAYS

THE SABBATH

God created the world in six days, and on the seventh day, God rested. On the seventh day of the week, beginning Friday night at sundown and continuing until sundown on Saturday night, Jews all over the world also enjoy a day of rest. Candles are lit, wine is sipped and braided egg bread, challah, is tasted. The Sabbath is filled with delicious family meals, often including guests, singing and storytelling, synagogue services, walks, much-needed naps, reading and studying.

JOSEPH
THE SABBATH LOVER

nce there was a man called Joseph the Sabbath Lover. He was not a wealthy man and saved his money every day of the week. But nothing was too good for his Sabbath table. He worked extra hard all week long so that he could purchase the best on the Sabbath in order to honor it.

"Here comes Joseph the Sabbath Lover," the woman selling eggs in the marketplace would call to her friend behind the poultry stall. "You will be able to sell that big plump chicken to him if to no one else."

"See how early he comes to market today," the fish merchant said. "He wants to be sure to buy only the best for the Sabbath."

"One would think he was a wealthy man."

"He isn't." The wine dealer joined in the chatter. "I have seen how hard he works in the fields, and how little he eats every other day."

Now Joseph had a wealthy neighbor who enjoyed mocking Joseph. "One day you eat like a king and the others like a pauper. I have never seen anything that made so little sense," he would say to Joseph. "You never get any richer because you honor the Sabbath. Whereas I, who never keep the Sabbath, do."

Joseph's honoring of the Sabbath and his wealthy neighbor's mocking of him went on for many years. Joseph paid little attention to his neighbor's words. He loved honoring the Sabbath, preparing his little house, his food, his clothing for the holy day. And all week long he looked forward to celebrating the Sabbath and sharing it with his friends. This was reward enough for Joseph.

Now it so happened that one day, when his neighbor consulted the astrologers and soothsayers, as he was often accustomed to do, he heard this fortune: "We have read in the stars that all your wealth will soon become Joseph the Sabbath Lover's."

Very shaken by these words, the wealthy neighbor thought and thought until came up with a plan that he was sure would prevent these words from ever becoming true. He sold everything he owned, and purchased one perfect jewel which he sewed into his turban. Then he secretly boarded a ship bound for a distant land, a land far away from his neighbor, Joseph the Sabbath Lover.

He was several days out to sea when a storm rocked the ship and waves higher than the ship rolled over and over it. It happened that the winds blew the neighbor's turban right off his head and into the sea.

In the course of the next few days, and unbeknownst to the neighbor, a large fish swam by the jewel and swallowed it.

Then, days later, a fisherman near Joseph's village caught this same big fish in his net and brought it to market. It was the day before the Sabbath and as was usual, Joseph came early to buy food for his Sabbath meals.

"See that man coming into the marketplace?" the grain merchant called to the fisherman. "He will buy that most beautiful fish and give you a price you deserve."

"He does not look wealthy," said the fisherman.

"He isn't. Haven't you heard of Joseph Who Loves the Sabbath?" said the grain merchant.

The fisherman had. He brought this beautiful fish up to Joseph who did indeed give him a good price for it, just as the grain merchant said he would.

Joseph, happy to have such a fine fish to prepare for the Sabbath, quickly bought what else he needed and hurried home.

When he opened the fish so as to ready it for cooking, Joseph stood back in amazement and joy. There inside was the largest and finest jewel he could have ever imagined. What a joyous Sabbath Joseph enjoyed, singing praises to God and sharing his good news with his friends.

And a few days later, when Joseph found a buyer for the jewel, he discovered that he was a very wealthy man indeed, as wealthy as his neighbor had been, his neighbor who had so mysteriously disappeared.

Then one Friday, not long after this, Joseph went, as had always been his custom, to the marketplace early to buy the finest foods for the approaching Sabbath. On his way, he met an old man, a stranger.

The man greeted him. "You must be Joseph the Sabbath Lover," he said.

"Yes, I am," Joseph said, not very surprised, for he knew that many called him this and knew him when he did not know them. But he was surprised by the next words the old man spoke, and happy to hear them as well.

"To the person who lends to the Sabbath," the old man said, "the Sabbath repays many times. May God continue to reward you, Joseph the Sabbath Lover."

SABBATH IN PARADISE

by Jane Yolen

 here was a rabbi who traveled from town to town teaching Torah. But this one day, the longer he traveled, the less he seemed to get anywhere. The path led to no city, no village, no town. Frustrated, he sent his assistant on to find the right road.

One hour passed. Then another. And still the assistant did not return. As darkness crept up on him, the rabbi became worried. It was almost sunset on Sabbath eve.

So forgetting his journey, he prepared for the Sabbath and began to say his prayers with such great passion there in the country air that every syllable went up to the heavens.

At first the rabbi's eyes were closed as he prayed. But for some reason he opened them and saw a man coming down the road toward him. At this the rabbi smiled. *A man,* he thought, *and where there is one man—there will be more. And where there are more—is a settlement.*

When the man got close, he said to the rabbi, "Will you spend the Sabbath with me, Rabbi?"

The rabbi answered simply, "Why not?"

"But you must promise me," the man said, "that when we get to where we are going you will not ask a single question. In fact, no matter what passes before your eyes, you will not make the slightest sound. You must give me your word on thls."

The rabbi thought for a moment. *To give a promise when you don't know what will befall . . . But I have no other choice,* he thought. So he agreed.

The man held out his hand and the rabbi took it. And they had walked only a short way when ahead the rabbi saw a wonderful palace.

The rabbi opened his mouth to speak, but the man put a finger to his lips. "Not a sound," reminded the man. "You promised."

And indeed he had, so the rabbi was silent.

They went up to the palace and the man opened the door. When they went in, the beauty of the entrance hall dazzled the rabbi's eyes and, for a moment, he shut them. But then he heard the high wail of a horn and the sweet voice of a fiddle – the rollicking sounds of a klezmer band. He opened his eyes again just as the man pushed open an inner door.

There was a temple, but more beautiful than any temple the rabbi had ever seen: adamantine floors and walls of alabaster and an Ark interlined with gold and jewels too numerous to count. And marvelous, too, were the men who prayed in that magnificent room.

At the altar an old man with a long white beard recited the words of the Sabbath service so sweetly, the rabbi was entirely overcome. It was as if he were hearing the prayers for the very first time, so straight and sure did they go to his heart.

The rabbi turned to his guide and was about to ask him where they were and who the people were, but the man held his finger to his lips. "Remember your promise," his gesture said. So the rabbi was silent.

When the prayers were done, they went into a room even more beautiful than the first, where on a table of dark ebony wood were set plates and chalices of silver and gold.

The rabbi turned once more to his guide, but this time the man did not need to raise his finger to his lips, for the rabbi was silent and just smiled.

They ate and drank, they drank and ate, each bite and each swallow a revelation. It was as if the rabbi had never eaten bread or drunk wine before.

"And now I will show you where to sleep," his guide said in a low voice. Then he led the rabbi to a fragrant bed in a room in which the sheets were of satin and the pillows of silk.

The next morning at prayers, when it was time for the Torah readers to be called up, the rabbi thought, *Now I will know where I am, for each will be called by his name.*

The first was summoned: "Moshe, son of Amram, the sixth portion."

The rabbi began to tremble.

And the second: "David hameylekh—David the king."

He trembled some more.

And the third: "Shlomo hameylekh—King Solomon."

The rabbi was trembling so hard he feared he would fall down.

"Avraham ovinu—our father Abraham," called the voice.

The poor rabbi's knees were suddenly so weak he knew he could not stand. But, as he had been warned, he was silent. He said nothing, only listened.

As night fell at last, and the patriarch Abraham said the blessing to mark the close of the Sabbath, King David accompanied him in song after song on his harp. The rabbi felt tears falling from his eyes. But still he was silent.

Then a voice cried, "Quiet. The celestial council of justice is about to convene."

Hearing that, the rabbi gave a deep sigh. "Ah," he said aloud. Only that one syllable. "Ah."

The moment it was uttered, everything disappeared and the rabbi found he was standing alone at night in an empty field.

ROSH HASHANAH

Rosh Hashanah, meaning the head or beginning of the year, comes in the fall, and is the anniversary of the day the world was created. Customs include sending New Year cards to family and friends wishing all a happy year, and dipping apples in honey in the hopes of a sweet year. It is a time to reflect on the past year, and think about changes that could be made in the year ahead. Much of the two-day holiday (one day in Israel) is spent in the synagogue where the shofar, the ram's horn, is blown at intervals throughout the service. "Wake up! Wake up!" the shofar calls.

To Heaven? If Not Higher!

This happened during the last week of the Hebrew month of Elul, just before Rosh Hashanah. It was the time for saying the special penitential prayers called *selichot*, the prayers asking for forgiveness. In Sassov, the village beadle walked from house to house at dawn with his lantern and a hammer shaped like a *shofar*, a ram's horn. He knocked on each door calling, "Wake up! It is time to wake up!" and the Jews got up to go to synagogue to say their prayers asking for forgiveness.

During these days, a man came to Sassov to visit his cousin. He had never been there before, nor had he ever met Sassov's Rabbi. One morning, he rose early, like the others, to go and say his prayers.

But he noticed that the Rabbi was not there.

"So, where is this sainted Rabbi of yours?" he asked his cousin. "This Rabbi I have heard so much about. He isn't here leading us all in our selichot prayers. Doesn't he himself need to ask forgiveness, too? Or is he so righteous and perfect?"

"We think he is up in Heaven," answered his cousin, "pleading with God to forgive all our sins before the solemn Day of Judgment."

"He is probably saying in our defense that we are good people," whispered someone. "He is telling God that we try very hard. But we are only human and make mistakes."

"Nonsense," said the cousin. And he laughed at them both.

"Well, where do you think he goes?" they asked him. "He is not in the House of Study or at home or . . ."

"I don't know. But I will find out," said the cousin who came up with a daring plan. Late one evening, when most people were asleep, he quietly entered the Rabbi's house, went into his bedroom, and hid under the bed where the Rabbi slept soundly. In this way, he planned to see exactly where the Rabbi went, and he was sure it wasn't up to Heaven. He was so determined to prove himself right, and the townspeople wrong, that he managed to stay awake there under the Rabbi's bed all through the long and dark night.

Very early the next morning, while it was still dark outside, Rabbi Moshe stirred. He said his morning prayers, washed, dressed in peasant clothes, and left the house.

Ah, look at those clothes, thought the cousin. *Surely he isn't going to meet God in an old shirt and patched pants.*

As soon as the door shut, the cousin squirmed out from under the bed. He felt stiff all over, but he only took a few stretches. He wanted to be able to follow the Rabbi.

When he caught up with the Rabbi, the cousin could see that this Rabbi Moshe carried an ax, tucked into his belt.

A peasant's clothes? An ax? the cousin thought. *Where is he going? To heaven, no. To the House of Study to pray and study, no. But where?*

He followed the Rabbi through the still quiet streets of the town. A few lights were on in the windows as people prepared to go to the House of Study to say the *selichot* prayers.

He followed the Rabbi into the forest at the edge of the town. He stopped when the Rabbi stopped to take out his ax and chop down a small tree. Then Rabbi Moshe split the tree into logs and kindling wood. He tied all the wood into a bundle with some rope from his pocket, and walked back into town with the cousin not far behind.

Down a narrow, muddy street the Rabbi walked. And so did the cousin, far enough behind to hide if the Rabbi should turn around. But the Rabbi didn't.

The Rabbi stopped at a broken down hut and knocked at the window.

"Who's there?" said a frail voice.

"It's Vassili," said the Rabbi, in a voice that made him sound like a peasant.

"What do you want? You know I have no money to pay you for your wood."

"And you know I trust you to pay me when you are well."

The Rabbi entered the poor hut and the cousin crept closer, hiding out of view by the side of the house. He could see a sick peasant woman lying under a thin blanket. There was no fire in her stove, and the hut was cold and damp.

"Do you see how sick I am?" said the woman. "Do you think I will be able to repay you?"

"I'm not worried about that," said Rabbi Moshe in his peasant's gruff voice.

"But I can't even get up to light my own fire," said the woman. "I'm a widow and my son is already at work."

"Ach, what trouble is it for me to light the fire?" said Rabbi Moshe, and he stooped down to put the wood in the stove and light it. The cousin could hear him whispering the *selichot* prayers asking for forgiveness as he worked at the fire.

The cousin decided he had seen enough. Quietly, he crept away from the hut and to the House of Study, where by now, all the townspeople were gathered, saying their morning prayers before going off to work.

And after the prayers, when the townspeople talked about their Rabbi Moshe not being there because he was in Heaven pleading for their sakes, the cousin did not cry "Nonsense" or laugh at them. No. Instead he said quietly, "To heaven? If not higher."

And this same cousin stayed in the town of Sassov, to become one of Rabbi Moshe's most devoted students.

THE SHOFAR

Before one Rosh Hashanah, Rabbi Levi Isaac of Berditchev was interviewing a number of candidates for the position of blowing the *shofar* before the congregation. He asked each one this question, "What will you be thinking about when you blow the shofar?"

Reb Shlomo, the grain merchant, answered first. He had blown the *shofar* for Rabbi Levi Isaac each of the past five years and always gave the same answer. "I will be thinking of how each note I blow is rising to the heavens, carrying our prayers."

"I will block out all thoughts of the everyday world if I blow the shofar," answered Reb Meir, the butcher. "My notes will not only carry the prayers of the congregation. They will be prayers themselves!"

And so it went. One answer was holier than the next, until the Rabbi came to Reb Menachem, the water carrier, who said, "Rabbi, I am a poor and simple Jew. I have four daughters and each one has already reached marriageable age and then some. I must find a match for each of my daughters. That means providing each with a dowry. You know how expensive that will be. When I will blow the shofar, I will be thinking of my four daughters. *Oh Merciful One*, I will be thinking. *I am fulfilling the commandment You gave of blowing the ram's horn. Please listen to this shofar crying out to You and fulfill your obligation of providing dowries for my four daughters."*

Rabbi Levi Isaac much preferred the sincere honesty of this poor Jew to the many pious words of the other applicants. And so that year, he chose the poor, simple Jew to blow the *shofar* before his congregation on Rosh Hashanah.

The *shofar,* the ram's horn that is blown on the High Holidays, on Rosh Hashanah and Yom Kippur, dates back to biblical times. Then the ram's horn was used to announce the beginning of a new month. Its call warned of danger, and it was blown at the inauguration of a king. The *shofar* sounded when the Israelites gathered at the base of the mountain to receive the Torah, the laws from God. And Joshua blew the *shofar* around the walls of Jericho.

The ram's horn also has an important place in the story of Abraham and the binding of Isaac. Abraham brought Isaac up on the mountain to offer him to God, as God had called him to do. Just as Abraham took out his knife, though, the angel of God called out to Abraham, and told him not to lay a hand on his son, that this was only a test of Abraham's faith. As the relieved Abraham looked up, he saw a ram caught in the bushes by its horns. Abraham took this ram and offered it up as a burnt offering in place of his son.

Saadia Gaon, a great scholar and leader of Babylonian Jewry over a thousand years ago, gave ten reasons for sounding the *shofar* on Rosh Hashanah. One reason was that this day was the beginning of creation, when God created the world and reigned over it. Just as trumpets and horns are blown in the presence of kings at the beginning of their reign, so should the shofar be blown to announce God the Creator on this day. Another one of Saadia Gaon's reasons was to remind us of the words of the prophets which were compared to the sounds of the shofar. They were warnings to the people of how they should be living and acting. Another reason was that when we hear the sounds of the *shofar* they will make us tremble, and we will humble ourselves before the Creator.

In modern times, in Israel, the *shofar* is blown in Orthodox neighborhoods to announce the coming of the Sabbath on Friday afternoons. And during the swearing in of a new president, the *shofar* is blown.

A *shofar* can be made from the horns of any kosher animal except cattle because of the incident of the golden calf. The horn is boiled for several hours. Then the cartilage is taken out and the horn is shaped. Often the horn is shaped with a curve to symbolize people's submission, their bowing to God. When the shaping is completed, the *shofar* is left to cool and harden.

It is not easy to blow the *shofar* and takes much practice. There are three different sounds made on the *shofar* on Rosh Hashanah and Yom Kippur. One is called Shevarim which has three notes, Teruah has nine quick notes, and Tekiah is one unbroken long sound. On Rosh Hashanah there are up to one hundred blasts sounded on the *shofar* in different groupings.

When the *shofar* sounds, awesome and clear on these holiest of days, people listen and pray that these sounds will carry their prayers for the new year up, up, up to the highest realms, to God.

YOM KIPPUR

Yom Kippur is the solemn Day of Atonement, a day of fasting, prayer, and intro-
spection, of coming closer to God. It is a day to ask forgiveness for any sins com-
mitted in the past year, and to think of how to return to God's ways. The holi-
day starts at sundown and ends at sundown of the next day. Most of the day is
spent in synagogue. The traditional opening prayer of Yom Kippur is called Kol
Nidre, which has a sad and haunting melody.

THE RABBI WAS LATE

I t was getting dark on the evening of Yom Kippur, one of the holiest days of the year. All the people in the town of Sassov were gathering in the synagogue, ready to hear Rabbi Moshe chant the beautiful and haunting Kol Nidre prayer. Soon the synagogue was so crowded that people were standing in the back and on the sides, because on this day everyone, even those who did not attend regularly on the Sabbath and other holidays, came to pray.

People greeted one another.

"May you be written and sealed in the Book Of Life for a good year."

"May you have an easy fast."

"Happy New Year."

"How is your mother? The new baby?"

People spoke quietly because they felt the approach of the solemn Day of Judgment.

But soon there was a complete hush in the synagogue. And a sense of anxiety, concern, for Rabbi Moshe still had not come. The people of Sassov had not been surprised that he wasn't there in the synagogue when they first started to arrive. They all knew that before the Sabbath and holidays, it was his custom to visit those who could not come to synagogue to pray, the old and the sick. But never before had he been so late. It was time to begin the prayer, the Kol Nidre, and where was Rabbi Moshe?

People began to whisper.

"Should some of us look for the Rabbi?"

"Could something have happened to him, God forbid?"

"No. He's probably visiting someone who is ill and lost track of time," said another. "Or perhaps there were more sick to visit than usual."

"But on this holiest night of the year?" asked his neighbor.

One woman, Rachel, was especially concerned because she had left her little baby at home alone just to come hear the Kol Nidre prayer. She had planned to be away only a few minutes, and listen to the Rabbi chant this one beautiful prayer that began the solemn day of Yom Kippur. But now the Rabbi was late, and the minutes were growing longer and longer. Rachel knew she could not stay. Her baby was still so little. Maybe she should not have left it at all, she thought.

So she got up quietly, nodded to the people in the rows around her, and left the synagogue. Once outside, she ran as quickly as she could down the streets to her house. As she neared the house, she was relieved. All was quiet. There was no sound of crying. The baby must have stayed asleep, she thought.

But when she opened the door, she was amazed to see none other than Rabbi Moshe sitting there, cradling her baby in his arms and singing to it. Rachel stood frozen by the door of her little house unable to say a word!

"What could I do?" Rabbi Moshe said to Rachel. "I was on my way to synagogue to begin the Kol Nidre prayer, when I walked by your house and heard the baby crying. Of course, I had to come in and comfort it."

"But Rabbi," said Rachel, regaining her speech. "They are all waiting for you at the synagogue and worrying about where you are."

"What can be more important than this baby?" Rabbi Moshe answered her. "God will understand why we are a few minutes late starting our prayers. And may you and the little one be inscribed for a good year," he added as he left, hurrying just a little.

THE SHEPHERD'S PRAYER

Once there was a farmer whose custom was to spend every Yom Kippur praying with the Ba'al Shem Tov and his disciples. Usually he would leave his young son at home to watch the sheep, and not bring him on his journey to Medzibozh, a town in Poland. After all, the boy could not make any sense of the Hebrew letters or recite any of the prayers. His father had tried over and over again to teach him, but to no avail.

His son, however, was a good shepherd, and he trusted him with the sheep. With his little wooden flute, his son played such mesmerizing tunes, some slow and sad, some joyful and sweet, that the sheep would follow him anywhere, and he never lost a one.

But now the boy was thirteen and of the age of a bar mitzvah when he was expected to keep the commandments. His father worried that if he left his son home, he would forget about fasting the whole day of Yom Kippur and he would eat something. So this time, the father brought his son with him to pray with the Ba'al Shem Tov. And he left the sheep in a neighbor's care.

The boy sat quietly through all the prayers in the House of Study. The Hebrew words and melodies surrounded him and moved him so. By the time of the afternoon prayers, the boy could no longer just sit there and listen. He begged his father, "Please, father, I want to take out my flute and blow it."

The father was irate. "You brought your flute! You can't play it in the House of Study! And on Yom Kippur of all days!" His father grabbed the little wooden flute out of his son's hands, and put it into his own pocket.

But the boy continued to want very much to play his flute, and join in this music of praying that he heard around him. He could hear the sounds of the tunes he would play in his head. If only his father would let him have his flute!

The chanting grew louder, softer. The people swayed while they prayed for forgiveness from the Heavenly One. Some were even crying.

"It is Neilah," the Ba'al Shem Tov said. "And the gates are closing. It is the last chance for our prayers to be sent heavenward on this holy day. To ask for forgiveness for what we have done in this past year. And for life and blessings in the new one."

Everyone stood for the final prayers, including, of course, the shepherd boy's father. The boy saw his chance and, so carefully did he reach into his father's pocket to retrieve the flute, that his father never felt a thing.

When he had his precious flute in his hand, the shepherd boy played a soulful tune. Everyone around him was startled to hear the music. They had never heard of such a thing! It was forbidden to play an instrument on the holy day! And in the House of Study!

People all around the boy grumbled angrily. His father felt so ashamed and fearful of what the Ba'al Shem Tov himself would say and do. But the Ba'al Shem did not say a word. He did not even turn around and look their way. He kept on praying. And the father noticed that his chanting did not sound so sad, but lighter, more joyful.

The Neilah service ended sooner than usual, and the Ba'al Shem Tov came right over to the father and his son. The father was sure it was to reprimand him for allowing his son to bring a flute to the House of Study, and on Yom Kippur! But truly, he had not even known his son carried it.

Much to the father's surprise, however, this was not at all what the Ba'al Shem Tov did.

"Your son made my job easier," the Ba'al Shem said. "His flute playing carried all our prayers right up to God. And do not worry that your son cannot read the Hebrew words or say the prayers. The words of God burn in him like a fire. God can hear the words in his music and join them together into prayers. What God wants from us most of all is that we pray with all our heart, and so be assured that your son's playing was accepted with pure delight by the Holy One."

SUKKOT

Sukkot, which means booths or huts, is a week-long joyous holiday. Jews build little huts for this holiday for two reasons. The huts commemorate the time when the Israelites wandered in the desert after leaving Egypt and had to live in temporary shelters. They also remind us of when the Israelites were farmers in the land of Israel and built little huts near their fields to live in during harvest time. It is customary for Jews to eat and even sleep in their decorated huts. The next day after Sukkot is also a holiday and is called Simhat Torah. It means rejoicing in the Torah, the laws. It is the day Jews celebrate the completion of the yearly reading of the entire Torah scroll in the synagogue. On Simhat Torah, the reading ends and then begins again. It's a festive time with processionals, and much singing and dancing.

NEVER TOO QUIET

 very day people flocked to Rabbi Pinchas with their questions and their problems, their troubles and their sorrows. From morning 'til late at night, there was a line outside the rabbi's house.

Today was no different. Such a commotion! It was like the center of the marketplace before the Sabbath.

When Rabbi Pinchas looked out the window at the crowd of squabbling people, he groaned.

"Almost evening, and still a line. Not even on the Sabbath do they leave me alone. My head hurts and my eyes see double."

Rabbi Pinchas looked longingly at his books, piled all around on shelves, on the desk, on the floor. "Not a minute to think or study or pray."

The rabbi straightened up suddenly and banged his fist on the table. "Enough is enough!" he said, grabbing pen and paper. In bold black letters he printed the words, ABSOLUTELY NO VISITORS!

Rabbi Pinchas got up from the table and carried his sign to the front door. "There are other rabbis in Koretz," he told the people. "They can help you just as well as I."

Then he hung his sign on the front door and went to sleep.

Such a sleep I haven't had since I was a baby, Rabbi Pinchas thought as he washed his hands the next morning. He smiled, thinking of the many hours ahead of him to read and study and pray.

All day no one knocked, no one called, no one burst into the house. *What a simple thing, a sign,* he thought. *And how it works!*

Weeks went by, summer weeks filled with quiet hours. Rabbi Pinchas had time to read and to write. He had time to visit with other rabbis in far-away towns. And he had time to walk by the river near his house, watching the sky change above him and the birds swoop down for insects and worms.

But one evening, while Rabbi Pinchas sat eating his simple meal, he felt a little sad. The study, the house, the yard all seemed, well, too quiet.

He shook his head as if to shake off the thought.

"Too quiet?" He chuckled, remembering the commotion. "It can never be too quiet." He pushed the thoughts and the feelings away and picked up a book.

But his mind wandered as he read, and he found himself thinking of Shana, the egg lady. He remembered all the times she had brought him fresh eggs and herb teas and news of the marketplace.

He thought of Yonkel, the Hebrew teacher. Yonkel no longer walked home with him from the synagogue to argue over a Bible passage.

And Heshe—that nuisance of a boy! Who was he plaguing at this very moment?

The rabbi thought of how Heshe used to beg him for a story. Of how he would tell Heshe about the little village where he grew up, about times he had long forgotten and was amused to remember. He would become young again in the telling, as young as Heshe, and they would laugh together.

The rabbi shook his head. "It's never too quiet," he told himself once again and picked up his book.

The summer weeks passed, and autumn came with its cooler air, falling leaves, and holidays.

The rabbi's Rosh Hashanah was sweet with learning. But he dipped the apple into the honey alone.

On Yom Kippur, he prayed uninterrupted, but broke his fast by himself.

When the Feast of Tabernacles came, he put up his little sukkot without any help. He lifted the wooden boards for the walls and cut the pine branches for the roof. He hung the apples and the grapes, the pears and squash.

On his way to evening prayers at the synagogue, the rabbi felt those sad and lonely feelings, those thoughts about Shana and Yonkel and Heshe, bubble up. But this time the rabbi didn't push them down. *Maybe, just this once, I can have a guest or two,* he thought. *After all, what is a sukkot without guests? Like a wedding without a bride and groom.*

So after the prayers, he stopped Shana. "Come for some wine and cake," he said.

"All of a sudden I'm invited, Rabbi?" Shana shrugged her shoulders and held up her hands. "I can't come. I'm going to Rivka's."

Yonkel looked surprised, too, when the rabbi invited him.

"I'm sorry, Rabbi," he said. "I've made plans with Velvel."

And Heshe looked frightened and disappeared altogether as soon as he saw the rabbi coming.

Rabbi Pinchas returned to his sukkot alone and stood at the table singing the proper blessings over the candles and the wine. It was time to invite the ancestors to join him.

"O Abraham, my holy guest, you so full of kindness, may it please you to have all the holy guests together in this sukkot," Rabbi Pinchas chanted.

When he looked up from his prayer book, he thought he saw a movement by the door. *Perhaps it's Shana or Yonkel or Heshe come to join me after all*, he thought.

He looked more closely and could see a figure in the shadows, an old man wearing a long robe and carrying a walking stick. On his head was a turban and on his feet, sandals. He looked like a man newly come from the Holy Land.

"Come in, old man," Rabbi Pinchas said. "You are welcome."

"I was afraid to come in," the man answered in a deep, strong voice, surprising in one so old. He didn't move from the shadows. "I saw your sign."

"Oh, that," the rabbi answered wearily. "Day after day, it was people and problems and yelling and squabbling; I couldn't think. But tonight is a time to remember our journey in the desert and to celebrate the bounty of our harvests. What kind of a celebration is it when you are alone?"

The old man nodded in agreement. "Life is not just studying and praying and thinking. It is also teaching and listening, celebrating, working and giving," he said.

Rabbi Pinchas felt a shiver of shame. He knew the old man was right. What could he have been thinking? Closing himself in his study all these months! What kind of a rabbi was he?

"That sign," he said to the old man, "I am going to have to change that sign." But there was no one there. The old man was gone.

The next day, Rabbi Pinchas went to pray in the synagogue. He greeted everyone warmly and invited each person to join him in his sukkot after services. He also asked after the old man, but no one had seen him. Certainly they would have noticed a newcomer from the Holy Land.

"With a cane? And a robe? And a headdress?" questioned the rabbi's friend Yonkel. "You're sure you weren't dreaming?"

Rabbi Pinchas thought of the old man's words. "No," he said. "It wasn't a dream."

It was then that Rabbi Pinchas remembered the prayer he had recited just before he saw the old man, the prayer calling to Abraham. Could it be that the old man was not a newcomer from the Holy Land, but the wise old-timer himself?

As soon as the holiday was over, Rabbi Pinchas took down his wooden sign. He took his pen and to the bold black ABSOLUTELY NO VISITORS, he added, IN THE AFTERNOON.

Then Rabbi Pinchas hung the sign back on his door and went into his study to wait for the people with their squabbles and their problems, their troubles and their sorrows—and their laughter and joy.

A Tale of Three Wishes

by Isaac Bashevis Singer

rampol. This was the name of the town. It had all the things that a town should have: a synagogue, a studyhouse, a poorhouse, a rabbi and a few hundred inhabitants. Each Thursday was market day in Frampol, when the peasants came from the hamlets to sell grain, potatoes, chickens, calves, honey, and to buy salt, kero-sene, shoes, boots, and whatever else a peasant may need.

There were in Frampol three children who often played together: Shlomah, or Solomon, seven years old; his sister, Esther, six years old; and their friend Moshe, who was about Shlomah's age.

Shlomah and Moshe went to the same cheder and someone there told them that on Hoshanah Rabbah, which is the last day of the Feast of Tabernacles, the sky opens late at night. Those who see it happen have a minute's time to make a wish, and whatever they wish will come true.

Shlomah, Moshe, and Esther spoke of this often. Shlomah said that he would wish to be as wise and rich as King Solomon, his namesake. Moshe's wish was to be as learned in religion as was the famous Rabbi Moshe

Maimonides. Esther desired to be as beautiful as Queen Esther. After long discussions, the three children decided to wait until Hoshanah Rabbah, to stay awake the whole night together and, when the sky opened, to utter their wishes.

Children must go to bed early, but the three stayed awake until their parents fell asleep. Then they sneaked out of the house and met in the synagogue yard to wait for the miraculous event.

It was quite an adventure. The night was moonless and cool. The children had heard that demons lurk outside, ready to attack those who dare to go out on a dark night. There was also talk of corpses who after midnight pray in the synagogue and read from the Holy Scroll. If someone passed by the synagogue at such a late hour, he might be called up to the reading table, a most frightening event. But Shlomah and Moshe had put on fringed garments, and Esther had dressed in two aprons, one in the front and one in the back, all meant to ward off the evil powers. Just the same, the children were afraid. An owl was hooting. Esther had been told that bats flew around at night and that if one of them got entangled in a girl's hair she would die within the year. Esther had covered her hair tightly with a kerchief.

An hour passed, two hours, three, and still the sky did not open. The children became tired and even hungry. Suddenly there was lightning and the sky opened. The children saw angels, seraphim, cherubim, fiery chariots, as well as the ladder which Jacob saw in his dream, with winged angels going up and down, just as it is written in the Bible. It all happened so quickly that the children forgot their wishes.

Esther spoke up first. "I'm hungry. I wish I had a blintz."

At once, a blintz appeared before the children's eyes.

When Shlomah saw that his sister had wasted her wish on such a petty thing a a blintz, he became enraged and cried out, "You silly girl, I wish you were a blintz yourself."

In an instant, Esther became a blintz. Only her face looked out from the dough, pale and frightened.

Moshe had loved Esther for as long as he could remember. When he saw that his beloved Esther had turned into a blintz, he fell into terrible despair. There was no time to lose. The minute was almost over, and he exclaimed, "I wish her to be as she was."

And so it happened.

Immediately the sky closed again.

When the children realized how foolishly they had squandered their wishes, they began to cry. The night had become pitch black and they could not find their way back home. They seemed to be lost in some strange place. There were no mountains in Frampol; still, the children were climbing up a mountain. They tried to walk down again, but their feet kept climbing by themselves. Then there appeared an old man with a white beard. In one hand he held a stick, in the other a lantern with a candle inside. His robe was girded with a white sash. A strong wind was blowing, but the candle did not flicker.

The old man asked, "Where are you going; And why are you crying?"

Shlomah told him the truth, how they stayed awake all night and how they wasted their wishes.

The old man shook his head. "No good wish is ever wasted."

"Perhaps the demons confused us and made us forget our wishes, " Moshe suggested.

"No demons have any power in the holy night of Hoshanah Rabbah, " the old man said.

"So why did the sky play such a trick on us?" Esther asked.

"Heaven does not play tricks," the old man answered. "You were the ones who tried to play tricks on heaven. No one can become wise without experience, no one can become a scholar without studying. As for you, little girl, you are pretty already, but beauty of the body must be paired with beauty of the soul. No young child can possess the love and the devotion of a queen who was ready to sacrifice her life for her people. Because you three wished too much, you received nothing."

"What shall we do now?" the children asked.

"Go home and try to deserve by effort what you wanted to get too easily."

"Who are you?" the children asked, and the old man replied, "On high, they call me the Watcher in the Night."

As soon as he said these words, the children found themselves back in the synagogue yard. They were so weary that the moment they came home and put their heads on their pillows, they fell asleep. They never told anybody what had happened to them. It remained their secret.

Years passed. Shlomah had become more and more eager for knowledge. He showed so much talent and studied so many books of history, trade, and finance that he became the adviser of the King of Poland. They called him the King without a Crown, and King Solomon of Poland. He married the daughter of an important man and became famous for his wisdom and charity.

Moshe had always been deeply interested in religion. He knew the Bible and the Talmud almost by heart. He wrote many religious books and he became known as the Maimonides of Our Time.

Esther grew up to be not only beautiful but a learned and highly virtuous young lady. Many young men from rich houses sent matchmakers to her parents to ask for her hand in marriage, but Esther loved only Moshe, as he loved only her.

When the old rabbi of Frampol died, Moshe was made rabbi of the town. A rabbi must have a wife, and Rabbi Moshe married his Esther.

All the people of Frampol attended the wedding. The bride's brother, Shlomah, came to his sister's wedding in a carriage drawn by six horses, with grooms riding in front and on the back of the carriage. There was music and dancing, and the young couple received many gifts. Late at night, the bridegroom was called to dance with the bride, and so were all the guests, the bride holding one edge of the handkerchief and her partner the other, according to custom.

When someone asked if everyone had danced with the bride, the wedding jester said, "Yes, except for the night watchman." As he uttered these words, an old man emerged from nowhere with a stick in one hand, a lantern in the other hand, his loins girded with a white sash. The bride, her brother, and the bridegroom recognized the old man, but they kept silent. He approached the bride, placed the lantern and the stick on a bench nearby, and began to dance with her, all the people staring in amazement and awe. No one had ever seen this old man before. The band stopped playing. It became so quiet that one could hear the sputtering of the candles and the chirping of the grasshoppers outside. Then the old man lifted up his lantern and gave it to Rabbi Moshe, saying, "Let this light show you the way in the Torah." He offered the stick to Shlomah with the words. "Let this stick protect you from all your enemies." To Esther, who was holding the white sash, he said, "Let this sash bind you to your people and their needs forever."

After saying these words, the old man vanished.

In the years following, it happened quite often that the Jews came to ask Esther to intercede for them before the rulers of the land. She would fasten the white sash around her waist, and she never failed to help her people. Everyone called her Queen Esther.

Whenever Rabbi Moshe had difficulties in understanding some fine point of the law, he opened the ark where the lantern stood with its eternal light, and things became clear to him. When Shlomah was in trouble, he would take hold of the stick and his foes became powerless.

All three lived to a ripe old age. Only before his death did Rabbi Moshe reveal to the people of Frampol what had happened that night of Hoshanah Rabbah. The rabbi said, "For those who are willing to make an effort, great miracles and wonderful treasures are in store. For them the gates of heaven are always open."

ROUGH OR SMOOTH?

The people of Chelm were unique in all the world. Very wise they thought themselves. But truly their ways were a mystery to everyone else.

To give you just one example, there was the time the people of Chelm decided that their village needed a new synagogue. A project like this could take Chelmites years—no, generations—to decide upon, argue, and plan. And it did. Three generations to be exact.

First they argued about how tall the synagogue should be. Then how wide. What kind of wood should be used? How many seats should it contain?

But now, after generations of arguing back and forth, the groundbreaking ceremony was over, and the Chelmites were celebrating.

"Chelm will be known far and wide!" said Velvel.

"And the synagogue will be ready in time for the New Year!" put in Baila.

"How we will dance in it on Simhat Torah!" said Haim-Yonkel joyfully.

"Wait a minute!" shouted Velvel, his hand up, his finger pointing in the air.

The eating, the drinking, the dancing stopped.

"The floors," Velvel continued. "We have not yet discussed the floors."

"What is there to discuss?" said Itshe, groaning. "Floors are floors."

"Didn't you hear what Haim-Yonkel just said?" Velvel answered. "We will dance with the Torah scrolls on Simhat Torah." Velvel twirled around to demonstrate his point.

"We always dance with the Torahs on Simhat Torah!" interrupted Itshe. "So what's the problem?"

"The problem is we always worry," said Velvel. "Will we drop a Torah in our jumping and twirling? Forty days of fasting if we drop the holy scroll. No, this cannot be. We must leave the floors of the new synagogue unfinished, rough. That way we will not slip and fall when we dance."

Immediately, there was a murmur in the room.

"What a good idea Velvel has!"

"We never thought of that."

"No slipping and falling."

"How clever we Chelmites are to think of everything."

"Wait a minute!" This time it was Itshe who shouted, his hand up, his finger pointing in the air. "You forgot about Yom Kippur."

"So what about Yom Kippur?" said Velvel.

"We go to synagogue in our stocking feet, remember?" said Itshe. "With rough floors, what big splinters we will get in our feet! What infections! What sores! No, the floors must be sanded smooth."

Rough. Smooth. The arguments went back and forth. Splinters. Torahs. Dancing. Slipping. The words mixed around themselves and in and out until everyone was totally confused.

Days passed. Weeks. Months. The building of the synagogue was at a standstill. There was no sawing, no hammering in Chelm. The new building was merely a cornerstone.

"We must go ask our rabbi," Haim-Yonkel finally said. "This is too serious a problem even for us."

Everyone agreed. The rabbi would find the perfect solution. He always did. On to the rabbi's house.

"Rabbi, we have a problem," Itshe blurted out as soon as he saw the rabbi.

The rabbi looked up from his books. "There is always a problem," he said.

"This is a very big problem," said Velvel.

The rabbi listened to Velvel, and then he listened to Itshe. He listened to Haim-Yonkel and Baila and all the others.

"This is a big problem," he said. "I will consult the holy books for seven days and seven nights."

It was a troubled week in Chelm. The people who wanted a smooth floor wouldn't talk to the people who wanted a rough floor. No one could do business. Tempers flared. Words were said. There were even some punches and blows.

Finally, on the morning of the eighth day, the Chelmites gathered at the rabbi's house, eager to hear his judgment.

Was Velvel right or was Itshe? Today they would know.

The rabbi came out of his study. "For seven days and seven nights I have read and thought, looking for the answer to this problem. Then, in my dreams last night, I found a solution worthy of Chelm." He paused.

Not one of the Chelmites made a peep. No one coughed. It was quiet, a rare moment in Chelm.

"We will have both kinds of floors in the new synagogue!" the rabbi announced.

"Truly a remarkable solution!" cried Haim-Yonkel. "But—how is it possible?"

"The floorboards will be smooth on one side and rough on the other," explained the rabbi. "All we have to do is appoint a committee to turn them over. Before Yom Kippur, when we pray in our stocking feet, the committee will turn over the smooth side. Before Simhat Torah, when we dance and twirl, they will turn over the rough side."

"Who would have thought of such a thing!" said Baila.

"How smart our rabbi is!" said Haim-Yonkel.

Now Itshe was happy. And so was Velvel. No splinters. No worries. No more arguing in Chelm. At least, not until tomorrow.

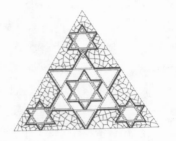

K'TONTON ARRIVES

By Sadie Rose Weilerstein

Once upon a time there lived a husband and a wife. They had everything in the world to make them happy, or almost everything: a good snug house, clothes to keep them warm, white bread, wine and fish for Friday night, and a special pudding—a kugel—every Sabbath. Only one thing was missing and that was a child.

"Ah," the woman would sigh, "if only I could have a child! I shouldn't mind if he were no bigger than a thumb."

One day—it was on Sukkot, the Feast of Tabernacles, she was praying in the synagogue, when she happened to look down. There at her side stood a little old woman. Such a strange, wrinkled old woman with deep, kind eyes peering up at her from under a shawl!

"Why do you look so sad," asked the old woman, "and why do you pray so earnestly?"

"I am sad," answered the wife, "because I have no child. Ah, that I might have a child! I shouldn't mind if he were no bigger than a thumb."

"In that case," said the little old woman, "I shall tell you what to do. Has your husband an etrog?"

"Indeed he has," said the wife, "an etrog, a mehudar." (That means that it was a very fine etrog, a perfect, sweet-smelling one, a citron that had come all the way from Israel.)

"Then," said the old woman, "on the last day of Sukkot you must take the etrog and bite off the end, and you shall have your wish."

The wife thanked the little old woman kindly. When the last day of Sukkot came, she bit off the end of the etrog just as she had been told. Sure enough, before the year had passed a little baby was born to her. It was a dear little boy baby, with black eyes and black hair, dimples in his knees, and thumbs just right for sucking. There was only one thing odd about him. He was exactly the size of a thumb, not one bit smaller or larger.

The wife laughed when she saw him. I don't know whether she laughed because she was so glad, or because it seemed so funny to have a baby as big as a thumb. Whichever it was, the husband said, "We shall call him Isaac, because Isaac in Hebrew means laughter." Then, because they were so thankful to God for sending him, they gave the baby a second name, Samuel. But, of course, they couldn't call such a little baby, a baby no bigger than a thumb, Isaac Samuel all the time. So for every day they called him K'tonton, which means very, very little; and that's exactly what he was.

The first thing they had to do was to find a cradle for the baby to sleep in.

"Fetch me the etrog box," the wife said to her husband. "It was the etrog that brought my precious K'tonton and the etrog box shall be his cradle."

She lifted the cover of the box, a curving, rounded cover. When she turned it over it rocked gently to and fro. Then she took the flax that the etrog had been wrapped in, and spun it and wove it into softest linen. Out of the linen she made a coverlet and sheet. Wherever she went and whatever she did, little K'tonton in his little cradle went with her. When she kneaded the dough for the Sabbath, she set the cradle on the table beside her.

"It will put a blessing in the bread," she said.

Often she placed the cradle in an eastern window. "Perhaps a sunbeam from Israel will steal down to him."

She fed him milk with honey in it—Israeli honey. "The Torah is like milk and honey," she said. "I will feed you milk and honey now, and when you grow older you will feed on Torah."

Sometimes K'tonton opened his tiny mouth and cried. You would never believe so loud a sound could come from so small a mouth. Then K'tonton's mother carried him, cradle and all, into the room where his father sat studying all day long in the big books of the Talmud. Back and forth K'tonton's father swayed reciting the Hebrew page. Back and forth K'tonton rocked in his cradle listening to the words and thinking them the pleasantest sound he had ever heard, even pleasanter than his mother's lullabies.

So K'tonton grew until he was as tall as his father's middle finger. By this time he wasn't a baby any longer. He was three years old, and wore trousers and a little shirt and a tiny arba kanfot of finest silk. You could see the fringes of the arba kanfot sticking out from under his shirt.

Now, when K'tonton's mother was cooking and baking for the Sabbath, there was no cooing baby to watch her from his cradle. No—there was a busy little chatterbox of a K'tonton, dancing about on the table, peeping into the cinnamon box, hiding behind the sugar bowl, asking a question, so many questions, that at last his mother would say, "Blessings on your little head, K'tonton. If you don't let me keep my mind on my work, I'll be putting salt in the cake and sugar in the fish." But before anything of the sort happened, K'tonton had a most exciting adventure. Only that is a story in itself.

HANUKKAH

Hanukkah is a joyous holiday usually celebrated in December. It commemorates the defeat of the Syrian-Greeks by the brave Maccabees and the restoration of the Holy Temple. Customs include lighting the candles of the menorah or hanukkiyah, eating potato pancakes and sufganiyot or jelly doughnuts, playing the spinning top or dreidel game, giving presents, and having parties. The oil of the candles and the different foods remind Jews of the miracle of the oil in the Temple. The Maccabees could not find enough oil to light the Temple lamps. There was only a small vial with one day's supply. But this supply miraculously lasted eight days, until new oil could arrive and that is why we celebrate Hanukkah for eight days.

THAT DAY IN MODIN
DAY ONE

Judea was a small land between two mighty empires and so it was important. Both Egypt and Syria fought to rule over Judea. In the year 198 B.C.E., Syria won this rule.

Now these Syrians had adopted the Greek culture and ways, their hairstyles, clothing, sports and gods. Some of the city Jews, the Jews of Jerusalem, also admired the Greek ways and became like the Greeks.

And for a while, the pious Jews in the city, and the pious ones working the land in the villages, were left alone to follow the ways of their ancestors.

Then Antiochus IV, who called himself "God Manifest," but whose people called him "The Madman," became the Syrian king. He had great ambitions, this Antiochus, of conquering Egypt and becoming a new Alexander the Great. He demanded even more money and loyalty from his border lands, from Judea.

"They must become more like us," he said, "this nation of philosophers who worship the sky. They must worship our gods. They must eat what we eat and do as we do."

Like the peoples of Tyre and Askelon, it seemed that the Jews would have to give up their ways. The end of the Jews as a people seemed near.

For what could those in the villages do when the Syrian soldiers came to enforce Antiochus' laws? The soldiers came with their horses and their swords and their spears to see that the holy books were burned, that the Jews tasted the meat of the unkosher pig, that they made offerings to the Greek gods, and left their baby boys uncircumcised.

And so when the Syrian soldiers came, some of the Jews did those things that were prohibited. Others did not and were killed. Others ran to the hills to hide. But those in the hills were not organized and could not hope to do more than keep themselves alive.

Until that day in Modin.

Modin was a village like many others in Judea and was not far from Jerusalem. It was here that the priest Mattathias and his five sons, Johanan, Simon, Judah, Eleazar and Jonathan lived.

Mattathias was in great pain over what had happened in Jerusalem. He saw with his own eyes the desecration of the Holy Temple, the Jews turned to Greeks, and the murder of the Jews who would not turn. In the village, he and his sons could live in the ways of the holy law. But for how long?

Soon the Syrian soldiers would come to Modin too, carrying the altar of the Greek gods, and force them to give up the old ways.

The thought was like a stone in Mattathias' heart for he knew he could never break the holy laws. Nor did he want his sons to do so. But how could they, the Judeans, such a small number of people, stand up to the mighty and numerous Syrian army?

He thought of taking his family to the hills, but didn't. Not yet. He waited with the others of Modin to see what would happen.

They had set a boy to watch in the hills above the town. And one day the boy came running down to find Mattathias, who was working among the olive trees.

"They're coming," the boy told him. "I see their armor shining in the sun. There are many of them. Horses too."

"Tell my sons to be ready," said Mattathias. And he left the trees to prepare himself for the soldiers.

The word spread through Modin. People hid the holy scrolls with the words sacred to them, but not to Antiochus' soldiers. They hid their babies and their children, their goats and sheep and donkeys.

The clamor of the soldiers marching and horses' hooves pounding came closer. Soon the foreign soldiers, clean shaven, with helmets and breastplates, stood before the Judeans. They were close now, closer than they had ever been. And Mattathias knew the old days were over. Whatever happened, their peaceful ways would change. Who knew for how long?

"Come Jews," the king's officer shouted to the people. "Today we bow down and make an offering to a god we can see."

He motioned for one of the soldiers to bring the Greek altar and place it before him.

"Who will be the first to make the offering of pig?" demanded the officer. No one moved.

The officer had no patience to wait.

"Where is the priest Mattathias?" His voice carried far in the silence.

The old man gathered his robes about him and stepped quietly but firmly forward. He knew what he had to say. But he would wait and hear the words of this officer first.

The officer nodded at this man who, though old, was tall and strong and commanded respect, even of a Syrian.

"You are a leader in this town," continued the officer. "And I am here at the king's command to carry out his laws. As you know, all over Judea, the people are accepting the new ways.

"You and your family will be honored with gifts of silver and gold. And it will go well with you if you do so. Be the first to bow down and make the offering on the altar that all citizens of Antiochus' empire honor!"

His words echoed in every Judean's ear and hung in the air. All the people, the soldiers too, waited for what Mattathias would say.

Mattathias spoke clearly, in his powerful voice. "Though all others forsake their ancestors, I and my sons and my villagers do not. We walk in the ways of our holy laws and in our covenant with the Almighty God.

"We cannot stray from our worship to bow down and make this offering that is unholy to us. We do not stray either to the right or to the left. But only do as our law commands."

Mattathias had spoken and a shudder ran through the people. All had heard what had happened in the other villages when the Jews did not accept the Greek gods. All had heard the tales of beatings and spears flying and fires burning. But they still stood.

Except for one. It was not a son of Mattathias, or a relative, or a friend, but a scared townsman of Modin who rushed forward to do the officer's bidding and put the unclean offering on the altar.

With that one man's movement, Mattathias saw the end of the Jews, forever. And for the first time in all these months, next to the pain in his heart he could feel a new sensation, a rousing of the spirit.

Mattathias reached inside his robe for his knife, ran up to the altar and with a swift motion felled the man and then the king's officer. Before the stunned Syrian soldiers and his people, he toppled the Greek altar and cried out, "Let everyone who cares for the holy law and would follow in the ways of our ancestors, come with me!"

And he and his sons and more fled Modin that day for the mountains to hide and build a resistance to Antiochus' harsh rule. Caves became their homes and the mountains of Judea that they knew so well, their allies. The world's first struggle for religious freedom had begun.

SOLDIERS BECOME BUILDERS

DAY TWO

I n the months after that day in Modin, many other Judeans joined Mattathias and his sons in the caves and hills. They formed a small army under the leadership of Mattathias' son, Judah, called the Maccabee, the Hammer.

Judah was a natural leader and comforted his people with his words. "Victory does not depend on the size of the army," he told them. "But on the strength that comes from heaven."

It was true that the Syrians were highly trained, well equipped and numerous. But the Jews fought for their very lives, their land and their religious freedom. And they knew all the hills and valleys of Judea.

With showers of arrows, they harassed the Syrian-Greek soldiers at night while they were sleeping. They sent spies into the enemy's camp and launched surprise attacks after learning of their plans. They trapped them in mountain passes and moved so swiftly up hills and behind rocks and trees that Antiochus' soldiers in their heavy armor could not follow.

The Maccabee's soldiers won the first battle against Antiochus' army. And the second. And then a third, even though each time the king sent more and more soldiers. Fifty thousand to Judah's thousand.

The Syrian-Greek soldiers either died or fled. Then there was a lull in the fighting. While Antiochus was distracted by an uprising in Parthia and led his army there, Judah took advantage of this break in the fighting. In 165 B.C. E., he marched his army into the holy city of Jerusalem to recapture it for the Jews, and rededicate it to the service of the One God.

Although the Maccabean War continued after this date until 141 B.C.E., the Jews were once again able to worship as they had for centuries in the Holy Temple from the date of this rededication until the Temple's destruction by the Romans in 70 C.E. This religious freedom, so hard won by the Jews, would last over two hundred years, about as long as the United States has been an independent nation.

*   *   *

There was great joy and gladness among the Maccabee's soldiers that day as they marched up the road to Jerusalem. It was a noisy group of thousands, laughing, singing, shouting.

But as they entered the city, they grew quiet. Disaster and destruction met their eyes. Where once there had been lively streets full of homes with children running about, artisans plying their trades, and marketplaces with oils and wines and the produce of fields, there was now decay and silence.

Even the houses of the Jews who still lived there were empty. They had fled to the fortress that the Syrian-Greeks had built, seeking the protection of Antiochus' soldiers. These were the Jews who adopted the Greeks' ways, wore their clothes, ate their foods and worshipped their gods.

Judah looked up, toward the Temple. He could see its beautiful gates hanging on their hinges, the wood slashed and burned, the silver and gold decorations gone.

And he remembered his promise to his father Mattathias to restore the Temple. He and his soldiers would do all they had to do to clean the Temple and beautify it so that it could once again be the people's holy place.

"Johanan! Eleazar!" he called to two of his brothers. "Bring a thousand and surround the fortress. We will not try to take it. Just hold it. Our work is there." And he pointed to the Temple.

He and the rest of the army climbed up to the Temple mount. Judah stood in the Temple square still and unmoving. All around him, men tore their clothes and fell on their faces onto the ground. They cried and mourned too.

Judah could remember standing here in this place as a boy with his father among throngs of people. They had come to serve God on the Sabbath and on the feast days, carrying their offerings of the best of their produce and animals without blemish.

Now all he saw were weeds as thick as a small forest, broken bits of holy objects, and pieces of columns and windows and doors.

He was afraid to step inside. It was easier to face the Syrian soldiers than this.

"Simon! Jonathan!" Judah called the two of his brothers who were not at the fortress to him.

Together with his brothers, he went through the yawning gate into the Temple court.

He noticed first the foul smell. On the once sacred altar and lying about the floors were the remains of unclean sacrifices of pig and who knew what else.

And there was a statue of Zeus where the priests once placed incense.

The brothers looked at each other and were sick.

"All the stories are true," whispered Johanan.

"Did you doubt them?" said Judah. "After you saw what happened in our little town of Modin? In all the other towns of Judea?"

"Where do we begin?" said Simon. "We will have to build a new altar. And the golden menorah is gone. The curtains are torn down. All this filth." The job was overwhelming.

Yohanan was the first to move. As he entered one of the side chambers, a wild dog and some little pigs scattered before him.

"The chamber is empty," he said. "Of all except swine."

They checked the other chambers. All was gone, the incense, the fine grains and wines and oils, the garments of the priests and the chests of coins, all the Temple vessels.

It was hard to imagine this was the same place where they had heard the trumpets sounding and the Levites singing God's praises. Now all they heard were the yelps and squeals of desecration.

Suddenly Judah turned to his brothers. "Come. We must gather the others and begin. Our soldiers will become builders now."

And the Temple became a busy place.

Those who had been priests were called to do the holy task of removing the old stones of the altar to build a new one.

Others sewed new and fine curtains, carved doors and gates, made new vessels.

They scrubbed until the foul smell was gone. They pulled weeds until the yard would have pleased a king's gardener.

As people near the holy city heard the news, they came up the mount too, to add their labor.

All that was burned and torn, broken and stolen was replaced.

Judah sent word with messengers throughout Judea that they were ready to rededicate the Temple on the twenty-fifth day of the month of Kislev. This was the very day three years before that Antiochus had come into the Temple proclaiming Zeus god.

"But Zeus is there no more," Judah's messengers told the people. "You will see for yourselves and sing Halleluyah!"

And on that day they came by the thousands to stand in the square and the courts once more, to hear the trumpets and the lutes and the cymbals and the singing of the Levites.

You have lifted me up
And turned my laments into dancing
That my whole being may sing hymns to You.
O God, I will praise You forever. (Psalm 30)

And they brought offerings and prayed and watched the lights being lit on the golden Temple menorah, including the westernmost one, the eternal flame which burned day and night.

Judah and his brothers rejoiced too, to see the Temple restored as in the days of their father.

After the Temple ceremonies ended, the soldiers, with Judah at their lead, danced and sang in the city streets, the streets they had walked through in silence a few weeks before. They carried their torches of light high above their heads. The lights could be seen twinkling in the darkness, almost as far away as Modin.

ADDING TO THE LIGHT

DAY THREE

Thousands of years ago in Jerusalem there was a court of rabbis called the Sanhedrin. People came to them with all sorts of troubles.

"His camel was carrying a load of flax and some flax fell into my shop and caught fire on my lamp and set my whole shop on fire." And so it went.

It was up to the rabbis to decide. Would the camel owner have to pay the shopkeeper for the damage? If so, how much and under what circumstances?

Was the shopkeeper's lamp inside or outside the shop? they would ask. Was it a Hanukkah lamp?

If it was a Hanukkah lamp, was it more than or less than the required ten handbreaths from the ground? And so on.

Now two of the seventy rabbis serving on the Sanhedrin were also leaders of two great schools, the school of Hillel and the school of Shammai. Back and forth they argued about the laws, citing customs, other rabbis, the Five Books of Moses, and all they had learned and studied in their days as students. So rarely did they agree that it was left to the rest of the Sanhedrin to decide whose ways the people should follow—that of Hillel's or that of Shammai's.

Lighting the Hanukkah lights was no different. Shammai said, "This is the way it should be done. Light eight lights for the first night of the holiday, seven for the second, six for the third, five for the fourth, four for the fifth, three for the sixth, two for the seventh, and one for the eighth."

But Hillel disagreed. "No. This is the way it should be done. Light one candle for the first night, two for the second, three for the third, four for the fourth, five for the fifth, six for the sixth, seven for the seventh, and eight for the eighth."

"All well and good," said the other rabbis. "But what are your reasons? We must have reasons to decide."

And Hillel and Shammai gave them reasons. Good ones too!

Shammai said, "The lights should correspond to the days of the holiday still to come. In this way, we will know how many days we have left to celebrate."

And Hillel said, "The lights should equal the days of Hanukkah that are gone. In this way we will know which day of the holiday we are celebrating."

A difficult choice.

"Any other reasons?" the other rabbis asked.

Of course there were other reasons. The rabbis settled in their seats. They were used to these arguments of Hillel's and Shammai's. These could go on for quite a while. Who knew how long?

Shammai argued, "The lights should be decreased because this is the way the young bullocks are sacrificed in the Temple during the Feast of Tabernacles. There are thirteen sacrificed on the first day, twelve on the second, eleven on the third, and so on. One less on each day. Surely, everyone knows this fact.

"And everyone knows that Hanukkah has so many similarities to the Feast of Tabernacles. This is because Judah the Maccabee and his army had to delay their celebration of the Feast of Tabernacles until they came down out of the hills and rededicated the Temple.

"And so they celebrated the eight days of the Feast of Tabernacles during that eight days of the first Hanukkah. And so the method of counting the bulls at the sacrifice can apply to the lighting of the Hanukkah candles."

"What Shammai says is true," the rabbis commented.

But Hillel had a quick reponse. And a shorter one. "The Hanukkah lights are holy," he said. "That is why we must not use them for any manner of work. But only to look at and remind us of the Maccabees and the miracles of the spirit. You all know this." Hillel paused.

The rabbis nodded in agreement.

"And you also know that we promote all matters of holiness. We do not reduce them or take away from them," Hillel added.

Of course the rabbis knew this too.

"Then this will be the way," Hillel concluded. "On the first night of Hanukkah, we will light one light, on the second two lights, on the third three lights. In this way, we will always be adding to the light and never diminishing it."

The rabbis agreed with Hillel. And so it was done and is done even today as Hillel said.

THE PAN OF OIL
DAY FOUR

by Chaver Paver

The little hills were already covered with snow, and the day itself was snow-laden. A wind swept out of the woods and tore at the roofs of the houses and the village.

The house that stood at the edge of the village was quiet like the others, the people in it were also asleep. It was dark in all the rooms, but the house was not completely dark. In the window that faced the broad winding road stood a pan of oil; there was a wick in the pan and it burned through the night. It shed a light far off toward the roads that fanned out from the village.

It was a thing of continual wonder to the village folk that with the coming of winter's snow and frost, the owner of that house placed the pan of oil in the window, lit the wick, and let it burn all through the night until daybreak. And it had been noted, too, that as soon as the winter was gone, when the snows melted and the hills turned green again, the light no longer burned in the window, and the house slumbered in darkness like all the rest.

The man who owned the house was named Abraham, and he had four children, two boys and two girls. He was the only Jew in the village, a man who loved work, who worked from sunup to sundown. He raised thousands of chickens, and he also had eight cows and a big dog. His children, when they were quite young, climbed over all the hills in the summer. In winter they stayed indoors and played with their dog. At first they paid no attention to the fact that their father lit the pan of oil every night during the winter, but when they grew a little older they wondered about it, but said nothing.

They said nothing, that is, until one night when they gathered to celebrate Hanukkah. Their father, Abraham, told them the story of the holiday and lit the menorah. It was then that the oldest of the children, consumed by curiosity, took advantage of the occasion to ask about the pan of oil.

"Father," he said, "I understand from all you have told us about the holiday that we light candles for each night of Hanukkah, for eight days, that is. But why do you burn a light in the window every night of the winter even when it is not Hanukkah?"

The question made Abraham thoughtful. He closed his eyes and was silent for a while. When he opened them there was a smile on his face, and he began to tell them the story.

"It all started twenty years ago," he said. "I was a young man then, nineteen years old. Both my parents died suddenly that year, in the same week, and I was left alone, without friends, without money and without a trade to work at. I was very worried, and after much thought I decided to leave my hometown and go out into the world and seek my fortune.

"It was wintertime. Snow lay over the fields, and it was so cold that my nose and ears froze as I walked. But I was lighthearted. I shrugged away all my cares and walked on for a whole day until night began to fall. I was then in the midst of a long stretch of woods and a snowstorm began to rage. By this time I was quite tired and began to worry that I would be swallowed up by the snow in the strange region. So I gathered up my strength and began to run, in the hope that I would soon come to an inhabited area.

"I ran for a long time until I could go no farther. My strength had given out and I fell in a heap of snow. Not a human was to be seen or heard anywhere. White fields enveloped me all around and the storm raged on. I stretched out on the snow. I was so tired and overheated from running that the snow seemed soft, like a pleasant bed.

"Suddenly I saw, as in a dream, a light shining from somewhere in the distance. I opened my eyes with difficulty and looked, but there was no light. I told myself that I had imagined it, so I closed my eyes again. But again the light appeared. I started into the distance; yes, there was really a light. The gleam seemed to be coming from a house; its glow seemed to he beckoning me to a warm, pleasant home.

"When the owner opened the door for me, I fell into a dead faint, and for two weeks I lay in bed with a high fever, practically unconscious. When I was finally able to understand what was going on around me, I saw an elderly Jewish couple and their young daughter, all of them deeply worried about my health.

"In time I became completely well. The old Jew told me that the night I arrived was the first night of Hanukkah. He had lit the first candle and he placed it on the windowsill. That was the light that had gleamed for me when I was lost among the white fields. It was the light that brought me to this house, my children, in which you now live.

"I told the owner all about myself. He listened to me and then said that if I liked I could stay with him and help out on the farm. I decided to stay with him. That was twenty years ago. The old man and his wife passed away a long time ago. I married their daughter. You probably guessed it— she is your mother.

"Since that time, as soon as winter descends and the snow, and frost arrive, I light the pan of oil. I put it in the window every night so it will shine far over the road, to give heart to those who might be out late in the night, so they will not get lost and perhaps be overcome in the snow."

That night, after the story, the children lay down on their beds but they could not fall asleep for a long time. When they finally dozed off they dreamed of snowy fields, of night, of a snowstorm roaring in the darkness and of a man all covered with snow, floundering about and crying. Then the gleam of a flame in a pan of oil appeared and the snow-encrusted man, overjoyed, ran with all his might toward the glow.

Translated by Benjamin Efron

EVEN IN THE DARKEST PLACES

DAY FIVE

It is Hanukkah. You may wonder how we know. Here in this most dreadful of places, this Auschwitz. And wonder why we would care. When our small candle of a life could be snuffed out at any time by the whim of a camp guard, an officer, the Kapo, or the fever that rages through the bunks.

But some of us do not forget, even here, the Hanukkah lights we lit in our homes it seems like forever ago, or the brave deeds of our Maccabean ancestors. Maybe here we remember these even more. The few against the many. The spirit mightier than the sword. Maybe even here a miracle could happen. Maybe even a small one.

There are only eight of us children in the camp. And I am the oldest. Rivka, who comes from Warsaw, looks after me. She is like a sister to me. She promises me we will have Hanukkah here.

"Even here," she says.

I believe her.

She already has managed to give us each a dreidel. Wooden ones carved with the letters nun, gimel, hay, shin, that stand for a great miracle happened there. I twirl my dreidel and then hide it. I ask Rivka, "Where from?" She doesn't answer.

But later I see Berel, the shoemaker from Vitebsk, walking outside. He hobbles along. I wonder what's wrong with him? Then I see. He's missing a shoe. One of his wooden clogs. And I know. I feel sorry for Berel for giving up his shoe. But when I look up at him, he smiles. And winks.

"I will get another," he shrugs. "It is for the holiday."

And I think, Berel's dreidel is the nicest one I've ever had.

Okay, dreidels from shoes. But candles? And menorahs? How is Rivka going to manage these. Still I am hopeful. For once in this camp I am hopeful. For doesn't Rivka smile like she has a secret?

It is getting dark and Rivka leads me very quietly to another bunk, one of the men's bunks. We creep close to the walls of the bunks, for we must not be spotted by the guards. We have never done this before – Rivka and me. I wonder at her bravery, our bravery. And I pretend for a moment that I am a Maccabee.

Now we're inside the bunk. Others have crept here too, praying they will not be discovered. The bunk is full. But quiet. Very quiet. I see Hershel and Chaim, and the other children. I count them. We are all here. And many more adults.

The rabbi is here too. It is he who remembered. It is he who keeps count of the holy days even here, where nothing seems holy.

He stands in front of a box. I look down and stare at what I see. There are nine tiny tins on the table. The kind used in making cloth buttons.

There is no sound as the rabbi pulls a homemade candle and then another from his pocket. Perhaps he is a magician as well as a rabbi, I think. Or maybe even the Prophet Elijah himself.

Rivka pokes my side. Her face says, I told you so. I squeeze her hand. I'm still holding it because the fear of coming here hasn't left me. Or the excitement.

She whispers, and nods toward the menorah and the candles. So softly I hardly hear. "Tins from inside coat buttons. The candles—fat from food rations. Saved bit by bit. Wicks . . . " She pulls on a thread of her thin dress. "Many threads twisted together."

So the rabbi isn't a magician or Elijah. But still the menorah and the candles are magical in the darkness of the bunk, our home now, our house of fear.

The rabbi sticks the candles to the tins by melting them a little, and then he lights them. First the shamash and then one candle. Their glow warms up the whole bunk and drives the fear away.

The rabbi is singing, his deep soft voice breaks the silence. The first blessing tells us how God has commanded us to light these Hanukkah lights. The second tells of the miracles God performed for us in the days of the Maccabees.

Some people begin to murmur. "That's what we need. A miracle."

When the rabbi sings the third blessing, people start to cry, soft cries. "Blessed are You, God, who granted us life and brought us to this season." We who are barely alive. We who have lost so many of our loved ones cry.

But the rabbi's words stay with us through the sobs. The words, the candles, the light. We stare and listen.

Even in the darkest of places, we have somehow found a way to kindle the lights. And, I will remember this Hanukkah forever. No matter what happens.

RIGHT SIDE UP

DAY SIX

n Hanukkah we play dreidel, spinning it round and round, hoping it will land on the letter gimel," the rabbi explained. "Then we claim everything in the pot. If it lands on hey, that's not such bad luck. We take half. But we groan if it turns up nun, nothing, or even worse, shin, put one in."

As Inna listened to the rabbi, she thought of how she had played the dreidel game with her father in Russia. In secret, of course. Of how her father carved a new one out of wood every year. Of her favorite dreidel, the one with Stars of David circling around a brave Judah the Maccabee. But since coming to America, her parents had been so busy finding them a place to live and working, they hadn't even unpacked the dreidels.

Suddenly, Inna realized the rabbi was still talking. "Our world, too, spins round and round just like a top, a dreidel," he was saying. "And we do not know how our luck will fall. Will we be wealthy or poor? Wise or a fool? Well liked or without a friend? Or perhaps wealthy one day, poor the next. Who knows?

"And there's another way that life is just like our little dreidel." The rabbi lifted up a see-through plastic one, the kind usually filled with choco-late coins. "See this central point on which the dreidel turns?" he asked. "So, too, does life have a central source—the Almighty. We mustn't forget that even as life seems to be spinning and spinning, taking us away with it, who knows where."

While she walked home from the synagogue, Inna remembered what the rabbi said. We've been lucky, and we haven't been lucky, she thought. We're lucky to be in America, in our own apartment, near our friends and relatives. And we don't have to be afraid to say we're Jewish out loud like we were in Russia. Papa doesn't have to smuggle in Bibles or carve our own dreidels in America. Here you see Bibles and dreidels in shop windows and watch Hanukkah shows right on television.

But as far as being wealthy, that dreidel was definitely landing on nuns and shins. Where were the jobs in the symphony for Mama, who played the violin, and Papa, who played the flute? Sometimes it seemed as if things had turned upside down for them. In Moscow, Mama and Papa had to work so hard to be Jewish. In America, they had to work so hard just to be musicians. Were Mama and Papa spinning and twirling away, just like the rabbi said?

During the eight days of Hanukkah, Mama no longer had the time to sit Inna and little Leo down to hear the story of brave Judah the Maccabee and how he led the fight for religious freedom long ago. She was teaching every kid in the neighborhood to squeak away on the violin. And for Hanukkah, Papa couldn't carve dreidels with them, big and little, fat and thin, to give to all their cousins. Secretly, of course. He was teaching every kid on the other side of town to make some decent noises on the flute.

And as the time in America passed, Inna could hardly remember Papa carving a dreidel or Mama's story about Judah the Maccabee. Leo thought Judah the Maccabee was a Jewish Superman and that all dreidels were pink and blue plastic and came from a store. But as the rabbi said, the world was always spinning in cycles, just like a dreidel, and one could always hope it would turn right side up again for them.

It was just before the first night of Hanukkah, their second in America, when Inna tapped her father on the shoulder as he was about to leave for the music school. "I know you don't have time to carve dreidels with us anymore, Papa," she said. "But couldn't we have a Hanukkah party and invite everyone and spin the ones we made in Moscow and play with pennies and give little presents and . . ."

"Whoa, Inna," Papa interrupted.

"Well, you don't want Leo to think all dreidels are pink and blue plastic and come from a store, do you? Or that Judah the Maccabee was Superman with a bow and arrow and a little hat on top of his head?"

"He thinks that?"

Inna nodded.

Papa laughed, but then he looked serious. "All right, Inna. We can have a party for the first night. After all, a big Hanukkah party was something we could never do in Russia. A party!" He snorted. "Why, we could never even light the menorah for fear of being reported. Did you know that little Ben and Rachel, our own cousins, had never even seen a dreidel!

"No, you are right, Inna. Mama and I will just cancel all our lessons for the night."

"Oh, Papa!" Inna was thrilled and gave her father a big hug. Then she went right to work. She telephoned all her relatives and neighbors to invite them to the party. "Bring a friend, too," she told them.

She dragged little Leo down to the basement, carrying the key to the storage closet in her pocket. They found their boxes still tied with rope, with Russian letters printed on the sides. They opened one and then another, looking for the old dreidels. One small box in the back had their Jewish things from Russia. The old prayer book and prayer shawl that belonged to great-grandfather was on top. Waiting underneath were all the wooden dreidels. Even in the dark of the basement, Inna could recognize the designs carved around the shins and nuns, heys and gimels, designs carved by Papa and grandpa and great-grandfather. There was her favorite dreidel and others with crowns and lions and birds, spears and elephants.

"Elephants?" asked Leo.

"The Syrian-Greeks used them to fight Judah and the Maccabees," said Inna. "Mama will tell you the whole story. Promise."

They wrapped all the dreidels in an old scarf and carried them upstairs, big ones and little ones, fat and thin ones—but no pink and blue plastic ones.

On the first night of Hanukkah, Mama and Papa made potato latkes in the kitchen while Inna and Leo answered the door and welcomed the guests. Once the doorbell started to ring, it didn't stop. There were aunts, uncles, and cousins, neighbors and friends, and friends of friends, too. When Inna and Leo lit the candles in the menorah, everyone sang the blessings. They ate the latkes and twirled the dreidels. And Mama told all about brave Judah and the Maccabees. And the elephants.

Of course, Mama and Papa brought out their violin and flute so they could play the Hanukkah melodies and everyone could sing along. Soon, though, everyone stopped singing to listen to the beautiful music. When Mama and Papa were done, they took a bow, smiles on their faces.

"It is so nice to play for friends and family," Mama said.

Suddenly someone they didn't know, one of the friends of a friend, stood up. "How would you like to play for more people? For an audience of people?" he asked.

Mama and Papa looked puzzled.

"I work for the symphony," he said, "and would like to recommend you two. As a matter of fact, we're auditioning right now. Would you be interested?"

"Interested?" repeated Mama, stunned.

"We would love to," said Papa. "It is what we did in Russia."

He turned to smile at Inna who held up the last wooden dreidel that Papa had carved before they came to America, her favorite, with the Stars of David circling around Judah the Maccabee. She held the dreidel right side up, the gimel and hey turned toward Papa, and smiled happily back.

In Honor of Judith

Day Seven

And why do some people eat cheese and cheese dishes on Hanukkah? Potato pancakes fried in oil, you know about those. But salty cheese? Well, there is a reason. And on this night of the new moon, the traditional time for the monthly women's holiday of Rosh Hodesh, sit back and you will hear the reason.

Judith's story takes place a long long time ago, even before the Maccabees. Some people think it was written down during the time of the Maccabees or soon after to inspire courage. Certainly the Maccabees needed courage to fight Antiochus. And certainly Judith had that kind of courage.

Judith was a young, lovely and wealthy widow who lived in the fortified city of Bethulia. Bethulia was an important city, because it stood on a mountain pass, and no one could go into Judea or its holy city of Jerusalem without passing through it.

An Assyrian commander-in-chief named Holofernes wanted to enter Judea with his army, and conquer all its lands and cities and peoples for his king Nebuchadnezzar. He had come as far as the walled city of Bethulia. News of the destruction his troops had brought traveled before him and spread fear among the people of Judea.

For thirty-four days, his army camped around Bethulia, until its inhabitants did not have a drop of water in their vessels or cisterns to drink. The
people, faint and dying of thirst, gathered against the elders of the city.

"We must talk peace with the Assyrians," they shouted desperately. "We
have no strength left. It is better that we be slaves and give up our ways
than helplessly watch our families perish."

"Have courage," Ozias their leader said. "Give me five more days. Surely
God will show mercy on us. If these five days pass and no help comes, then
I will do as you ask."

Judith heard what the people and Ozias had said. She called Ozias and
the elders of the city to her. "How dare you agree that in five days we will
give up our ways and become slaves to this Holofernes? You put God on
trial before the people with this oath."

"They will not last much longer without water," Ozias said. "Pray for all
of us, Judith, that the rains might fall and fill our cisterns."

Judith thought for a moment. "I will do that and more," she answered
Ozias. "But you must not ask me where I go or what I plan. Just stand at
the city gate tonight when my maid and I go out of the city."

After the elders left her, Judith fell on her face and prayed. "Creator of
heaven and earth, take my words and actions in place of the words You
heard from Ozias and the people. They are desparate and speak out of thirst
and fear."

When Judith finished praying, she took off her widow's clothes, and
dressed as beautifully as she had when her husband Manasseh lived. She
put on her sandals, her fine bracelets, rings and earrings and anklets. She
was dazzling in her beauty.

Next she gave her maid wine and her saltiest cheese, a pouch of barley
groats, fig cakes, oil, and loaves of fine bread. Dishes, too, for her to carry.

Judith and her maid walked to the city gates where Ozias and the elders waited.

"Give orders to open the city gate for us," Judith instructed. "So I may do as I have said."

Judith and her maid were not far from the city gates when an Assyrian guard saw them. He stopped them.

"Who are you? Where do you go?" the soldier demanded to know.

"I am a daughter of the Hebrews," Judith answered. "And I flee from them seeking Holofernes. I want to tell him how he can conquer all this hilly country."

The soldier was impressed with Judith's beauty. "You have saved your life today," he told her. "I will send you with some of my men to Holofernes' tent. Tell him what you have told me."

Judith and her maid walked alongside the soldiers and could hear questioning whispers all around them from the men in the camp.

When she reached Holofernes' tent, she was announced to the commander who lay resting under a canopy of purple and gold, woven with emeralds and other precious stones.

Judith fell upon her face and his slaves raised her up.

"Do not fear," Holofernes said to her. "I will not harm anyone who serves Nebuchadnezzar, king of all the earth. And I would not have harmed your people if they had not lifted their spears against me. Now tell me, why have you fled from them to us?"

"We have heard of your wisdom, and of your wondrous deeds in battle," Judith said, flattering Holofernes. "I have come to tell you how you may win these hills of Judea. My people are about to commit terrible sins against God. This will be their downfall and your gain. When their supply of food and water is gone, they have decided to disobey God's laws and eat that which is forbidden to them—the first fruits of wheat and the tithes of wine and oil which has been set aside for the priests at the Temple of Holies in Jerusalem. The day they do this will be their day of defeat.

"God has sent me because I, your slave, am God-fearing. I will stay with you and go each night, just before dawn, into the valley to pray to God. God will tell me when the people have committed these sins. Then I will bring you word that you may march your army forward and conquer Bethulia and all of Judea."

Judith's words pleased the commander. "You are not only beautiful but wise and well spoken. If you do as you have said, then your God shall be my God. You will sit in the house of the king and be famous throughout the land."

So it was that for three nights Judith was allowed to leave her tent before dawn to bathe in the spring of water near Bethulia. She prayed to God for the success of her mission.

On the fourth day, Holofernes invited Judith to his tent for a feast and to drink and make merry.

Judith accepted.

When she came into his tent, he was delighted to see her. She ate and drank the foods her maid prepared and fed these to Holofernes. The fig cakes and barley groats, the salty cheese and loaves of fine bread. And the wine, too.

So enraptured was Holofernes with Judith, and so salty was the cheese she had brought, that he drank more wine than he ever had in a day.

When it was very late, Holofernes' slaves and attendants left his tent to sleep. Judith told them that she would be leaving Holofernes' tent just before dawn to go to the spring and pray, just as she had done the three times before.

Judith was alone with him, having told her maid to stand outside the chamber and wait.

Now Judith prayed once more to God to look down with favor on her and give her strength. Then she went to Holofernes, who was lying down, drunk with wine.

Swiftly, so that she would not even think of hesitating, she took his sword from the bedpost. In one decisive motion, she seized the hair of his head, and beheaded him. Then she placed his head in her pouch to bring to her people, who, she knew, needed such strong proof as this to rise to action. As Judith had hoped, she and her maid were able to leave for the spring unnoticed. And from there, they climbed the mountain to the gates of Bethulia.

"Open the gate," she shouted. "God is with us this day."

The people at the gate heard her voice and called the elders. Everyone great and small heard too and ran there, amazed to see Judith and her maid alive. The people opened the gate and welcomed them, and lit a fire for light.

Then, before all the people, Judith drew Holofernes' head from the pouch and held it high.

"As soon as morning dawns," she said, "take up your weapons and go toward the camp of the Assyrians. They will see you and go to their camp to rouse their generals. When they rush to Holofernes' tent, they will see what I have done and run from you."

Her people did as Judith said, and indeed, chased the Assyrian soldiers from Judea. From all over the land, the people came to the mountain pass, to Bethulia, to see this brave Judith, and to praise her.

DON'T BLOW OUT
THE CANDLES
DAY EIGHT

 **I**ris sat by the window watching the candles burn in the Hanukkah lamp, the one that had belonged to her great-grandmother in Poland. This menorah was the only one Iris had ever seen with a lion carved onto its shiny golden sur-face.

Tonight three candles were burning, one on top near the lion's face, and two down below near the lion's feet.

Iris hummed a tune. It was a blessing her family chanted on each of the eight nights of Hanukkah before lighting the candles. Then she heard Benjy.

"Brum. Brum. Bruuuum." Her four year old brother raced into the living room.

"Oh, no," Iris groaned. "He's pretending he's driving a race car again."

While bobbing his head up and down and turning an imaginary steering wheel, Benjy circled the sofa. "Brum. Brum. Bruuuum."

"Screeech." He stopped in front of the menorah and put on his brakes.

"I can blow out those candles in one puff," he boasted.

"Oh no, you don't," said Iris. "No one blows those candles out."

"I can."

"No, you can't. I'll call Mama and Daddy," she threatened.

Benjy just stood there, eyeing first the flickering candles and then his sister.

"Why can't I?" he finally demanded. "You're not my boss."

"They have to burn down all by themselves so they can remind us of the Hanukkah story," Iris told him.

Benjy didn't budge.

"You liked the story last time Daddy told it," she tempted him.

"Does it have any car races in it?" Benjy asked.

"No," said Iris, exasperated. "It was before cars were invented. But there are bows and arrows and elephants in it."

"OK. Tell it to me." Benjy drove to the chair next to his sister's, got out of his imaginary car, and sat down.

"A long time ago," Iris began, "a lot of Jews were in a fight with a mean Syrian-Greek king and his soldiers. The king's name was Antiochus the Fourth. He was so mean that he wouldn't let the Jews eat what they wanted. He wouldn't let them celebrate the Sabbath. And he wouldn't let them do a lot of other things. But not all the Jews listened to the mean king."

"Not Judah Maccabee." Benjy waved his arm around in the air as if he were holding a sword.

"You remembered!" Iris said, glad to see Benjy as Judah instead of a race car driver.

Benjy nodded, pleased with himself. "Daddy said Judah was as brave as a lion, like the lion over there." He pointed to the lion on the menorah.

"And just like a real lion, he and his brothers and his father–all the Maccabees–had to hide in caves in the hills," Iris continued. "They threw rocks at Antiochus's soldiers. More and more Jews ran away to the hills and told Judah that they wanted to fight the king, too."

"Too bad they didn't have some race cars and some trucks and. . ." interrupted Benjy.

"Shh," said Iris. "Listen. Every time the king sent his soldiers into the hills, Judah and the Maccabees jumped out of hiding to surprise the king's army. The soldiers would be so surprised that they would drop their bows and arrows and swords and spears and run away. The king got madder and madder at the Jews."

Benjy scrunched up his face and clenched his fists. "I'm mad, too."

"I thought you were Judah. Are you the king now?"

"No, I'll be Judah," Benjy answered.

"Anyway, the king was so mad he sent bigger and bigger armies with horses and elephants. He couldn't understand why his big army wasn't winning when Judah had such a small army."

"Do you think Judah was ever scared fighting such a big army?" Benjy interrupted.

"Maybe, even lions get scared sometimes," Iris said. "But being brave means you keep trying even if you're scared. Judah didn't give up. He fought for three years and won!"

"Yay for Judah!" Benjy cheered. He patted something imaginary next to him.

"Is that still your car?" Iris asked.

"No. It's an elephant I captured from the soldiers," answered Benjy.

Iris smiled. "So," she continued, "Judah and his followers were happy when they marched into Jerusalem. They couldn't wait to say thank you to God in the Great Temple. But when they saw the Temple, they were sad. Everything was broken and full of garbage, and a statue of the Greek god Zeus stood in the holiest of places."

"Poor Judah," said Benjy, shaking his head.

"They cleaned up the Temple and made new curtains for the holy ark. Then they looked all over for the oil to light the Temple menorah."

"Did they find it? Did they?" Benjy sounded worried.

"They found only one jar of the special oil," said Iris. "They thought it would last for just one day. But it burned longer, for eight days. They had time to get more oil from the north where the olives grew. Everyone was happy because of the miracle of being able to pray in the Great Temple again. They danced and sang, and Judah called this holiday Hanukkah, the Feast of Dedication."

"Is that the end?" asked Benjy, hoping for more.

"Just that these lights on the menorah remind us of Judah's lights in the Temple. You won't try to blow out the candles now, will you, Benjy?"

"I won't," he promised, sitting quietly and staring at the menorah in the window. The slowly burning candles lit up the lion's face, and it seemed to be smiling.

TU B'SHVAT

Tu B'Shvat means the fifteenth day of the Hebrew month of Shvat and is the New Year of the Trees. This holiday emphasizes how important trees have been and are to the Jewish people. In Israel, it is around this date that the air is turning warm, the winter rains have ended, and trees seem to come to life. It is customary to eat fruits that grow in Israel such as figs and dates, carob and oranges on this holiday.

HONI AND THE CAROB TREE

by Eric A. Kimmel

Honi ha'Ma'agel—Honi the Circle Maker—lived in Galilee two thousand years ago. He talked to God and worked miracles. When people were in distress, Honi would draw a circle on the ground. Standing inside the circle, he would ask God for what was needed. He didn't always ask politely, but God never failed to answer his prayers.

One day Honi was walking along when he saw an old man planting a carob tree. Honi called to the man, "It takes a carob tree seventy years to bear fruit. Do you think you're going to live long enough to harvest carobs from that tree you're planting?"

The old man answered, "When I came into the world I found carob trees bearing fruit. I didn't plant them. Where did they come from? My father and grandfather and great-grandfather planted them for me. I know I will not live long enough to harvest fruit from this tree. I am planting it for my grandchildrern and great-grandchildren. As my forefathers provided for me, so do I provide for my descendants."

Honi felt humbled. "There is great wisdom in what you say," he told the old man. Afterwards, he went to a secluded place. He sat down on a stone and began thinking about what the old man had told him.

Honi thought and thought. He thought so hard that he fell into a deep sleep.

Days passed, then weeks and years. God caused the rock to grow up around Honi. It became a small hill. Honi sat inside, sheltered in a deep cave.

One day Honi woke up. He walked outside the cave, squinting in the bright sunlight. The world looked the same as before. He had no idea that a hundred years had passed.

Honi saw an old man harvesting fruit from a carob tree. "So you did live long enough to see that tree bear fruit!" he exclaimed.

The man turned to Honi. "What do you mean? I didn't plant this tree. It was planted a hundred years ago by my great-grandfather. He lived in Honi ha'Ma'agel's time."

"I'm Honi ha'Ma'agel!" Honi said. The old man laughed at him.

Honi continued walking, He came to a bridge crossing a stream. "When did they build this bridge?" he asked the people traveling along the road.

"It was built long ago, in Honi ha'Ma'agel's time," they told him.

"I'm Honi ha'Ma'agel!" Honi said.

All the peopie laughed at him.

Honi came upon a group of scholars studying the Torah. They were discussing a difficult passage and couldn't agree on what it meant. "I can explain that for you," Honi said. He explained the passage so clearly that the scholars praised him.

"Such wisdom has not been heard in Israel since Honi ha'Ma'agel's time!"

"I'm Honi ha'Ma'agel!" Honi said.

The scholars laughed at him, too.

Honi trudged back to the hill. "Now I see that the greatest curse is to live beyond your time," he said to himself. "God, take my soul from me. I no longer have a place in this world."

Honi went back inside his cave. The hill closed around him. But whether he lived or died, no one knows.

Honi ha'Ma'agel was never seen again.

PURIM

Purim is a very joyous holiday commemorating the story of the brave Queen Esther of ancient Persia who saved her people from the evil plot of the courtier Haman. It is celebrated in February or March, on the fourteenth day of the Hebrew month of Adar. Some of the customs of this holiday are to dress in costume, exchange gifts of food including hamantaschen, and hear the reading of the Book of Esther, the Megillah, in the synagogue.

ESTHER

King Ahasuerus reigned over one hundred and twenty-seven provinces from India to Nubia. In the third year of his reign, he gave a banquet for all his officials, nobles and governors in his palace in Shushan. For one hundred and eighty days he displayed the riches of his realm. At the end he gave a banquet for all who lived in Shushan. His Queen Vashti gave a banquet for the women.

On the seventh day, when the King was merry with wine, he ordered his servants to bring Vashti to display her beauty before all. But Queen Vashti refused to come. The King turned to his sages for advice about what should be done. They said that Vashti was setting a bad example for all the wives of Shushan, and should never again come into the King's presence. The King should choose a new Queen who was more worthy. The King did as his sages advised.

Some time later, the King's advisors said that officers in every province of his realm should gather all the most beautiful young maidens and bring them to Shushan. Let the maiden that most pleases the King be made Queen. The King liked the plan.

Now in Shushan there lived a Jew by the name of Mordecai. He was a foster father to Esther, his uncle's daughter. Esther was beautiful and shapely. When the King's order was announced, many girls were assembled in

Shushan. Esther was among them, though she did not reveal that she was a Jewess. Her cousin Mordecai had told her not to do so. Each day, Mordecai would walk about in front of the court of the harem to learn what was happening to Esther.

When Esther's turn came to go before the King, the King loved her more than all the other women. He set a royal crown on her head, and made her Queen instead of Vashti. He gave a great banquet for her.

Now one day, when Mordecai was sitting at the King's gate, for he still went every day to see how Esther was faring, he overheard two of the King's servants, Bigthan and Teresh, plotting to do away with the King. Mordecai told this to Esther, and Esther reported it to the King. The King arrested the two servants and had them killed. This was recorded in the book of annals.

Some time later, the King promoted Haman higher than any of the other officials. Everyone bowed down to Haman as he went by, all except Mordecai because he was a Jew and only bowed down to God. Haman found out who Mordecai was and plotted to do away with Mordecai and all of Mordecai's people, the Jews.

A lot was cast before Haman to determine the day of the killing. This day fell on the twelfth month of Adar. Haman told King Ahasuerus that there were a certain people in his realm whose laws were different from everyone else's, and who did not obey the King's laws. He advised the King to draw up an edict for their destruction, and he would pay the King ten thousand talents of silver for doing this. The King took off his signet ring so that Haman could seal the edict.

And so the decree was issued to the governors of every province to destroy the Jews on the thirteenth day of the twelfth month. The King and Haman sat down to a feast, but the city of Shushan was dumbfounded.

When Mordecai learned all that had happened, he tore his clothes, and went to inform Esther of the edict through her servants. He asked that she go before the King and plead with him for her people.

"Tell Mordecai that if anyone comes before the King unbidden, he or she shall be put to death," Esther told her servant. "Only if the King extends the golden scepter may the person live."

"Do not think that you, Esther, will escape this decree by being in the King's palace," Mordecai said in his message to Esther. "Perhaps you have risen to this position of Queen just so you can rescue your people."

Esther replied to her cousin. "Gather all the Jews who live in Shushan and ask them to fast on my behalf. I will not eat or drink for three days either. Then I shall go to the King. If I am to die, then I will die."

On the third day, Esther put on the royal dress, and went to the King. As soon as he saw her standing in the court, he extended the golden scepter to her. "What troubles you, Queen?" he asked. "What is your request? Even to half the kingdom, it shall be granted."

"If it please your Majesty," she said. "Let your Majesty and Haman come to the feast that I have prepared."

The King agreed. But that night he couldn't sleep and ordered the book of records to be brought to him. He found written there that Mordecai had saved his life, and asked what honor had been given Mordecai.

"Nothing has been done for him," replied his servants. Just then Haman entered the court. The king asked him, "What should be done for a man whom the king desires to honor?"

Haman thought the King was talking about him, and said that the man the King wished to honor should be dressed in royal clothes, sat upon a horse, and led around Shushan by one of the King's noblemen who would proclaim, "This is what is done for the man whom the King desires to honor!"

"Quick then," said the King, "and do as you have said to Mordecai the Jew, for he is the one I wish to honor for saving my life."

So Haman had to take the royal clothes and the horse to Mordecai, and paraded him through the city.

Soon after this, Haman and the King came to the feast with Queen Esther. Again the King asked Esther, "What is your wish?"

"If it pleases your Majesty, let my life be granted me and my people's also. For someone has paid to have us destroyed."

"Who is this that dares do such a thing?" demanded the King.

"The enemy is this evil Haman," answered Esther.

Haman cringed in terror before the King and Queen. The King in his fury left the feast, while Haman remained to plead with Esther for his life.

The King ordered that Haman be hung on the very gallows that Haman had set up for Mordecai.

Mordecai presented himself to the King, for Esther had revealed that he was her cousin. The King slipped off his ring, which he had taken back from Haman, and gave it to Mordecai. Esther spoke to the King again, pleading with him to avert the evil plotted by Haman.

"You may write what you see fit with regard to your people," the King told Esther and Mordecai. "Write it in the king's name and seal it with the King's signet ring."

Mordecai left the King's presence in royal robes of blue and white and with a crown of gold. On hearing his news, the city of Shushan rang with joyous cries. The Jews enjoyed light and gladness, happiness and honor.

The day had been transformed for them from one of grief and mourning to one of festive joy. They were to observe this time every year as a time of feasting and merrymaking, and an occasion for sending gifts to one another and presents to the poor.

BRAVE LIKE MORDECAI

hat's that?" Benjy asked his big sister.

"My costume, silly," Iris answered, holding a long, blue dress up under her chin. "Don't you know it's Purim tonight? Now, leave me alone. I have to find my crown."

"Crown?"

"Uh, huh. I'm going to be Esther, the brave queen who risked her life to save her people. Whenever the rabbi reads her name on Purim, everyone claps."

"I'm brave," said Benjy. "I'll be Esther, too."

"Oh, no, you don't. You can't copy me. Let's see. How about being King Ahasuerus? Then you could wear a crown, too."

Benjy smiled and waved his arms. "I'll be the brave king."

"Uh-oh," muttered Iris. "Sorry Benjy. This king wasn't brave, and he wasn't very wise either. He always asked everybody else what he should do."

Benjy sat down and pouted. "Then I'll be Esther like you."

"Wait a minute. How about Haman? You could be the king's prime minister. The wicked Haman who tried to kill all the Jews. We could make you a three-cornered black hat and a black moustache. You could wear Dad's black pajamas."

"Will everyone clap when the rabbi reads my name?" Benjy asked.

"Are you kidding? Everyone boos at Haman. They stamp their feet, and they shake their noisemakers, their graggers. You could be the bad guy."

"No. I'm brave."

"Then how about Mordecai, Esther's cousin?" Iris said. "He helped Esther save the Jews from the mean Haman. Everyone claps when the rabbi says Mordecai's name."

"Good. I'll be Mordecai."

"And I'll call you Cousin," said Iris.

"What do I wear?" asked Benjy.

"How about Dad's brown bathrobe and the beard he wore last Purim?"

Iris helped Benjy get into his costume. Then she got into hers. "Let's go find Mama, Cousin," she said.

"What strangers do I have here?" Mama said when she saw Iris and Benjy.

"We're Esther and Mordecai," said Iris.

"We're brave," muttered Benjy through his beard.

"I'm glad you're ready," Mama said. "Benjy, will you take the Purim gifts, the mihloach manot, to Mrs. Abrams next door? We have to deliver them early, since she will be at her son's house for Purim."

"Can I peek?" he asked.

"Just a peek. No bites."

"How come I don't get any mishloach manot?" Benjy complained.

"You'll get plenty later," Mama said. "By the time you get home, dinner will be ready and Dad will be here. Then we'll go hear the rabbi read the Megillah, the story of Esther."

"Will everyone clap for me and Iris?"

"You bet."

Benjy took the plate with the green cloth on top. He peeked and saw a stack of hamantaschen, those three-cornered cakes Mama filled with raspberry jam.

"Just one?" Benjy begged.

"Benjy, they're for Mrs. Abrams," Mama insisted. "You wouldn't eat her present, would you? Mordecai wouldn't do that."

Benjy trudged off to Mrs. Abrams's house. Mrs. Abrams answered the door.

"Well, who is this?" Mrs. Abrams said. She took the plate of mishloach manot. "A distinguished visitor. A king perhaps? Maybe Ahasuerus?"

"No crown," Benjy said.

"Then you must be Haman."

"No. Haman's too mean. He wouldn't bring you mishloach manot."

"You can't be Queen Esther."

""No." Benjy laughed and pointed to his long, brown beard.

"Then you must be Mordecai!"

"Right!" Benjy shouted.

"Oh, such a brave man. For such a man as Mordecai I have a special treat. Here's a plate of goodies for your family. And a plate just for you."

Benjy clapped his hands in delight. A plate of cookies all his own!

"I like you, Mrs. Abrams."

"I like you too, Mordecai."

"I'm really Benjy."

"Little Benjy from next door? I don't believe it."

Benjy took his sticky beard off.

"See?"

"You make a handsome Mordecai."

"And you make a yummy cookie," said Benjy, taking a bite of Mrs. Abram's double chocolate chip.

PASSOVER

The name of this holiday, Passover, refers to the tenth plague in ancient Egypt when the Angel of Death passed over the houses of the Israelites and took the lives of the Egyptian first-born. The week-long holiday celebrates the Exodus of the Israelites from Egypt and their freedom from slavery. Houses are cleaned from top to bottom before the holiday begins. Instead of bread and other leavened products, Jews eat only matzah, unleavened bread during Passover. On the first two nights of the holiday (only one in Israel), families and friends gather for sedarim, *special meals which take the participants through tangible steps that enable them to reenact the story of liberation. A book called a* haggadah *is the guide for the* sedarim.

PASSOVER HERBS

L ong ago in the city of Fez there lived a wise and great rabbi named Jonathan Siriro. Rabbi Jonathan's beadle, the man who took care of his synagogue, was poor but honest and named Joseph. He was a faithful man who truly believed that the synagogue was God's temple and treated it so. The Rabbi knew that all of Joseph's deeds were for the sake of Heaven.

It so happened that this beadle, Joseph, had a large family. Since his wages as a beadle were small, the Rabbi would help him with extra money whenever Joseph needed it, especially for the Sabbath and holidays when there were always extra expenses. It was Joseph's custom to always repay these gifts if he could, though the Rabbi gave them to him freely without any expectation of a return.

With the passing of the years, the righteous Rabbi grew older, and one winter passed away, much to the sorrow of the entire community. It was a great loss, but perhaps Joseph, the beadle, felt it most, for whom could he turn to now when he needed help? He especially missed the Rabbi as the holiday of Passover approached when he would need to buy the matzah, wine and herbs for the seder table.

Though Joseph hated to do so, he went to the wealthier members of the community to ask for a loan for his holiday purchases. He promised to repay the loan, but he was turned down.

During the very last week before Passover, Joseph did not know what to do. How would his family celebrate this most important of holidays? With an empty table? In his desperation, he sat down and wrote a letter to the Rabbi asking him to help him as he always had when he was alive. Joseph carried his letter to the cemetery and placed it on the Rabbi's gravestone, praying all the while. He put a stone over the letter so the wind wouldn't carry it away. When Joseph left the cemetery, he felt much more hopeful.

It happened that this year there was a shortage of the herbs needed for the Passover table. People searched the marketplaces and farms of the surrounding villages and towns, but no such herbs were available anywhere.

Imagine Joseph's surprise when, on the day before the festival was to start, a stranger knocked at his door at dawn. Behind him was a donkey laden with these very same herbs.

"I have to come to you, Joseph, because you have a reputation for hard and honest work. And thorough, too. As you can see, I have a large quantity of the herbs to sell that the Jews in your city need for the holiday. I have many more loads to bring in such a short time, but only this one donkey with which to carry them. I need someone to sell my herbs in the marketplace while I bring one donkey load and then another into the city. Would you do this work for me? I will pay you well."

Although Joseph did not know who this stranger was, he agreed at once to do the work, overjoyed at the prospect of being able to buy what his family needed to celebrate the holiday.

It did not take long for the news to spread that the Passover herbs were available in the market. Joseph's table was soon surrounded by eager customers willing to pay a high price. Joseph stood by the table and sold, while the stranger went back and forth, bringing one load of herbs, then another, then another, all day long. Word continued to spread through all parts of the city and customers came from every corner. Joseph and the stranger were so busy, they did not even have time for one conversation between them.

Then as suddenly as the stranger had arrived, he disappeared, leaving Joseph with all the money from the sales of the herbs and the donkey as well. People still came to buy the herbs, but the stranger did not reappear with more, and so there were no more to be had.

Joseph waited and waited for the stranger to come back. Finally, he led the donkey to his home and fed him and went out to look for the stranger. He asked at inns and eating places, in the streets and the markets, but no one could give him any information. Joseph was very sad and worried about the kind stranger, worried something had happened to him.

The next day, Joseph took his agreed upon wages from the profits of the sales of the herbs and bought everything he and his family needed for the Passover celebration. He put the rest of the money aside to return to the stranger when he came back to claim it.

It was a joyous festival that year for Joseph and his family after all, celebrated with full hearts and a full table.

When the holiday was over, Joseph continued to wait for the stranger, sure he would appear for his money and his donkey. And Joseph very much wanted to thank him, too. But weeks went by and he did not come.

As the time passed, Joseph became more and more certain who the stranger was and one day he went to the cemetery, to Rabbi Jonathan's grave.

"Thank you, dear Rabbi," he said, his voice filled with gratitude and tears. "Thank you for helping me in my time of need and recommending me as an honest and faithful worker to the Prophet Elijah."

THE MAGICIAN

By Y.L. Peretz

To a little town in Wolin there once came a magician. And despite the fact that it was in the trying days just before Pesach, when every Jew had plenty of work, his coming caused a great stir. The man was a puzzle. He was raggedy, wore a crushed high hat, had strongly-marked Jewish features, and a shaven face. No one knew anything about him, and no on had ever seen him eat – kosher food or not. Just try to figure out a man like that! If asked "Whence?" his answer would be "From Paris." And "Whither?" "To London." "How did you get here?" "I just strayed." He never joined a minyan, not even on the Sabbath before Pesach; when an attempt was made to prevail upon him to do so, he vanished as though the earth had swallowed him, and turned up on the other side of the market-place.

He rented a hall and began to demonstrate his tricks. Such magic! He would swallow burning coals as easily as though they were barley. He pulled yards and yards of colored ribbons from his mouth. From the leg of a boot he produced sixteen turkeys – and such turkeys, the size of bears – which fluttered about all over the hall. He scraped gold coins off the souls of shoes. When his public applauded, he whistled and lo and behold! Loaves of bread sprang about in dance formation overhead! Again he whistled and everything disappeared: bread, ribbons, turkeys, and all!

Of course it was common knowledge that not only we have our magicians. No doubt, there were magicians in ancient Egypt who could produce even greater marvels. But why, in Heaven's name, was this magician such a pauper? Though he could scrape gold coins from the bottom of his shoes, he was unable to pay his inn bill. Though he produced turkeys and loaves of bread from the air, he himself was thin and looked half starved. People began to whisper; this was truly strange. But before we come to our Pesach tale, let us leave the magician and talk about Chaim-Yoneh and his wife Rivka-Beile. Chaim-Yoneh had once been a timber merchant but had been badly fooled in business and lost everything he owned. He then became a forest clerk, but soon lost his position. It was now many months since he had been given any work. His past winter he would not have wished on his worst enemy. But after the winter comes Pesach! And there was nothing left in his house to pawn.

Said Rivka-Beile to her husband, "Go to the Council and ask for a loan from the Pesach fund." But Chaim-Yoneh replied that he had faith, that God would come to their aid, and he refused to humble himself by asking for a loan.

Rivka-Beile searched in every corner of the house and found an old, tarnished silver spoon. Miraculous find! For years she had believed the spoon lost. But Chaim-Yoneh sold the spoon and contributed the meager proceeds to the Pesach fund. The needs of paupers, he exclaimed, come first.

Time flew by and now only a few weeks were lacking to Pesach. Still Chaim-Yoneh had faith. "God will not desert us," he assured his wife. In the quiet of the night she would weep into her pillow so that Chaim-Yoneh would not hear. This was a comfort denied her during the day, when she would pinch her cheeks to make them look healthy. The neighbors cast pitying glances her way. Some even asked when she was going to bake her matzos, if she had a sufficient supply of beets, and so on. Her closest friends

exclaimed, "What ails you, Rivka-Beile? If you lack anything we will glad-
ly lend it to you."

But Chaim-Yoneh rejected the help of man, and his wife had to follow
his example. So she made all kinds of evasive excuses.

When their neighbors appealed to the Rabbi in their concern, he sighed
and said that since Chaim-Yoneh had so much faith, there was nothing
anyone could do for him.

Rivka-Beile had not a single candle left, over which to make a blessing… and here it was already Pesach!

Chaim-Yoneh, returning home from the synagogue, saw all the windows in the market-place alight with holiday brightness, and just his house
looking like a mourner at the feast. Still, he was not discouraged.

"If God wills it, we shall yet have a good Pesach," he mused, and enter-
ing his home called out a cheerful "Gut Yom-tov to you, Rivka-Beile."
From a dark corner came her tearful reply, "Gut Yom-Tov. Gut Yor."

Chaim-Yoneh came to her and asked, "Rivka-Beile! Do you know what
day this is? The day of the Exodus from Egypt! No tears now. What is there
to weep about? If God has not chosen to let us have out own Seder, then
we shall accept His will and go to a neighbor. Everyone's door is open to
us. They are saying: let him who is hungry enter. Come, put on your shawl
and we shall go to the first good neighbor."

Rivka-Beile, who had always obeyed her husband, choked back her
tears and wrapped herself in her old, torn shawl.

At that moment, the door opened and someone entered, calling out,
"Gut Yom-tov!"

They both replied, "Gut Yom-tov," though they were unable to see
whom they were addressing.

Said the newcomer, "I should like to be a guest at your Seder."

Chaim-Yoneh replied that they themselves had no Seder, to which the unseen guest retorted that he had brought the Seder along with him.

Rivka-Beile could not contain herself and burst out, through her sobs, "In the dark?"

"I should say not; we'll have light," came the response. "Hocus-pocus!" And two silver candlesticks with candles all aflame appeared hovering in the air. The room lit up. Chaim-Yoneh and Rivka-Beile saw the magician before them and were struck mute by the wonder and fright of what they had witnessed.

The magician addressed the table which had been pushed into a corner: "Well, there, my lad, get your cover on and come here!" In the twinkling of an eye, a gleaming snow-white table-cloth dropped from the ceiling and the table began to move. It stopped directly beneath the candlesticks, which settled down on the center of the cloth.

"Now," said the magician, "we need Pesach thrones. Let there be Pesach thrones!" And from three corners of the room, chairs moved over to three sides of the table. The magician commanded them to grow wider, and they became arm-chairs! "Softer," he cried, and lo, the chairs were padded with red velvet. Pillows descended from the ceiling to settle on the chairs, and there were the Pesach thrones!

Then, at his command, a Pesach platter with all the herbs appeared on the table, as well as ruby glasses, beakers of wine, matzo, and everything else which goes to make up a Seder – even gilt-edged Haggadahs!

"If you had no water with which to wash, I can produce that, too," cried the magician.

At that, both dumb-stricken people came to life. Rivka-Beile whispered close to her husband's ear, "May we touch all these things?" Chaim-Yoneh was at a loss to know what to answer. She advised him to ask the Rabbi, but he told her to go instead, since he was afraid to leave her alone with the magician.

"No," said Rivka-Beile, "the Rabbi would question the babblings of a foolish woman and would only think her mad."

So they both went to the Rabbi, leaving the magician alone with the Seder.

The Rabbi told them that whatever a magician produces is only an illusion, and is not real. Therefore, they were to go home, and, if the matzo could be crumbled, the wine poured, and the pillows felt, they would know this was all a gift from Heaven, sent for their enjoyment.

With thumping hearts, they returned to their home. They entered to find the magician gone and the Seder still standing as they had left it. The pillows were soft to the touch, the wine poured, and the matzo crumbled. Then they knew that their guest had been the prophet Elijah, and they spent a happy Pesach!

YOM HASHOA

Yom Hashoa helps us remember the Holocaust when many many Jews were persecuted, rounded up and killed in concentration camps by Adolf Hitler's German Nazi army during World War II. Yom Hashoa is a day for gathering in synagogues, saying prayers, and lighting candles, so that the six million who died in the Holocaust are not forgotten.

The following poems are from I Never saw Another Butterfly: Children's poems from Terezin Concentration camp 1942-1944

AT TEREZIN

"Teddy," 1943

When a new child comes
Everything seems strange to him.
What, on the ground I have to lie?
Eat black potatoes ?
No! Not I! I've got to stay? It's dirty here!
The floor—why, look, it's dirt, I fear!
And I'm supposed to sleep on it?
I'll get all dirty!

Here the sound of shouting, cries,
And oh, so many flies.
Everyone knows flies carry disease.
Oooh, something bit me! Wasn't that a bedbug?
Here in Terezin, life is hell
And when I'll go home again, I can't yet tell.

THE BUTTERFLY

Pavel Friedmann, 1942

The last, the very last,
So richly, brightly, dazzlingly yellow.
    Perhaps if the sun's tears would sing
    against a white stone...

Such, such a yellow
Is carried lightly way up high.
It went away I'm sure because it wished to
    kiss the world goodbye.

For seven weeks I've lived in here,
Penned up inside this ghetto
But I have found my people here.
The dandelions call to me
And the white chestnut candles in the court.
Only I never saw another butterfly.

That butterfly was the last one.
Butterflies don't live in here,
    In the ghetto.

ON A SUNNY EVENING

Anonymous, 1944

On a purple, sun-shot evening
Under wide-flowering chestnut trees
Upon the threshold full of dust
Yesterday, today, the days are all like these.

Trees flower forth in beauty,
Lovely too their very wood all gnarled and old
That I am half afraid to peer
Into their crowns of green and gold.

The sun has made a veil of gold
So lovely that my body aches.
Above, the heavens shriek with blue
Convinced I've smiled by some mistake.
The world's abloom and seems to smile.
I want to fly but where, how high?
If in barbed wire, things can bloom
Why couldn't I? I will not die!

HANNAH SENESH

Hannah Senesh was born in Hungary in 1921. Her father was a popular writer for Budapest's main newspaper and he also wrote humorous plays. Hungary's most famous artists, writers and actors would often gather in the Senesh's apartment and fill it with exciting conversation, laughter, and music. But her father had a weak heart because of the rheumatic fever he had as a child and died when Hannah was only six years old.

After her father's death, Hanna discovered that she too was a writer. She found comfort in pouring her heart out in her poetry. Then in 1933, life changed for Hanna again. Hitler rose to power in Germany, and by 1934, German Nazis were already in Budapest, standing on the street corners wearing their brown shirts and swastika armbands.

The growing anti-Semitism reached her beloved school where she was not allowed to hold office in the Literary Society of which she was a member because she was Jewish. Conditions for the Jews in Hungary continued to grow worse and worse. Many Jews became jobless with the passing of the First Anti-Jewish Bill. Anti-Semitic activities became more acceptable. Teachers said terrible things about the Jewish students, and students spit at them. Hannah's brother George decided to leave Hungary and go to France to avoid being drafted.

During this time, Hannah was very moved by the writings of Theodor

Herzl, who had also been born in Budapest. She liked his idea that the Jews should return to Zion, their ancient homeland in Palestine, where they could become a nation once again and be proud of being Jewish. She joined the Hungarian Zionist Youth Society and talked to people who had already been to Palestine. They told her of the life of the pioneers in Palestine who worked hard to make the dry land productive once again. She wrote to her brother George in France about Zionism and found out that he, too, wanted to move to Palestine and become a pioneer. He was already studying Hebrew!

In 1939, the Second Anti-Jewish Bill was passed by the Hungarian parliament. Among other things, it said that Jews could not hold government positions, could not be editors or writers, could not teach in schools, and could not get business licenses. At this same time, Hannah graduated with honors from high school and decided to go to Palestine. She studied Hebrew and worked in the garden in the hot sun so she could get used to outdoor work. Her mother tried to convince her not to go, but when Hannah received a letter of acceptance to the Nahalal Girls School of Agriculture in Palestine, she was even more determined. At the age of eighteen years old, Hannah Senesh left Hungary to help rebuild the Jewish homeland.

Hannah loved the freedom of her new life in Palestine and threw herself into her studies and work in the agricultural school. But it grew increasingly difficult for Hannah to remain in Palestine when she heard what was happening in Hungary. She read letters from home about The Third Anti-Jewish Bill which forbid all relationships between Jews and non-Jews. Hitler demanded that the Jews of Hungary wear an identifying yellow Star of David band, that all their money and possessions be confiscated, and that they be "resettled" by the Germans. Hannah decided to go back to Hungary to help young people escape to Palestine and to rescue her mother.

At this time, the Haganah, a Jewish defense organization that defended the settlements, as well as the major cities in Palestine, expanded its defense to include those Jews in Nazi-occupied areas. The Haganah established the Palmach strike force, which parachuted its members into areas near Nazi-occupied zones. After being parachuted into these places, the Haganah members entered the Nazi zones, trained Jews in resistance and helped Nazi victims.

After Hannah enlisted in the Haganah, she was trained in judo techniques, in the use of different kinds of knives, and in how to fire captured German arms. She overcame her fear and learned how to parachute out of planes. After all her training, Hannah joined a brave group of thirty-two young Jews who parachuted into areas near those occupied by the Nazis.

Several of the members of this group managed to enter Hungary and steal the uniforms of Hungarian soldiers. When Hungarian mobs rounded up Jews, these Palmach members pretended to be Hungarian soldiers. They took charge of the arrested Jews and smuggled them to safety.

Hanna parachuted into Italy and managed to reach Yugoslavia successfully. When she tried to enter Hungary, though, she was captured by the police at the border. Her Nazi captors tortured her in an effort to force her to reveal information about Jewish underground resistance activities. They even brought in her mother who begged Hannah to reveal what she knew to save her own life. But Hannah would not tell them anything and was killed by the Hungarian police in November of 1944.

In 1950, Hannah's remains were brought to Israel where she was buried on Mount Herzl. Hannah Senesh's poetry and journals have survived her, as has her personal story of courage and self-sacrifice, and she continues to be an inspiration to many. One of her most famous poems begins with the line, "Blessed is the match consumed in kindling flame."

YOM HA'ATZMAUT: ISRAEL'S BIRTHDAY

What happened during the Holocaust convinced many Jewish people that they needed a homeland. They felt that if there had been a homeland before World War II, the Holocaust may never have happened. Jews would have had a place to escape to, and a government that spoke up for them and fought for them.

The place Jews have long looked to as their homeland is the Land of Israel. Jews first settled there after the Exodus from Egypt over three thousand years ago. When the Romans destroyed their Temple in Jerusalem and drove the Jews out in 70 C.E., only a few remained in the Land of Israel. For two thousand years, the Jews lived scattered all over the world in what is called the Diaspora. They yearned to return to the homeland. They did not have a country of their own all these years, and much of the time were persecuted in the lands where they had settled.

Then, over a hundred years ago, a movement began to resettle Jews in the Land of Israel, which was called Palestine then. The movement had the goal of establishing a Jewish country once again. This movement was called Zionism, since the word Zion, a hill and fortress in Jerusalem, often came to stand for Jerusalem in poetry and prayers. The "father" of this movement was Theodor Herzl.

The early days of the Jewish pioneers in the Land of Israel were tough ones. The land they worked on was desert or swamp. They had little money or skills, but they were living their dream of reclaiming the land and building their own country where they could be free. The Turkish government, which then ruled Palestine, did not want to establish a Jewish state, however. And the surrounding Arab countries did not welcome these new settlers or the idea of a Jewish country. In 1920, the British took Palestine over from the Turks. In the Balfour Declaration, the British promised the Jews that they would have their own country one day, just as the British had created Jordan, Syria, Iraq and Lebanon for the Arabs.

When Hitler rose to power, many Jews tried to escape to Palestine, but the British were very strict about letting Jews in and allowed only a few to enter. After the war, when the refugees who had survived the Holocaust wanted to move to the Land of Israel, the British would not let them in either. The British were afraid of the reaction of the neighboring Arab countries.

A famous incident of this period, that showed the plight of the European Jews to the world, involved the ship called the Exodus. It was an old ferryboat carrying four thousand five hundred Jewish displaced persons that sailed for Palestine in 1947. Seven British ships attacked it. They captured the boat by ramming and boarding it, using machine guns and tear gas. Once captured, Ernest Bevin, the British Foreign Secretary of State, decided to make an example of the Exodus. He wanted no further Jewish immigration into Palestine and no Jewish country. And so he ordered that the ship be sent back to Europe. It made its way to France and docked there, but the Jews refused to get off. They said they wanted to go to Palestine. The British sent them to Germany where they again refused to get off. The British used clubs to force the Jewish refugees of the Holocaust off the ship. This incident raised an outcry all around the world.

In April of 1947, the British government gave up, and turned the responsibility for Palestine over to the United Nations. Their decision was to divide Palestine in half, giving half to the Jews and half to the Arabs.

After all the British officials and troops left the country, on May 14, 1948, in Tel Aviv, David Ben-Gurion read the Declaration of Independence that proclaimed the independent State of Israel. All over the new state, Jews danced happily in the streets. At long last, Jews had a home and could live in freedom!

On the very next day, the new state was invaded by powerful armies from the Arab nations. The fighting of this War of Independence was hard and long, but after a year, the Jews were able to stop the Arab advance. It seemed like a miracle! On March 11, 1949, the blue and white Israeli flag with its Star of David was raised at the United Nations in New York City. That six-pointed star, which Jews had worn during the Holocaust to mark them for the Nazis, was now part of the flag of the new Jewish state.

One of the first acts of the Jewish state was to open it doors to Jews from all over the world. The population of the new state doubled over the next five years. One group to "come home" were the Yemenite Jews. As soon as they heard about the new state, they packed up and walked to the city of Aden, which had the nearest airport. It took the Israelis about a year to bring the forty-five thousand Yemenite Jews to Israel via what was called Operation Magic Carpet. The Yemenite Jews had never seen an airplane, but were not afraid. They remembered the words from the prophet Isaiah that the Jewish people would return to Zion on wings as eagles. When they saw the big metal birds, they felt as if they were witnessing a miracle!

Israelis have established a holiday to celebrate their independence, but they also have a holiday that directly precedes it called Yom Ha-Zikaron.

On this day Israelis remember all the men and women who died defending their country. There are two minutes of silence on this day when all work stops, and cars pull over to the side of the road to remember. People bring flowers to cemeteries and war memorials. And then, right when this Day of Remembrance ends, Independence Day begins. Without those who fought to bring independence to Israel, there would be no independence to celebrate! Israelis tie the bitter together with the sweet, as on Passover when Jews make a sandwich of the sweet apple and nuts mixed with the bitter horseradish to remember the bitterness of slavery and the hope of freedom.

At sundown of the Day of Remembrance, the sirens blast across Israel and Yom Ha-Atzmaut, Israel's birthday, begins. Torches are lit on Mt. Herzl in Jerusalem and bonfires are lit all around the country. There is dancing, parades, air displays by the jets belonging to the Israeli air force, and a Bible quiz on television with participants from all over the world. The day if full of happy celebration.

LAG B'OMER

Lag B'Omer means the thiry-third day of the counting of the Omer, the period between Passover and Shavuot. The fifty days when Jews count the Omer is a quiet, serious time. For the ancient Israelite farmers it was a watchful time when they worried about their crops. After fifty days, the wheat crop would be ripe and the farmers would know whether they faced a time of plenty or a time of famine.

Lag B'Omer became a holiday after the destruction of the Second Temple by the Romans. This thirty-third day during the Omer is a break from the other quieter Omer days. Stories are told about the brave military leader Bar Kochba, and the rabbis Shimon bar Yohai and Akiva who managed to study and teach even under Roman rule. It is a day of picnics and bonfires, outdoor play and fun, especially for schoolchildren.

THE CAVE OF SHIMON BAR YOHAI

by Howard Schwartz

Near the village of Peki'in in the Galilee there is a cave known as the cave of Shimon bar Yohai. That is the cave in which Shimon bar Yohai and his son, Eleazar, hid from the Romans after they passed a decree calling for his execution. Shimon bar Yohai and his son remained in that cave for thirteen years, devoting themselves to the study of the Torah.

Many miracles took place while they lived in that cave. During the first night they spent there, a well of living water formed inside the cave and a large carob tree grew outside it, filled with ripe carobs, that completely hid the entrance. When Shimon bar Yohai and his son discovered the spring and the tree that had appeared overnight, they drank from the water and tasted the fruit. The water was pure and delicious and the fruit was ripe, and they knew that their faith had been rewarded and that the Holy One, blessed be He, was guarding them. And they gave thanks.

After that, Rabbi Shimon and his son cast off their clothes and spent each day buried in the sand, studying the Torah. Only when it was time to pray did they put on their white garments, and in this way they preserved them through the long years of their exile.

Then a day came when Elijah the Prophet arrived at the cave to study with them. Elijah revealed great mysteries to them that had never been known outside of heaven. And in the days that followed Elijah often returned, and Shimon bar Yohai wrote down those mysteries on parchment that Elijah brought them, which came from the ram that Abraham had sacrificed on Mount Moriah in place of Isaac. Now that was an enchanted parchment, for it expanded to receive his words as Shimon bar Yohai wrote. And every letter he inscribed there burned in black fire on white. And the name of the book that he wrote down there, filled with the celestial mysteries, was the *Zohar*.

One day, as they watched from inside the cave, Rabbi Eleazar saw a bird repeatedly escape from a hunter, and he recognized this as a sign that they were free to leave the cave, for the Emperor had died and the decree had been annulled. But before they left, they hid the book of the *Zohar* in that cave, for they knew that the world was not yet ready for its secrets to be revealed.

There the book of the *Zohar* remained for many generations, until an Ishmaelite who happened to find it in the cave sold it to peddlers. Some of its pages came into the possession of a rabbi who recognized their value at once. He went to all the peddlers in that area and found that they had used the pages of the book to wrap their spices. In this way he was able to collect all of the missing pages, and that is how the *Zohar* was saved and came to be handed down.

Shavuot

Shavuot, which means weeks, comes at the end of the period of the counting of the Omer and is an early summer festival. It commemorates two different events. One is the time when the first fruits of the harvest were brought from all over the land of Israel to the Temple in Jerusalem. The other is the giving of the Ten Commandments to Moses and the people on Mount Sinai. It is customary to decorate houses and synagogues with flowers and greens on this holiday, to read the story of Ruth, and to eat blintzes, pancakes filled with cheese.

MOUNTAINS OF BLINTZES

by Sydney Taylor

anny snuggled happily beneath the coverlet. It was story time. He felt comfy-cosy, and drowsy, and full to bursting. "Daddy," he murmured, "Shavuot's a swell holiday 'cause Mommy always makes lots of cheese blintzes."

"I know," replied Daddy, laughing. "You ate enough blintzes tonight to make a mountain."

Danny grinned and patted his stomach. "It feels like a mountain."

"Want to hear a Shavoot story about mountains?"

"Uh-huh!" Danny flip-flopped on his pillow a couple of times, getting settled. "All right, Daddy. I'm ready."

"Well, after the Jews left Egypt, they wandered about in the desert for seven weeks. One day they came to a mountain, and it was here, the Bible tells us, that Moses went up to receive the Ten Commandments from God.

"The Commandments are God's laws. They teach us how to be good. To remember this wonderful gift God gave us, we celebrate Shavuot.

"Now when the mountains first heard about this, they began to quarrel. Each mountain wanted the Law to be given on its peak.

"Mount Tabor spoke up proudly. 'I should be the favored one, for I am the tallest! In the time of Noah, when the great floods came, all you other mountains were covered up by water. Only my head remained safely above!'

"That made Mount Hermon very cross. 'Huh! Just being the biggest doesn't count! You've got to do something important! Like me, for instance!'

"'And what did you do that's so important?' asked Mount Tabor.

"Mount Hermon huffed and puffed with pride. 'When the Jews fled from Egypt, the waters of the Red Sea divided. I got down between the two shores so the Jews could cross over safely.'

"Meanwhile foxy Mount Carmel plopped itself down near the sea. 'If I stay right here I'll surely be the lucky one. For if God wants to give the Law on the sea, then I am on the sea! If on land, then I am also by the land.'

"'Stuff and nonsense!' shouted the other mountains.

"But little Mount Sinai said nothing. I'm so very little, he sighed. Nothing wonderful ever happens to me.

"Suddenly a voice rang out of heaven. 'The Lord will not choose any of the tall, proud mountains that boast and quarrel. The Lord chooses a humble mountain—Mount Sinai!'

"And that's how little Mount Sinai became the place where the Ten Commandments were given to the Jews."

Danny yawned sleepily. "I'm glad God picked Mount Sinai, Daddy. All the other mountains were so stuck on themselves."

"Good night, Danny," Daddy whispered, kissing him.

Danny lay quietly in the soft darkness thinking about the mountains. All at once his bed started to quiver and shake! Danny sat upright. What was the matter? He stared around. The walls were moving away! Danny jumped out of bed and raced after them, trying to catch up. It was too late! They were gone!

Danny stopped running. He felt all mixed up. He was outdoors! All around him were big rolled-up yellow things, and from their tops oozed squashy, creamy stuff. "Ooh! They're blintzes! Mountains and mountains of blintzes!" yelled Danny. But as he spoke, the shapes changed. No, they were really mountains! Mountains with faces, all angry and scowling! Now they were galumping toward him, groaning and muttering.

"So!" roared one of them, "you think we're stuck up, do you?"

A second mountain swept its head back and bellowed. "Look at the size of him! And he dares to criticize us! Ha! Ha! Ha!"

"He thinks 'cause he's so full of blintzes, he's as big as we are!" shouted another.

"Say, Mount Carmel, let's have a little fun with this Blintze Boy!" yelled a medium-size mountain. It bent its crown and suddenly Danny was lifted high. "Catch!" cried the mountain. WHOOSH! . . . Danny flew through the air. Smack! He landed sprawling atop Mount Carmel.

"Oh, please, please Mister Mountain!" he gasped. No one paid him any attention. "Your turn, Mount Hermon!" screamed Mount Carmel, shaking Danny like a small puppy. WHOOSH! . . . He whirled inro space again! Crash! He was flat on his face atop Mount Hermon!

"This is fun! Send that Blintze Boy on to me!" And Mount Tabor set its peak all ready for the catch.

"Oh please, Mount Tabor! I'm sorry for what I said. I didn't mean . . ." The only answer the mountains gave was WHOOSH . . . WHOOSH . . . WHOOSH! Danny was being tossed back and forth like a rubber ball.

Danny's stomach began to hurt terribly from all the shaking. "Oh please! Stop!" he cried.

Suddenly as he flew over Mount Carmel, Danny spied a low mountain waddling toward him. It had a kind face and was smiling. "Danny," it called out, "I'm Mount Sinai! I'll save you. Quick, land on me! I'll send you straight on home again!"

With his heart in his mouth, Danny twisted and turned until he toppled right onto the peak of little Mount Sinai. "Good boy! Now, hold on tight!" Mount Sinai took a running start. "One-two-three! Let go!

Danny felt himself falling and falling. From far away, he could hear Mount Sinai calling after him. "Remember Danny, remember! If you ever come to Israel, come and visit me! Don't forget! Don't forget...."

There was the sound of running feet. Danny blinked his eyes wonderingly. He was stretched out on the floor of his own little bedroom! Over there was his bed and here were Mommy and Daddy standing over him.

"Danny, you fell out of bed!" Mommy's voice sounded a little alarmed. "Are you hurt?"

"Oh no!" Danny tried to explain. "I didn't fall. It was little Mount Sinai that threw me home."

Mommy and Daddy looked at each other. "Oh, it was only a bad dream," Daddy said.

"I warned him not to eat so many blintzes," Mommy added, laughing.

And they all laughed together.

BIBLIOGRAPHY

Ausubel, Nathan, ed. *A Treasury of Jewish Folklore.* New York: Crown Publishers, 1965.

Bamberge, David. *My People: Abba Eban's History of the Jews.* New York: Behrman House, Inc., 1979.

Bialik, Hayyim Nahman. *And It Came To Pass: Legends and Stories about King David and King Solomon.* New York: Hebrew Publishing Co., 1938.

Bin Gorion, Emanuel, ed., Micha Joseph Bin Gorion, coll., I.M Lask, trans. *Mimekor Yisrael: Selected Classical Jewish Folktales.* Bloomington, Indiana: Indiana University Press, 1990.

Burstein, Chaya M. *A Kid's Catalog of Israel.* Philadelphia: The Jewish Publication Society, 1988.

Buber, Martin. *Tales of the Hasidim.* New York: Schocken Books, 1991.

Certner, Simon, coll. *101 Jewish Stories: A Treasury of Folk Tales from Midrash and Other Sources.* New York: Board of Jewish Education of Greater New York, 1983.

Encyclopedia Judaica. vol.4: 564-569, 6: 1078-1099, 7: 1242-1243, 8: 407-421, 10: 379-383, 451-459, 15: 1410-1413. New York: Macmillan, 1972.

Ginzberg, Louis. *The Legends of the Jews.* Philadelphia: The Jewish Publication Society of America, 1968.

Goldin, Barbara Diamond. *The Family Book of Midrash.* Northvale, New Jersey: Jason Aronson, Inc. 1990.

Goodman, Philip. *The Hanukkah Anthology.* Philadelphia: The Jewish Publication Society of America, 1976.

Harlow, Jules, ed. *Lessons From Our Living Past.* New York: Behrman House, Inc. 1972.

Henry, Sondra and Emily Taitz. *Written Out Of History: Our Jewish Foremothers.* Sunnyside, New York: Biblio Press, 1988.

Kaplan, Rabbi Aryeh. *The Living Torah: The Five Books of Moses.* New York: Maznaim Publishing Corporation, 1981.

Kerdeman, Deborah and Lawrence Kushner. *The Invisible Chariot: An Introduction to Kabbalah and Jewish Spirituality.* Denver, Colorado: Alternatives in Religious Education, Inc., 1986.

Kimmel, Eric A., ed. *A Hanukkah Treasury.* New York: Henry Holt and Company, 1998.

Noy, Dov. *Folktales of Israel.* Chicago: The University of Chicago Press, 1963.

Patai, Raphael. *Gates to the Old City: A Book of Jewish Legends.* Northvale, New Jersey: Jason Aronson, Inc., 1988.

Patterson, David. *The Greatest Jewish Stories Ever Told.* New York: Jonathan David Publishers, Inc., 1997.

Prose, Francine. *Stories from Our Living Past.* New York: Behrman, Inc., 1974.

Sadeh, Pinhas. *Jewish Folktales.* New York: Doubleday, 1989.

Schram, Peninnah, ed. *Chosen Tales: Stories Told by Jewish Storytellers*. Northvale, New Jersey: Jason Aronson, Inc., 1995.

Schur, Maxine. *Hannah Szenes: A Song of Light*. Philadelphia: The Jewish Publication Society, 1986.

Serwer-Bernstein, Blanche L. *In The Tradition of Moses and Mohammed: Jewish and Arab Folktales*. Northvale, New Jersey: Jason Aronson Inc., 1994.

Serwer-Bernstein, Blanche L. *Let's Steal the Moon*. New York: Shapolsky, 1987.

Simon, Solomon, and David Morrison Bial. *The Rabbis' Bible*. New York: Behrman House, Inc. 1966.

Tanakh: A New Translation of the Holy Scriptures. Philadelphia: The Jewish Publication Society, 1985.

Weissman, Rabbi Moshe. *The Midrash Says*. New York: Benei Yakov Pub., 1980.

Wiesel, Elie. *Somewhere A Master: Further Hasidic Portraits and Legends*. New York: Summit Books, 1981.

Wiesel, Elie. *Souls on Fire: Portraits and Legends of Hasidic Masters*. New York: Summit Books, 1972.

Winkler, Gershon. *They Called Her Rebbe: The Maiden of Ludomir*. New York: Judaica Press, Inc. 1991.